中国矿业大学"十四五"规划教材（立项编号：GHJC23104）

2021年度国家级一流本科专业（英语）建设点成果

中国矿业大学"基础、人文与新兴交叉—外国语言文学"学科建设

英译中国文化

理论与实践

TRANSLATING CHINESE CULTURE

THEORY AND PRACTICE

唐书哲　徐　剑　编著

刘婷婷　苗　燕　刘会民　参编

南京大学出版社

图书在版编目(CIP)数据

英译中国文化：理论与实践 / 唐书哲，徐剑编著.
南京 ：南京大学出版社，2024.8. — ISBN 978 - 7 - 305
- 28275 - 1

Ⅰ．H315.9

中国国家版本馆 CIP 数据核字第 2024CB7402 号

出版发行　南京大学出版社
社　　址　南京市汉口路 22 号　　　　邮　编　210093
书　　名　**英译中国文化：理论与实践**
　　　　　YINGYI ZHONGGUO WENHUA；LILUN YU SHIJIAN
编　　著　唐书哲　徐　剑
责任编辑　张淑文　　　　　　　　编辑热线　(025)83592401
照　　排　南京南琳图文制作有限公司
印　　刷　南京玉河印刷厂
开　　本　787 mm×1092 mm　1/16 开　印张 13.75　字数 424 千
版　　次　2024 年 8 月第 1 版　2024 年 8 月第 1 次印刷
ISBN 978 - 7 - 305 - 28275 - 1
定　　价　55.00 元

网址：http://www.njupco.com
官方微博：http://weibo.com/njupco
官方微信号：njupress
销售咨询热线：(025) 83594756

Introduction

Translation is closely associated with the development of linguistics and cultural theories. Prior to the 1990s, translation was primarily understood from a linguistic perspective. Catford, a leading figure of the linguistic approach to translation, defines translation as "the replacement of textual material in one language (SL) by equivalent textual material in another language (TL)."[①] The linguistic notion of translation as a process of language transference is later challenged by scholars who regard translation as a cross-cultural activity as language is inseparable from culture. Though cultural awareness has long been demonstrated in translation, it is not until the 1990s that scholars like Bassnett, Lefevere, and Venuti declared the cultural turn in translation studies, which was spurred by cultural studies. According to the cultural school of translation studies, translation is not simply a process of language shift, but also a process of cross-cultural communication. The current book is largely written in accordance with such a view and discusses the theories, principles, methods, and practices of cultural translation, aiming to improve readers' cross-cultural and translation competence.

To attain this aim, we adopt the triple angles of theory, history, and practice in writing the book. The first two chapters are primarily theory-oriented, focusing on a historical review and critical explication of the background, major theories, and core concepts of cultural translation with specific examples so as to help mediate between theory and practice. The rest 14 chapters discuss the translation of 14 aspects of Chinese culture, namely, traditional Chinese clothing, Chinese cuisine, traditional Chinese architecture, Chinese relics, traditional Chinese medicine, traditional Chinese festivals, traditional Chinese thoughts and philosophies, Chinese classics, Chinese literary works, tourism publicity materials, Chinese idioms, color terms, animal terms, and movie titles.

In Chapters 3—16, we follow the structure of introduction, theory, and practice.

---

① Catford, John C. *A Linguistic Theory of Translation*. London: Oxford University Press, 1965, p. 20.

First，we offer a brief introduction to the discussed aspect of culture；then we trace its translation history with reference to the major translators and translated works；and finally，we discuss translation criteria，principles，strategies，and methods with specific examples. Some of the major translation and linguistic theories and concepts are expounded and exemplified in our discussion，such as cultural equivalence，manipulation theory，translation as resistance，*skopos* theory. Meanwhile，the contested strategies of domestication and foreignization and debated methods of literal translation and free translation are also revisited in the context of cultural translation with examples.

Another notable feature of this book is that we quote the original words of scholars and translators wherever possible and have them properly cited so that readers can make their own judgements and locate the original texts if they want further readings.

Before introducing the major contents of the book，we'd like to justify our selection of the 14 particular aspects of Chinese culture. We have to firstly admit that there is indeed a certain degree of subjectivity and personal preferences involved as politics，religions，rituals，etc.，are also important aspects of Chinese culture and that we are personally acquainted with and inclined towards the 14 chosen aspects. We select the 14 aspects for discussion mainly out of two considerations. For one thing，since the aspects of Chinese culture are numerous，it's simply an impossible task to discuss the translation of each aspect of it，and there is bound to be a selection，which is often affected by the authors' personal preferences and background knowledge. Besides，we deem that the chosen 14 aspects can present a panoramic view of Chinese culture. For another，the theories，criteria，principles，strategies，and methods of translating culture，no matter what aspect of it，are essentially identical，and it is easy for readers to transfer them to the translation of any other aspect of Chinese culture.

The main content of each chapter is summarized as follows.

Chapter 1 offers a workable definition of culture and cultural translation，discusses the relationship between language and culture，and exemplifies the role of culture in translation. Culture is defined as the "spiritual wealth" created by a group of people，including values，thoughts，literature，morals，customs，etc.，and cultural translation is used in several of its senses—the translation of culture，an adaptation-like approach to translation，and the translation of culture-specific terms. The translation of culture，with its origin in anthropology，means that one culture is taken as a text and re-expressed in a way that is understandable to another culture. Used as an adaptation-like strategy，cultural translation refers to the process "in which the content of the message is changed to conform to the receptor culture in some way， and/or in which information is introduced which is not linguistically implicit in the original. "[1] In a narrower sense, cultural translation usually refers to the translation of culture-specific terms by using the strategies of domestication or foreignization. The cultural turn of translation studies is partly based on the inseparable relationship between language and culture. Since language is one of the most important mediums of culture, the role of culture has to be accorded sufficient attention in translation.

Chapter 2 first explains the social and cultural background for the cultural turn in translation studies and then elucidates the theories and concepts proposed by Susan Bassnett, André Lefevere, and Lawrence Venuti with examples. Like the paradigm shift in any other discipline, the cultural approach to translation studies doesn't appear out of nowhere. Instead, it is deeply rooted in Marxism, cultural studies, and post-colonialism which discuss the role of ideology and culture in shaping our subjectivity and power relations. According to Bassnett, translation is a process of cross-cultural communication that emphasizes the role of culture and aims to attain dynamic cultural equivalence. Lefevere proposes the theory of manipulation and contends that a translator's activity is manipulated by ideology, poetics, and patronage. Venuti's theory is also ideology-bound. He unleashes criticism at the tacit translation norm of fluency rooted in Anglo-American centrism and advocates the introduction of heterogeneous language and cultural elements into translated texts to resist Anglo-American centrism. Venuti's theory is a continuation of the polemics between domestication and foreignization in a postcolonial context and largely remains theoretical, as the norm of fluency still predominates. It is also notable that the cultural turn called for by Bassnett and Lefevere helps to establish translation as an independent discipline.

In the next 14 chapters, we discuss the translation of 14 aspects of Chinese culture. In each of the 14 chapters, we offer a brief and informative introduction to the topic under discussion so that readers can familiarize themselves with the topic and acquire the topic-related vocabulary which is important to their ability of retelling Chinese culture in English.

Chapter 3 focuses on the translation of traditional Chinese clothing (TCC). We first expound the relationship between TCC and Chinese culture, elucidate the aesthetic tradition of TCC, and analyze the relationship between clothing and identity. Influenced by traditional Chinese culture, particularly Confucianism and Taoism, TCC lays emphasis on the preservation of social hierarchy, draws inspiration

---

[1] Nida, Eugene & Charles R. Taber. *The Theory and Practice of Translation*. Leiden: E. J. Brill, 1982, p. 199.

from nature, uses various items to cover and decorate the body, and forms its own distinctive aesthetic tradition—emphasis on ethics, naturalness, and the balance between completeness and variety. Clothing is an outward expression of the wearer's identity, such as his/her cultural orientation, ethnicity, gender, class, profession, age, and education. As clothing is an important aspect of Chinese culture, TCC translation is a form of cross-cultural activity that involves the negotiations between SL and TL cultures from the angles of mindset, sociocultural background, values, social psychology, geohistorical tradition, etc. Translators often adopt the methods and skills of free translation, addition, omission, loan translation, transliteration, and translation with illustration in the translation of TCC.

Chapter 4 is devoted to the translation of Chinese cuisine. The first section makes a survey of Chinese cuisine, including its history, qualities, elements, and major culinary traditions. Chinese national cuisine upholds the qualities of color, flavor, taste, shape, and meaning, emphasizes the elements of ingredients, cutting technique, heat control, and flavor, and each of the major culinary traditions, i.e., Shandong cuisine, Sichuan cuisine, Guangdong cuisine, Jiangsu cuisine, Fujian cuisine, Zhejiang cuisine, Hunan cuisine, and Anhui cuisine possesses unique features and has its typical dishes. In the second section, we investigate the relationship between food and culture, and maintain that food, as an important aspect of culture, plays a pivotal role in reflecting and maintaining cultural identity. Section three discusses the challenges and methods of translating Chinese cuisine. The challenges concern both dish names which are sometimes figurative and culturally codified and publicity materials of cuisine which tend to use decorative language. The first challenge can be resolved by adopting the methods of transliteration and free translation, and the second one can be addressed by drawing theoretical support from *skopos* theory which holds that the purpose of translation justifies the process. In this case, a reproduction of the meaning of the source text will suffice as foreign readers care more about the factual information of Chinese cuisine such as ingredients and preparation methods rather than its history and cultural origins.

Chapter 5 discusses the translation of traditional Chinese architecture (TCA). The first section offers a brief introduction to the nine unique features of TCA as summarized by Liang Sicheng. These features, embodied in composition of single construction, layout, structure, brackets, purlin raising, roof, color and colored drawings, artistic treatment of component junction, and building materials, distinguish TCA from other architectural systems in the world. The second section examines the relationship between TCA and Chinese culture, and argues that TCA reflects the philosophical views and aesthetic taste of Chinese people. The site, layout, and landscape design of TCA reflect the traditional thought of harmony between man and nature and Confucian ethical relations. The third section analyzes the difficulties of TCA translation in terms of terminology and stylistics, and the fourth section explains the principles of TCA translation—communication-friendliness, conciseness, and clarity. In the last section, we exemplify the commonly used methods and skills in the translation of TCA, namely, loan translation, transliteration plus annotation, free translation, translation plus illustration, addition, and omission.

Chapter 6 focuses on the translation of Chinese relics. Section one discusses the relationship between relics and culture, believing that relics reveal a lot about the ways of living of different historical periods and possess great historical, cultural, artistic, technological, and educational values. Section two analyzes the difficulties of translating Chinese relics and holds that the lack of background information and cultural differences make the translation of Chinese relics a challenging task. Section three examines five common types of errors in the English translation of Chinese relics—spelling mistakes, grammar mistakes, misinterpretations, losses of key information, and inconsistencies. Sections four and five exemplify the principles and methods of Chinese relics translation. Guided by the principles of faithfulness, readability, and nationality, translators often use the methods of free translation, transliteration, and half transliteration in the translation of Chinese relics.

Chapter 7 discusses the translation of traditional Chinese medicine (TCM) from six aspects—significance, history, difficulties, principles, methods, and standardization. TCM translation can serve to alleviate ailments and promote cultural exchange, and its history can be traced back to the 17th century. The history of English translation of TCM witnesses the English translation of major Chinese medical classics like *The Yellow Emperor's Classic of Internal Medicine*, *Compendium of Materia Medica*, and *Nan-Ching*, and the standardization of TCM nomenclature. As evidenced by translation history and practice, the difficulties of TCM translation chiefly lie in the lack of philosophical context and equivalents, misunderstanding, and polysemy, which can be addressed by explication of the philosophical foundations of TCM, and the methods of loan translation, literal translation, free translation, and transliteration plus free translation. Chinese scholars like Li Zhaoguo have set some of the basic principles for the English translation of TCM—natural principle, national principle, back-translation principle, and prescriptive principle, which aim at the positive interaction of TCM and Western medicine, as well as the standardization and dissemination of TCM. In the last section, we analyze the standardization of TCM nomenclature which influences the internationalization of TCM.

Chapter 8 discusses the translation of traditional Chinese festivals. In section one，we analyze the relationship between festivals and Chinese culture，believing that Chinese festivals have their roots in various aspects of Chinese culture like myth，legends，astronomy，and lunar calendar，and that they reflect Chinese people's way of living and their wish for love，family reunion，and harvest. Section two offers brief introductions to major traditional Chinese festivals—the Spring Festival，the Lantern Festival，Tomb Sweeping Day，Dragon Boat Festival，and Mid-Autumn Festival. In the last two sections，we exemplify the challenges and methods of translating major traditional Chinese festivals. The culture-specific expressions and customs of festivals constitute a major challenge for translators as they have to explain them in English to help readers make sense and get the cultural connotations of festivals. To successfully translate traditional Chinese festivals，translators usually use the methods of transliteration，transliteration plus annotation，literal translation，literal translation plus annotation，and free translation.

Chapter 9 concentrates on the translation of Confucianism，Taoism，and Buddhism which are the cornerstones of Chinese culture. We first offer an overview of each of the three schools of thoughts and philosophies in terms of their histories，tenets，core terms，and cultural influences，and then discuss their translations from the angles of translation purposes，principles，and methods，and list the generally-accepted translations of some of the key terms. A large proportion of this chapter is devoted to Buddhism translation which is a peak of translation in ancient China. We discuss the translation principles，methods，and practices of some major Buddhism translators，particularly those of Xuan Zang（玄奘）whose "five guidelines for not-translating a term" are of profound and continuing influence on translation. [1]

Chapter 10 discusses the translation of Chinese classics，particularly literary classics. We begin this chapter by defining classics as works of art that are of recognized and established values and arguing that classics play an irreplaceable role in sustaining cultural identity and enlightening our mind. Then we offer a relatively comprehensive and detailed history of classics translation from the 17th century to the present. In each of the four historical periods，we offer a critical discussion of the translation thoughts and practices of major translators like James Legge，Arthur Waley，David Hawks，Stephen Owen，and Howard Goldblatt，and special attention is paid to the knotty issue of fidelity versus readability，which hinges upon translation purpose and translator's cultural orientation. If the translator orients towards target

---

[1] Cheung，Martha P. Y. *An Anthology of Chinese Discourse on Translation Volume One: From Earliest Times to the Buddhist Project*. London and New York: Routledge，2014，p. 92.

culture and aims to come up with smooth translations, he/she will be likely to place readability over fidelity. On the contrary, if the translator intends to introduce heterogeneous cultural elements into target culture, he/she may take fidelity as the top priority. The translation history of Chinese classics can help readers grasp the genealogy and landscape of English translation of Chinese classics. The last section of this chapter is devoted to analyzing some of the typical difficulties and solutions in classics translation. First, culture-loaded terms can be translated by using makeshift equivalents, transliteration, or transliteration plus annotation. Second, polysemes can be translated by checking their meanings and consulting reference books. Third, Chinese characters borrowed to replace characters that should be used can be translated by ascertaining their real meanings in the contexts. Fourth, passive structures can be converted into English passive structures or active voices. Fifth, Chinese paratactic structures can be rendered to English hypotactic structures. And finally, repetition in Chinese can be replaced by substitution in English.

Chapter 11 concentrates on the translation of Chinese literary works. The first section draws theoretical support from Shklovsky's distinction between literary language and everyday language, and discusses the self-referential, indirect, and fictional features of literary language and their implications for translation, arguing that literary translation should bring out the information and aesthetic effects of the source text. The second section explains the elements of literary texts by using graphology and Ingarden's strata theory which divides a literary text into four interconnected strata, namely, the stratum of linguistic sound formations, the stratum of meaning units, the stratum of represented objects language and the stratum of schematized aspects, and exemplifies their implications for literary translation. We believe that a superior translation should reproduce all the strata of the TL texts faithfully, but oftentimes, some of the strata are compromised or even left out in translation either because they are irreproducible or the translator leaves them out intentionally or out of incompetence. In the last section, we discuss the qualities of a successful translator of literary works. Besides professional ethics, bilingual proficiency, and encyclopedic knowledge which are required of all translators, a qualified literary translator should also possess language sensitivity, rich imagination, and aesthetic ability.

Chapter 12 discusses tourism translation, particularly the translation of Chinese tourism publicity materials like brochures and tour guide manuals. We first analyze the features of tourism publicity materials and hold that they are usually multifunctional, rich in genre and content, and that they possess a high level of literariness. The last two sections of this chapter focus on the principles and methods of translating tourism publicity materials. Guided by the principles of fidelity and readability, translators often adopt the methods and skills of transliteration, half transliteration, free translation, addition, omission, rewriting, and cross-cultural substitution in translating Chinese tourism publicity materials.

Chapter 13 focuses on the translation of Chinese idioms. We first define Chinese idioms as linguistic chunks made up of phrases or sentences whose real meanings cannot be obtained by adding the meanings of their constituents and then discuss the differences between Chinese culture and English culture as embodied in idioms from the angles of ecological culture, linguistic culture, religious culture, material culture, and social culture. The last section exemplifies the commonly used methods and skills in the translation of Chinese idioms—literal translation, literal translation plus annotation, free translation, substitution, and addition.

Chapter 14 discusses the translation of color terms. In this chapter, we first examine the classification of language meaning from linguistic and semiotic perspectives, and believe that language meaning can be classified into referential meaning, structural meaning, and pragmatic meaning which can be further classified into associative meaning, interactive meaning, and representational meaning. The translation of color terms is fundamentally a cross-cultural activity as different colors and their related expressions usually have different cultural associations. Then we discuss the cultural associations of white, black, red, green, yellow, and blue and provide lists of color-related terms and their generally accepted translations.

Chapter 15 focuses on the translation of animal terms. Like colors and color terms, animals and animal terms oftentimes also possess different cultural connotations. We exemplify the cultural associations of some animals, such as fox, tiger, dragon, and dog, and then group animals and animal terms into four categories: animals with similar cultural connotations, animals with different cultural connotations, different animal terms with similar meanings, and animal terms without equivalent animal terms in the TL culture. For each category, we offer a list of some animal-related terms and their generally accepted translations.

Chapter 16 discusses the translation of movie titles. The first section discusses the importance of movie titles from the perspective of paratext and argues that the title of a movie can influence readers' perception of it and serve as a threshold through which readers can access and interpret the movie. The second section explains the translation of movie titles as a cross-cultural activity that requires the mediation between SL culture and TL culture. Section three elucidates the four principles of translating movie titles—value of information, value of culture, aesthetic value, and commercial value. In the last section, we illustrate the methods and skills of translating movie titles with specific examples—transliteration, half transliteration, literal translation, free translation and addition.

We conclude the book by revisiting some of the key issues of cultural translation. We first analyze the paradigm shift in translation studies and its implications for translation practice. What we advocate is not a discussion of cultural translation to the exclusion of language; rather, we believe translation is essentially an activity that involves text-based transference of one language into another and that the adoption of different paradigms usually leads to a comprehensive and deepened understanding of translation. We also review the core issues involved in cultural translation— domestication versus foreignization and literal translation versus free translation. These contested issues are related with each other and rooted in the purpose of translation and the translator's ideology and cultural orientation. To put it simply, the purpose of translation and a translator's ideology and cultural orientation determine his/her choice of translation strategy which in turn decides his/her adoption of specific translation methods.

Tang Shuzhe, Xu Jian, Liu Tingting, Miao Yan, and Liu Huimin collaborated in compiling and writing the book. Tang Shuzhe wrote the first draft of Introduction, Chapters 1—16, and Conclusion; Xu Jian designed the framework and layout; Liu Tingting saw to project approval; Miao Yan proofread Introduction and Chapters 1— 8; and Liu Huimin proofread Chapters 9—16 and Conclusion.

We hope this book can help readers acquaint themselves with Chinese culture and improve their ability of introducing Chinese culture and telling China stories to English readers. In using this book, teachers can break the current arrangement of chapters and pick up chapters based on necessity and teaching schedule. The authors are responsible for any mistakes in the book.

Contents

Chapter 1

Culture and Cultural Translation

 Objectives

➤ Understand the definitions of culture

➤ Understand the definitions of cultural translation

➤ Understand the relationship between language and culture

➤ Understand the role of culture in translation

➤ Maintain a cultural awareness in translation

1. The Definitions of Culture

To define cultural translation, we have to define culture first. According to *The American Heritage Dictionary of the English Language*, culture refers to "the totality of socially transmitted behavior patterns, arts, beliefs, institutions, and all other products of human work and thought."[1] In *Primitive Culture*, Edward Tylor defines culture from an ethnographic perspective, maintaining that "culture or civilization, taken in its wide ethnographic sense, is that complex whole which includes knowledge, belief, art, morals, law, custom, and any other capabilities and habits acquired by man as a member of society."[2] Though its definitions vary, culture is usually used in a collective sense, referring in particular to the totality of the "spiritual wealth" produced by a group of people, including but not limited to its food, clothing, tradition, habits, social customs, morals, education, laws, politics, values, religion, mode of thinking, social relations, etc. Chinese culture refers to the total spiritual wealth created by Chinese people. It is different from Western culture and unique to the Chinese nation. For example, the culturally unique expression 红双喜 would remind Chinese people of marriage, happiness, and good luck while in English the color red is usually associated with evil and sin. Even within Western culture, the reserved inclination of a British gentleman differs from the dashing spirit of an American cowboy.

2. The Definitions of Cultural Translation

Like culture, cultural translation also elicits different definitions. Let's review and exemplify some of the major ones.

2.1 Cultural translation as the translation of culture

The translation of culture is believed to be a branch of anthropology that describes the cultures of ethnic groups, particularly non-Western ethnic groups. [3] In this sense, cultural translation means the translation of culture, i. e. , taking one culture as a text

---

[1] Soukhanov, Anne H. et al. *The American Heritage Dictionary of the English Language* (3rd edition). Boston: Houghton Mifflin Company, 1996, p. 1836.

[2] Tylor, Edward. *Primitive Culture: Researches into the Development of Mythology, Philosophy, Religion, Art, and Custom* (Volume 1). London: John Murray, 1871, p. 1.

[3] Evans-Pritchard, E. E. *Anthropology and History*. Manchester: Manchester University Press, 1961, p. 17.

and re-expressing it in a way that is understandable to another culture. For instance, in her autobiography *Fifth Chinese Daughter*, Jade Snow Wong regards Chinese culture as a text and puts various aspects of it into English. Take calligraphy as an example. Wong explains the holding of brush in English. "The illustration showed that one's fingers should be curved in a continuous fluid line, with the brush held flexibly between the thumb and third finger, while the index and middle finger rested gently on it. In fact, it was much like holding a chopstick."[①] By expressing the posture of holding a brush in English, English readers can get a glimpse into Chinese calligraphy.

2.2   Cultural translation as an adaptation-like translation strategy

Nida and Taber define cultural translation as a translation strategy "in which the content of the message is changed to conform to the receptor culture in some way, and/or in which information is introduced which is not linguistically implicit in the original."[②] Let's illustrate this definition with two frequently cited examples. In China, we often greet people by asking "你吃了吗?". But in English, this greeting, if literally translated as "Have you eaten yet?" would sound strange to foreign ears. By putting it into "How are you doing?", we actually change the content of the original expression. For a similar reason, the Chinese idioms 明珠暗投 and 对牛弹琴 are usually rendered into the biblical expression "cast pearls before swine." In the process of translation, new information is sometimes added to the original text. Some translators are not in favor of this strategy, deeming it unfaithful to the original text, but as a useful and effective way of cross-cultural communication, it is justified and frequently used by many other translators.

2.3   Cultural translation as the translation of culturally unique elements

Culturally unique elements, sometimes synonymous with culture-specific terms or culture-loaded terms, refer to the cultural elements that are unique to a certain culture. 红尘, 缘分, and 天命, for example, are expressions that are unique to Chinese culture. In translating these culturally unique elements, translators usually adopt the strategy of domestication or foreignization. As a translation strategy oriented towards the target culture, domestication advocates the substitution of elements that are unique to the source culture with culturally equivalent terms. For

---

① Wong, Jade Snow. *Fifth Chinese Daughter*. Seattle: University of Washington Press, 1989, p. 16.

② Nida, Eugene & Charles R. Taber. *The Theory and Practice of Translation*. Leiden: E. J. Brill, 1982, p. 199.

example，by translating "spring up like mushrooms" into 雨后春笋，we are using domestication by substituting 笋 with "mushrooms." Domestication can also be used on a macro-level. Lin Shu（林纾），a renowned translator of the late Qing dynasty，"translated" over a dozen foreign novels into fluent classic Chinese by making substantial adaptations to the content，culture，and style of the original works.

Contrary to domestication，foreignization is a source-culture-oriented strategy in which the foreignness of source culture is retained，sometimes to the extent of disrupting the norms of target culture. Lu Xun（鲁迅）was an ardent advocator of foreignization. He believed that the Chinese language can be enriched and modernized by borrowing expressions from foreign languages. Let's review the polemic between Lu Xun and Zhao Jingshen concerning the translation of "the Milky Way." In translating the English version of Chekov's short story "Vanka"，Zhao put "the Milky Way" first into 牛奶路 in 1927 and later into 天河 in 1930. After reading Zhao's translation，Lu Xun composed a critical essay titled "Wind，Cow，and Horse" in 1931，alluding to the Chinese expression 风马牛不相及 which means totally unrelated. He criticized Zhao for wrongly translating "the Milky Way" as 牛奶路 and proposed the "right" translation 神奶路. He told a Greek myth to justify his translation.

> The supreme god Zeus in Greek mythology is a philanderer. One day，he went to the mortal world and fathered a child with a girl. When Zeus' jealous wife Hera heard about the affair，she flew into rage and brought the child to heaven，seeking to kill him. Ignorant of his imminent death，the child touched Hera's nipple and sucked it with all his strength. Hera was startled and flung him away. The child tumbled into the human world and grew into a hero. Due to his sucking，Hera's milk spewed into heaven and formed the Milky Way，the so-called 牛奶路. No，actually it was 神奶路.[①]

As we can see，domestication and foreignization are two contending strategies with larger political，social，and cultural agenda behind them. Supporters of domestication value the norms of target language and culture，and emphasize the readability of translated works while advocators of foreignization intend to rejuvenate and vitalize national language and culture by loaning foreign elements. The polemics between supporters of the two strategies have long existed and will continue into the future.

---

① 鲁迅：《鲁迅全集：第四卷》，北京：人民文学出版社，2005 年，第 355 页。

2.4 Cultural translation as a postcolonial literary phenomenon

Some scholars define cultural translation from a postcolonial perspective. In *The Location of Culture*, Bhabha endows cultural translation with two new meanings. Firstly, he uses it to describe the postcolonial literary phenomenon that integrates translating with writing. Secondly, he uses it as a metaphor for the postcolonial migration experience, meaning the transference and adaptation of migrants and their culture to a new land and culture. [1] Let's exemplify the first meaning here.

For most migrant Chinese American writers whose mother tongue is Chinese and Chinese American writers who know about Chinese culture, they usually merge translating with writing and their English works are marked with an obvious trace of translation. Ha Jin (哈金) in his novel *Waiting* integrates writing with translating. Let's quote a paragraph to illustrate it.

> As the cart came to a stop at the front gate, Hua dropped a bulging burlap sack to the ground and jumped down. "Thanks, Uncle Yang," she called out to the driver. Waving at the plump girl atop the load, she cried, "See you this evening." Then she brushed bits of straw from her shirt and pants. [2]

In the quoted paragraph, the protagonist Kong Lin's daughter Kong Hua was taking a ride on an oxcart. Chinese readers would knowingly nod their heads at Ha Jin's writing. Neither would they lose sight of the trace of translation, nor would they turn a blind eye to the expressions with strong Chinese characteristics like "burlap sack" and "Uncle Yang." It is partly due to the blending of translating and writing that Chinese readers feel at home reading Jin's novels.

There are other definitions of cultural translation, but for the purpose and scope of this book, it's unnecessary to review all of them. As you may have felt, the four definitions of cultural translation explained here are to a certain extent overlapping. In this book, we define cultural translation as the translation of various aspects of Chinese culture. And in translating texts pertaining to Chinese culture, we will adopt the strategies of domestication and foreignization, and resort to various methods and skills such as literal translation, free translation, addition, omission, substitution.

---

[1] Bhabha, Homi K. *The Location of Culture*. London and New York: Routledge, 1994, pp. 212 – 235.

[2] Jin, Ha. *Waiting*. New York: Vintage International, 1999, p. 5.

3. The Relationship Between Language and Culture

We might have known or heard about the assertion that language and culture are inseparable, but why and in what sense are they intertwined? Language is perhaps the most important medium for the origination, development, preservation, innovation, and transmission of culture. Ngugi wa Thiong'o argues:

> Culture embodies those moral, ethical and aesthetic values, the set of spiritual eyeglasses, through which they come to view themselves and their place in the universe. Values are the basis of a people's identity, their sense of particularity as members of the human race. All this is carried by language. Language as culture is the collective memory bank of a people's experience in history. Culture is almost indistinguishable from the language that makes possible its genesis, growth, banking, articulation and indeed its transmission from one generation to the next ... [1]

Thiong'o's argument indicates that every language belongs to a certain culture and that language and cultural identity are inseparable. Let's illustrate this with an example from Amy Tan's "Mother Tongue." Tan used to be ashamed of her mother's broken English. She identified with "Standard English" and the values behind it:

> I was ashamed of her English. I believed that her English reflected the quality of what she had to say. That is, because she expressed them imperfectly, her thoughts were imperfect. And I had plenty of empirical evidence to support me: the fact that people in department stores, at banks, and at restaurants did not take her seriously, did not give her good service, pretended not to understand her, or even acted as if they did not hear her. [2]

Growing up in the United States, Tan used to perceive the world through the "spiritual eyeglasses" of Caucasian Americans and associate English with identity, believing "perfect" English is a marker of one's social and cultural identity. The underlying meaning of Tan's words is that if you can speak "perfect" English, you are

---

① Thiong'o, Ngugi wa. "The Language of African Literature." *The Post-colonial Studies Reader*. Eds. Bill Ashcroft, Gareth Griffiths & Helen Tiffin. London and New York: Routledge, 1995, p. 289.

② Tan, Amy. *The Opposite of Fate*. New York: G. P. Putman's Sons, 2003, p. 274.

Americanized and well-educated. This, as argued by Ashcroft et al., reflects a form of "control over language", i.e., the "imperial education system installs a 'standard' version of the metropolitan language as the norm, and marginalizes all 'variants' as impurities."[①] Through an American education, "standard" English and the culture behind it were instilled into Amy Tan's mind, causing her to be ashamed of her mother's English.

4. The Role of Culture in Translation

As language and culture are inseparable, we have to consider the cultural factor in translation. According to Susan Bassnett, "translation is not just the transfer of texts from one language into another, it is now rightly seen as a process of negotiation between texts and between cultures, a process during which all kinds of transactions take place mediated by the figure of the translator."[②] Obviously, culture plays a significant role in translation and translator is accorded the role of a language and cultural mediator. As for cultural translation, the role of culture can never be overemphasized and negligence of culture can lead to misunderstanding or even conflict.

An anecdote about Li Hongzhang (李鸿章), a high-ranking official of the late Qing dynasty can exemplify the role of culture in translation. During his stay in the U.S., Li hosted a banquet in a popular American restaurant to show his gratitude for the hospitable American officials. Before starting the banquet, Li stood up and made some opening remarks.

今天承蒙各位光临,不胜荣幸。我们略备粗馔,聊表寸心,没有什么可口的东西,不成敬意,请大家多多包涵……

The interpreter "faithfully" put Li's words into English,

I am very happy to have all of you here today. Though these dishes are coarse and not delicious and good enough to show my respect for you, I hope you will enjoy them ...

When the translated version of Li's words was seen by the restaurant owner in the

---

① Ashcroft, Bill, Gareth Griffiths & Helen Tiffin. *The Empire Writes Back* (2nd edition). London and New York: Routledge, 2002, p. 7.

② Bassnett, Susan. *Translation Studies* (4th edition). London and New York: Routledge, 2014, p. 6.

local newspaper, he felt insulted and demanded an apology from Li, insisting that he produce the evidence of which dish was poorly made and which dish was unpalatable; otherwise, he would sue Li for damaging the restaurant's reputation.

The misunderstanding arises from the failure of cultural negotiation. Li's self-effacing words are formulaic polite expressions in China and convey respect in Chinese culture. Like the formulaic greeting "你吃了吗?", Li's words show discrepancy between form and content, a phenomenon that is not rarely seen Chinese culture. However, America values individualism and American people tend to express themselves directly. As a result, the restaurant owner failed to grasp the real meaning of Li's words and interpreted them as open insults. The misunderstanding could have been avoided if Li's words were put like this, "The cuisine of your country is really great. It is my great honor to have a chance to entertain you with them ..."

A Short Summary

In this chapter, we've mainly discussed the definitions of culture cultural translation, the relationship between language and culture, and the role of culture in translation. Culture is the "spiritual wealth" created by a certain people. It includes food, clothing, values, morals, laws, politics, and many other aspects. Cultural translation in this book is mainly defined as the translation of various aspects of Chinese culture. Since language and culture are inseparable, we need to regard translation as a process of cross-cultural communication and fully consider the role of culture in it.

Reviewing Questions

1. What is Chinese culture in contrast with Western culture?

2. What are the definitions of cultural translation? Please illustrate them with examples.

3. What is the relationship between language and culture?

4. In what sense is "standard" English related with British colonialism and American racism?

5. Why do we need to pay attention to culture in translation?

Chapter 2

The Cultural Turn of Translation Studies

 Objectives

➢ Understand the sociocultural context for the cultural turn of translation studies

➢ Understand the key ideas of Marxist literary theory

➢ Understand Susan Bassnett's concept of cultural translation

➢ Understand André Lefevere's manipulation theory

➢ Understand Lawrence Venuti's theory of translation as resistance

➢ Be able to apply theories of cultural translation in research and practice

1. The Sociocultural Background for the Cultural Turn of Translation Studies

Regarded as an era of theory explosion, the 20th century witnessed the emergence of various theories in humanities and social sciences like Marxism, new criticism, feminism, structuralism, deconstructionism, cultural studies, colonialism, post-colonialism. These theories contribute to a paradigm shift in the study of humanities and social sciences, leading to the emergence and development of interdisciplinary studies. It was against such a background that translation studies broke loose from the traditional linguistic paradigm and adopted an interdisciplinary approach. Translators found inspiration in the theories, concepts, key ideas, and research paradigms of comparative literature, linguistics, hermeneutics, semiotics, anthropology, sociology, etc., and applied them in translation studies. Of all these theories and disciplines, Marxism and post-colonialism seem to have the most extensive and profound influence on the cultural turn of translation studies. Scholars emphasize the subjectivity, systematicness, and openness of translation studies as a discipline and exhibit an increasing interest in the impact of ideology on translation studies.

1.1 The definitions of ideology

As Chinese college students, we must have gone through courses on Marxism and are not unfamiliar with the key terms of Marxism, such as ideology, class struggle, economic base, superstructure. In this chapter, let's focus on "ideology," a core idea of Marxism and illustrate it with examples. According to Raymond Williams, there are three common versions of the concept in Marxist writings: 1) a system of beliefs characteristic of a particular class or group; 2) a system of illusory beliefs—false ideas or false consciousness—which can be contrasted with true or scientific knowledge; and 3) the general process of the production of meanings and ideas. [1] Since the systems of beliefs are "in part or wholly false," Williams believes the first and second definitions of ideology can be combined. A scrutiny of the definitions reveals that the term "ideology" in Marxism is used both in a theoretical and a practical sense, referring to a system of beliefs specific to a certain class or group and the formation of it. Lefevere defines ideology in relation with translation studies and regards it as "the conceptual

---

① Williams, Raymond. *Marxism and Literature*. Oxford and New York: Oxford University Press, 1977, p. 55. Though a core concept in Marxism, "ideology" doesn't originate in Marxism. It was first coined in the late 18th century by the French philosopher Destutt de Tracy, meaning the "science of ideas."

grid that consists of opinions and attitudes deemed acceptable in a certain society at a certain time, and through which readers and translators approach texts."[1] Compared with Marxist definitions of ideology, Lefevere's definition is much broader, thus expanding and consolidating the theoretical foundation for the cultural turn of translation studies.

1.2   The influence of ideology on translation studies

Now, let's turn to the role of ideology in translation studies.

To begin with, ideology can influence and even determine the selection of source texts. Let's illustrate this with the example of Salman Rushdie's *The Satanic Verses* which narrates the illusionary experience of an Indian movie star who becomes a prophet and founds a new religion. When first published in 1988, the novel was declared sacrilegious and banned by the Islamic world. The writer was even signed a death warrant (*fatwa*) by the religious leader Khomeini, and on 12th, August 2022, Rushdie was shot by a Lebanese American named Hadi Matar during a literary seminar. Due to ideological factors, the translation of *The Satanic Verses* is a highly sensitive and even dangerous thing. It is hard to imagine the translation of the novel in the Arabic world.

Ideology can also affect translators' translation practices. In dealing with materials that are ideologically sensitive, translators usually need to work as a negotiator between ideologies of the source text and target text and resort to the strategies of omission, adaptation, rewriting, and/or abridgement. Let's examine the translation practice of the famous sinologist Howard Goldblatt who has translated many modern and contemporary Chinese novels into English. In his translation, Goldblatt situates the texts in a Western ideological context and translates them in a way that caters to Western readers' Orientalist expectations of China. For example, he translates the title of A Lai's novel 《尘埃落定》 as "Red Poppies", obviously a reincarnation of the persistent stereotypical image of Chinese as opium eaters. Goldblatt's example epitomizes the powerful influence of ideology on translation practice.

Having explained the sociocultural background for the cultural school of translation studies, let's turn our attention to some of the leading figures in this school and elucidate their theories and key concepts. These advocators of cultural translation

---

① Lefevere, André. "Translation Practice(s) and the Circulation of Cultural Capital: Some Aeneids in English." *Constructing Cultures: Essays on Literary Translation*. Eds. Susan Bassnett & André Lefevere. Clevedon: Multilingual Matters, 1998, p. 48.

may differ in their specific views, but they agree on the general principles that translation is a historical and cultural phenomenon and that translation studies should focus on the interaction between culture and translation.

2. Susan Bassnett and Her Concept of Cultural Translation

Susan Bassnett, born in Britain in 1945, is Emeritus Professor of Comparative Literature at the University of Warwick and author of over 20 books on translation studies. In her seminal work *Translation Studies*, Bassnett reviews the development of translation studies and discusses the cultural turn of it. According to Bassnett, the role of culture in translation has been procuring increasing attention since the late 1980s. "The 'cultural turn' that Translation Studies underwent in the 1990s drew attention to the fact that translation involves much more than the transfer of texts produced in one language to another." It also has the social-cultural dimension that is gaining more attention in a postcolonial and global context.① Bassnett and Lefevere regard translation as "a rewriting of an original text" and a manipulation act in their coauthored preface to *Translation, History, Culture: A Sourcebook*.②

Susan Bassnett presents her concept of cultural translation through a historical discussion of translation studies and a special discussion of literary translation. Readers can get a panoramic picture of her views by reading *Translation Studies*, but for the purpose of this book, a summary of Bassnett's concept would suffice. Her concept of cultural translation has the following major tenets. First, translation should neither be text-bound nor language-bound; rather it should consider the role of culture and achieve cultural equivalence. Second, translation is not merely a process of language decoding and recoding, it is also a process of cross-cultural communication. Third, the principles and norms of translation are dynamic rather than static, varying from language to language and from period to period. Finally, translation should shift from description of source language texts to cultural equivalence, but equivalence does not mean sameness "since sameness cannot even exist between two TL versions of the same text, let alone between the SL and TL version."③ Actually, we can further summarize Bassnett's concept in a single sentence: Since language and culture are

---

① Bassnett, Susan. *Translation Studies* (4th edition). London and New York: Routledge, 2014, pp. 11 - 12.

② Bassnett, Susan & André Lefevere. "General Editors' Preface." *Translation, History, Culture: A Sourcebook*. Ed. André Lefevere. London and New York: Routledge, 1992, p. xi.

③ Bassnett, Susan. *Translation Studies* (4th edition). London and New York: Routledge, 2014, p. 39.

inseparable, translation is a cross-cultural process that relies on various forms of equivalence to achieve cross-cultural exchange and understanding. ①

Let's exemplify the use of equivalence in translation. As we've discussed in Chapter 1, many expressions are culture-specific and the translation of them involves a process of cross-cultural transference. Strategies of foreignization and domestication and skills of substitution and addition are usually employed to achieve culturally functional equivalence. For example, if we translate the idiom 班门弄斧 as "show off one's proficiency with the axe before Lu Ban, the master carpenter," we are using the strategy of foreignization and the skill of addition. However, if we put it into "teach one's grandma to suck eggs," the strategy of domestication and the skill of substitution are used. Though both strategies can attain the goal of functional equivalence, domestication and foreignization are different in cultural orientation and significance. Generally, domestication places target culture over source culture and can increase the readability and acceptability of TL texts by reducing or removing cultural barriers; whereas foreignization is source culture oriented and aims to introduce new elements to target culture. The larger social and cultural implications of foreignization and domestication will be further addressed when we come to our discussion of Lawrence Venuti later in this chapter.

3. André Lefevere and His Manipulation Theory

Born in Belgium in 1945, André Lefevere is another representative figure of the cultural school of translation studies and is known for his rewriting and manipulation theory. He abandons the traditional text-bound paradigm of translation studies and investigates translation activity in the larger social and cultural context which he refers to as ideology. For Lefevere, translation is an act of rewriting and a translator often rewrites the original text because he/she is manipulated by ideology, poetics, and patronage. Bassnett and Lefevere regard translation as a form of rewriting in the preface to *Translation, Rewriting, and the Manipulation of Literary Fame*.

Translation is, of course, a rewriting of an original text. All rewritings,

---

① Bassnett mentions several forms and levels of equivalence by referring to translators like Anton Popovič and Eugene Nida. Popovič distinguishes four types of equivalence—linguistic equivalence, paradigmatic equivalence, stylistic equivalence, and textual equivalence. Nida distinguishes two types of equivalence—formal equivalence and dynamic equivalence. Bassnett, Susan. *Translation Studies* (4th edition). London and New York: Routledge, 2014, pp. 35 – 36.

whatever their intention, reflect a certain ideology and a poetics and as such manipulate literature to function in a given society in a given way. Rewriting is manipulation, undertaken in the service of power, and in its positive aspect can help in the evolution of a literature and a society. [1]

It's easy for us to notice that rewriting and manipulation are two key words of Lefevere's translation theory, which can serve as the threshold to the core of his theory. First, let's focus on translation as rewriting. For Lefevere, plot summaries, reviews, critical articles, stage performances, and translations are all forms of rewriting which have a nonnegligible impact on the evolution of literature and culture. Of all the forms of rewriting, translation "is the most obviously recognizable type" and "potentially the most influential," "because it is able to project the image of an author and/or a (series of) work(s) in another culture, lifting that author and/or those works beyond the boundaries of their culture of origin."[2] For average Chinese readers who cannot read in French, their knowledge of Balzac is mainly from various forms of rewriting, translation in particular. It is chiefly through the translation of Fu Lei that Balzac and his works transcend the borders of France and French culture.

Translation as a form of rewriting is subject to the influences of ideology, poetics, and patronage. Since ideology has already been discussed, we'll focus on poetics and patronage here. "A poetics can be said to consist of two components: one is an inventory of literary devices, genres, motifs, prototypical characters and situations, and symbols; the other a concept of what the role of literature is, or should be, in the social system as a whole." The two components of poetics exert influence on translation in different ways. "The latter concept is influential in the selection of themes that must be relevant to the social system if the work of literature is to be noticed at all."[3] For example, Liang Qichao associated the selection of source texts with the social milieu of the late Qing dynasty and advocated the translation of books on Western law, politics, history, education, agriculture, mining, technology, business, academics, etc. to strengthen and rejuvenate the Chinese nation. Poetics is the other component that affects translators' practices. Lefevere quoted from Earl

---

[1] Bassnett, Susan &. André Lefevere. "General Editors' Preface." *Translation, Rewriting, and the Manipulation of Literary Fame*. Ed. André Lefevere. London and New York: Routledge, 1992, p. xii.

[2] Lefevere, André. *Translation, Rewriting, and the Manipulation of Literary Fame*. London and New York: Routledge, 1992, p. 9.

[3] Lefevere, André. *Translation, Rewriting, and the Manipulation of Literary Fame*. London and New York: Routledge, 1992, p. 26.

Miner to show the conforming power of poetics:

> A systematic poetics emerges in a culture after a literary system proper has been generated and when important critical conceptions are based on a then flourishing or normatively considered genre. The coinciding of major critics with the considered genre generates the critical system. [1]

Once the poetics and its corresponding critical discourse are established, all parties involved in the fields of writing, reading, translating, studying, and criticizing are influenced by them. Take genre as an example. Conceived "as a set of constitutive conventions and codes altering from age to age, but shared by a kind of implicit contract between writer and reader,"[2] genre can affect writers' creation, readers' expectation, and translators' rewriting. A translator may demonstrate strong subjectivity, but seldom to the degree of totally neglecting genre conventions. Lin Shu made substantial changes to the stylistics of the original novels, but his translations, centering on the depiction of characters, still conformed to the basic conventions of fiction. If the genre of the original work is changed, the title or preface of the translation would have the change rightfully marked. Charles Lamb adapted Shakespearean plays into short stories, and he properly marked the change of genre in the title of the book *Tales from Shakespeare*. Fu Donghua translated Homer's epics *Iliad* and *Odyssey* into prose and acknowledged the change of genre in the preface. Translators' transgression of genre conventions and their acknowledgement of it attest to the power of poetics.

Patronage is another factor that manipulates translation. Lefevere defines patronage as "something like the powers (persons, institutions) that can further or hinder the reading, writing, and rewriting of literature." Patronage can be exerted by persons, "groups of persons, a religious body, a political party, a social class, a royal court, publishers, and, last but not the least, the media, both newspapers and larger television corporations."[3] According to Lefevere, patronage has three components— the ideological, the economic, and the status. Ideology "would seem to be that

---

[1] Miner, Earl. "On the Genesis and Development of Literary Systems, Part I. " *Critical Inquiry* 5. 2 (1978), p. 350.

[2] Abrams, M. H. *A Glossary of Literary Terms* (9th edition). Boston: Wadsworth Cengage Learning, 2009, p. 135.

[3] Lefevere, André. *Translation, Rewriting, and the Manipulation of Literary Fame*. London and New York: Routledge, 1992, p. 15.

grillwork of form, convention, and belief which orders our actions."① As to the economic component, the patron would see to it that the translator is financially provided either in the form of pension or a job. Samuel Johnson received an empty pecuniary promise from Lord Chesterfield for the compilation of *A Dictionary of the English Language* and ventilated his vengeance in "Letter to Lord Chesterfield," denouncing him for fishing for fame and declaring the independence of intellectuals. Patronage also operates in the form of status. "Acceptance of patronage implies integration into a certain support group and its lifestyle."② After World War I, Hemingway, Fitzgerald, Anderson, Pound, and other notable American writers sojourned in Paris and clustered around the famous patron Gertrude Stein, forming the famous "Lost Generation." They expressed disillusionment with social reality and indulged in hedonism, seeking support and solace from each other.

As an originative translation theorist, Lefevere regards translation as a form of rewriting and manipulation, providing scholars with a new perspective into translation, but his theory also possesses limitations. First, his theory may work well for literary texts but not texts on science, technology, and business, which, as informative texts, are relatively objective and the translation of them demands faithful reproduction of information. Second, ideology, poetics, and patronage are all exterior factors that influence translators' subjectivity. The interior factors impacting translators' subjectivity have not been investigated.

4. Lawrence Venuti and His Theory of Translation as Resistance

Another leading figure of the cultural school of translation studies is Lawrence Venuti. Born in Philadelphia in 1953 and Emeritus Professor of English at Temple University, Venuti is credited with the theory of "translator's invisibility" and the strategy of foreignization as resistance. In his monograph *The Translator's Invisibility*, Venuti traces the history of English translation from the 17th century to the early 1990s and finds that the translators are invisible in contemporary British and American culture. He defines translator's invisibility as follows:

"Invisibility" is the term I will use to describe the translator's situation and

---

① Jameson, Frederic. *The Prison-House of Language: A Critical Account of Structuralism and Russian Formalism.* Princeton: Princeton University Press, 1974, p. 107.

② Lefevere, André. *Translation, Rewriting, and the Manipulation of Literary Fame.* London and New York: Routledge, 1992, p. 16.

activity in contemporary British and American cultures. It refers to at least two mutually determining phenomena: one is an illusionistic effect of discourse, of the translator's own manipulation of the translating language, English in this case; the other is the practice of reading and evaluating translations that has long prevailed in the United Kingdom and the United States, among other cultures, both Anglophone and foreign languages. [1]

According to Venuti, all the parties involved in translation—translators, publishers, reviewers, and readers "conspire" to make the translator invisible. On the part of publishers and reviewers, they prefer translations that are fluent and without linguistic or stylistic peculiarities. A fluent translation seems transparent and plausibly reflects the writer's style and the essential meaning of the original work. Tacitly conforming to the expectations of publishers and reviewers, translators adhere to the current usage of English and doctor linguistic and stylistic peculiarities "to insure easy readability." [2] Readers also have a role to play in effacing the translator's presence. They tend to read for meaning and grudge against language use that may interfere with fluent reading. The concordant efforts and expectations of all parties involved in translation result in the translator's invisibility and the writer's visibility. "The more fluent the translation, the more invisible the translator, and, presumably, the more visible the writer or meaning of the original text." [3] The demand for fluent translation forms a powerful constrictive tradition and impedes the exchange between languages, literatures, and cultures. The author's style and voice is veiled and erased in translation on the one hand. On the other hand, new elements fail to be introduced into target language and culture, making culture a one-way flow. Suppose Lu Xun's short story "The True Story of Ah Q" (《阿Q正传》) were translated in the style of fluent English identical with that of "Degradation" (《沉沦》) by Yu Dafu, the distinctive styles of the two writers would be concealed and Chinese linguistic and cultural elements would be subdued by English and Anglophone culture.

Venuti's theory of translator's invisibility offers an implicit criticism of Anglo-American centrism as embodied in the formidable normative and disciplinary power of "Standard English," which is closely associated with British colonialism and American

---

[1]   Venuti, Lawrence. *The Translator's Invisibility: A History of Translation* (2nd edition). London and New York: Routledge, 2008, p. 1.

[2]   Venuti, Lawrence. *The Translator's Invisibility: A History of Translation* (2nd edition). London and New York: Routledge, 2008, p. 1.

[3]   Venuti, Lawrence. *The Translator's Invisibility: A History of Translation* (2nd edition). London and New York: Routledge, 2008, p. 1.

racism. Maintained through the institutional forces of education, writing, translation, publication, etc., "Standard English" is used as a tool to subjugate other races and languages. Ashcroft et al. argue:

> One of the main features of imperial oppression is control over language. The imperial education system installs a "standard" version of the metropolitan language as the norm, and marginalizes all "variants" as impurities. [1]

America duplicates the hierarchical relationship between "Standard English" and its variants. Though American people do not speak one single language, American culture "presents itself as an English-language culture," "espouses a single-language ethos," and "strives very actively to assert a monolingual identity."[2] Consequently, the use of other languages in English translations and writings is restricted, either explicitly or implicitly. For example, Ha Jin's manuscripts were once rejected for not using correct and fluent English. Obviously, the establishment of fluent English as the norm and the repellence of other languages and varieties of English is a form of oppression. "The translator's invisibility is symptomatic of a complacency in British and American relations with cultural others, a complacency that can be described—without too much exaggeration—as imperialistic abroad and xenophobic at home."[3]

Venuti attributes the translator's invisibility to the translation strategy of domestication that has long been dominant in Britain and U. S. "An illusionism fostered by fluent translating, the translator's invisibility at once enacts and masks an insidious domestication of foreign texts, rewriting them in the transparent discourse that prevails in English and that selects precisely those foreign texts amendable to fluent translating."[4] The overreliance on domestication, according to Venuti, is detrimental in several ways. It hinders the translation of foreign texts that are difficult to render into fluent English and masks the writer's original style. It ignores the translator's contribution and talent. It blocks cultural exchange and consolidates British and American cultural hegemony. Then what should translators do to make

---

① Ashcroft, Bill, Gareth Griffiths & Helen Tiffin. *The Empire Writes Back: Theory and Practice in Post-colonial Literatures* (2nd edition). London and New York: Routledge, 2002, p. 7.

② Arteaga, Alfred. *Chicano Poetics: Heterotexts and Hybridities*. Cambridge: Cambridge University Press, 1997, p. 72.

③ Venuti, Lawrence. *The Translator's Invisibility: A History of Translation* (2nd edition). London and New York: Routledge, 2008, p. 13.

④ Venuti, Lawrence. *The Translator's Invisibility: A History of Translation* (2nd edition). London and New York: Routledge, 2008, pp. 12 – 13.

themselves visible and offset the negative consequences of domestication? The antidote prescribed by Venuti is foreignization.

Venuti begins his discussion by quoting German theologian and philosopher Friedrich Schleiermacher's words on the two strategies of translation. "Either the translator leaves the author in peace as much as possible and moves the reader towards him; or he leaves the reader in peace, as much as possible, and moves the author towards him."① Of the two strategies, Schleiermacher opts for the former and his argument is taken as an ethics of translation that is "concerned with making the translated text a place where a cultural other is manifested."② Situating his discussion in the larger postcolonial context, Venuti loads foreignization with political and cultural critique, taking it as a way to resist Anglo-American colonialism and racism. "Foreignizing translation in English can be a form of resistance against ethnocentrism and racism, cultural narcissism and imperialism, in the interests of democratic geopolitical relations."③ Venuti advocates the strategy of foreignization to highlight the heterogeneity of foreign texts and shield them from the ideological manipulation of target culture. He seeks theoretical support from French philosophers Deleuze and Guattari and emphasizes the translation of foreign texts that are "excluded by the standard dialect, by literary cannons, or by ethnic stereotypes in the United States (or in the other major English-speaking country, the United Kingdom)."④ In translating these texts, particularly "texts that are stylistically innovative," Venuti appeals to translators to "create sociolects striated with various dialects, registers and styles, inventing a collective assemblage that questions the seeming unity of standard English."⑤ As a matter of fact, by introducing foreign elements through translation, the English language and culture can also gain heterogeneity and vitality. King-Kok Cheung thus comments on Ha Jin's using of non-standard English in his writing.

On a metanarrative level, by infiltrating American English with his peculiar

---

① Venuti, Lawrence. *The Translator's Invisibility: A History of Translation* (2nd edition). London and New York: Routledge, 2008, p. 15.

② Venuti, Lawrence. *The Translator's Invisibility: A History of Translation* (2nd edition). London and New York: Routledge, 2008, p. 15.

③ Venuti, Lawrence. *The Translator's Invisibility: A History of Translation* (2nd edition). London and New York: Routledge, 2008, p. 16.

④ Venuti, Lawrence. *The Scandals of Translation: Towards an Ethics of Difference.* London and New York: Routledge, 1998, pp. 10 - 11.

⑤ Venuti, Lawrence. *The Scandals of Translation: Towards an Ethics of Difference.* London and New York: Routledge, 1998, p. 11.

conceits，Jin has already answered the editor's sardonic question. He has engendered a form of linguistic deterritorialization by adapting Chinese lines into English lyrics and by imbuing oft-quoted lines by Faulkner，Frost，and Emerson with shades peculiar to his own struggle as an émigré writer，thereby inflecting "standard" lexicons with singular tonalities. Weaving Chinese poetry into English texts and infusing an immigrant sensibility into the common understanding of the American literary canon dissolve cultural borders，keeping the ethnic legacy alive while expanding the American heritage. [1]

Venuti's theory of foreignization as resistance is theoretically powerful in resisting the dominance of Anglo-American centrism and introducing new elements to "Standard English" and Anglophone culture，yet it fails to draw the support of average readers，reviewers，and publishers who still favor fluent translation.

A Short Summary

In this chapter，we've discussed the influence of ideology on translation and explained the theories and key concepts proposed by Bassnett，Lefevere，and Venuti. Consisting of opinions and attitudes that are deemed acceptable in a certain society，ideology exerts a considerable influence on translation. Translators usually choose texts that conform to the dominant ideology of the target culture and make adaptations to the contents that are ideologically sensitive. Susan Bassnett regards translation as a cross-cultural activity that needs to fully consider the role of culture. For André Lefevere，translation is an act of rewriting which is manipulated by ideology，poetics，and patronage. Lawrence Venuti advocates the translation of "minor" literary works into English and the use of non-standard English studded with dialects.

Reviewing Questions

1. What is ideology and its influence on translation?

---

[1] Cheung，King-Kok. *Chinese American Literature without Borders*. New York: Palgrave，2016，pp. 248 - 249.

2. How do you understand the cultural turn of translation studies?

3. What is Susan Bassnett's concept of functional equivalence in terms of culture?

4. In what ways are translators manipulated and how are they manipulated?

5. Why does Venuti advocate foreignization?

Chapter 3

Translation of Traditional Chinese Clothing

 Objectives

➢ Understand the aesthetic features of traditional Chinese clothing（TCC）

➢ Understand the relationship between clothing and identity

➢ Understand TCC translation as a form of cross-cultural negotiation

➢ Understand the cultural elements affecting TCC translation

➢ Grasp the strategies，methods，and skills of TCC translation

➢ Be able to maintain a cross-cultural awareness in TCC translation

➢ Be able to translate simple TCC texts into proper English

1. Aesthetic Features of TCC

According to archaeological relics，the earliest fabric clothing in China dated back to the period of Yangshao Culture about 5,000 to 7,000 years ago. During its long history，traditional Chinese clothing（TCC）has been affected by Chinese culture and formed its distinctive aesthetic features.

1.1 Emphasis on social relations

TCC has long been associated with social relations. In *I Ching*（《易经》），it records that "Hwang Tî，Yâo，and Shun（simply）wore their upper and lower garments（as patterns to the people），and good order was secured all under heaven"（皇帝、尧、舜垂衣裳而天下治）.[1] This is supposedly the earliest comment on the relationship between clothing and social order. In ancient China，clothing played an important role in preserving social order. What one wore was not solely based on his/her personal preference；rather，it depended on his/her place in the society and was subject to ritual codes，which were both explicitly stated and tacitly agreed. Zhou Xibao argues that once the ritual and ethical codes for clothing are established，people wear clothes in accordance with these codes and social order naturally ensue.[2] The social and governing function of clothing in ancient China was maintained at the cost of personal preference and one was not at liberty to wear whatever he/she liked，otherwise the social order would be breached and chaos or even disasters might follow. For instance，a peasant wearing a yellow imperial robe would be regarded as a fatal violation of the social hierarchy，which might lead to the imprisonment or execution of the wearer. As a result，the match between one's clothing and his/her social status constituted the primary aesthetic feature of TCC and the style of clothing was of less importance compared with its social function. When Qi Qingfeng，the Prime Minister of the state of Qi drove an exquisite carriage and wore a fancy garment，Shusun Bao commented that "when a man's fancy clothing does not fit his status，disaster will follow"（"服美不称，必以恶终"）.[3] In general，clothing that fits one's social position is regarded beautiful while garment that mismatches one's social status is deemed undesirable.

---

[1] Legge，James，trans. *The I Ching: Book of Changes*（2nd edition）. New York：Dover Publications，1963，pp. 383 – 384.

[2] 周锡保：《中国古代服饰史》，北京：中国戏剧出版社，1984 年，第 3 页。

[3] 杨伯峻：《春秋左传注（下）》，北京：中华书局，2018 年，第 974 页。

1.2   Emphasis on naturalness

Though the official ideology in ancient China placed overriding importance on the social function of clothing, ancient people expressed their love of beauty through the color, pattern, and style of clothes. They incorporated the principle of unity between man and nature in clothes designing and held naturalness as a key aesthetic principle. Nature with its kaleidoscopic scenes, rich hues, and diverse animals and plants is an inexhaustible source of inspiration for people in designing clothes. According to Zhou Xibao, the choice of color reflects people's perception and imitation of the universe. "As the sky before dawn is black, the upper outer garment adopts the color of black, and since the earth is yellow, the lower outer garment is chiefly black."[①] Ancient Chinese also reproduced celestial bodies, natural objects, animals, and plants in the patterns of clothing. The coronation robe of an emperor, for example, was sewn and dyed with colored patterns of the sun, the moon, mountain, dragon, fire, etc. And the Chinese idiom 衣冠禽兽, a derogatory expression meaning "a gentleman in appearance but a beast in conduct" was derived from the fact that the robes of officials in Ming and Qing dynasties were decorated with the patterns of animals like crane, *kylin* (麒麟), and rhino according to the wearers' rankings. Pomegranate skirt (石榴裙) and "hundred birds blouse" also reflect the role of nature in the development of TCC. However, as we've mentioned in the previous section, the color, pattern, and style of clothing were not to be liberally used in the past, they had to conform to the established ethical codes. Take color as an example. Yellow garments used to be the privilege of emperors and the garments of noblemen were usually red, purple, emerald, and crimson. For commoners, they could only wear cool-colored clothes. [②] Ancient Chinese had to satisfy their aesthetic demands for clothing in accordance with the established ethical codes.

1.3   Balance between completeness and variety

Another prominent aesthetic feature of TCC is the balance between completeness and variety. Lan Yu and Qi Jiahua contend that the balance between completeness and variety of TCC originates from ancient Chinese's aesthetic tendency to cover and decorate the body. Unlike Western clothing which is characterized with exposure of the beauty of the body, TCC aims to cover the body with a whole set of garments and accessories. A typical ancient Chinese robe, referred to as 深衣 in Chinese, was

---

① 周锡保:《中国古代服饰史》,北京:中国戏剧出版社,1984 年,第 2 页。
② 兰宇,祁嘉华:《中国服饰美学思想研究》,西安:三秦出版社,2006 年,第 13 - 14 页。

usually made as a whole piece and covered the entire body, achieving a sense of uniformity and completeness. Even a set of garments consisting of the upper garment and the lower one aimed to realize a sense of uniformity. The sizes, colors, and patterns of the upper and lower garments are usually so well matched that they achieve an aesthetic balance between completeness and variety. [①]

Going with the main garments are various other items and accessories. In the Ming dynasty, for example, a bride usually wore a phoenix coronet, an embroidered vest, a red veil, a pair of red embroidered shoes, bracelets, and various other accessories to match the main wedding garment which usually consisted of a red round-collar blouse and a red pleated skirt. These assorted pieces formed a complete set of well-matched attire for the wedding, also showing a balance between completeness and variety.

The three basic aesthetic features of TCC coexist and interact with each other, forming the aesthetic tradition of TCC that values fitness, naturalness, completeness, and variety.

2. Clothing and Identity

Clothing is an outward reflection of one's various forms of identity, including but not limited to his/her cultural identity, ethnicity, gender, class and profession.

2.1 Clothing and cultural identity

Clothing is rooted in culture and can be a marker of the wearer's cultural identity. A handy example is from *Bound Feet and Western Dress* by Pang-Mei Natasha Chang, a grandniece of Zhang Youyi who was the ex-wife of Xu Zhimo. In the biographical novel, the author indicates Xu Zhimo's Western cultural orientation by describing his Western dress. When Zhang Youyi went to France to unite with her husband Xu Zhimo, she saw him standing on the Marseilles pier, "dressed in a long, narrow, black wool coat with a white silk scarf around his neck."[②] Xu's Western attire was an outward marker of his cultural orientation. Actually, the title of the novel itself is indicative of the conflict between Chinese culture and Western culture as "bound feet" and "Western dress" are symbolic of ancient Chinese and modern Western cultures respectively. It needs to be pointed out that Zhang Youyi never had bound feet as her mother's attempt at binding her feet was thwarted by her brother. The author

---

① 兰宇,祁嘉华:《中国服饰美学思想研究》,西安:三秦出版社,2006 年,第 14 - 16 页。
② Chang, Pang-Mei. *Bound Feet and Western Dress*. New York: Bantam Books, 1997, p. 103.

deliberately takes advantage of the obstinate and stereotyped association between Chinese women with bound feet to arouse the Western readers' interest by catering to their Orientalist imagination of China.

2.2　Clothing and ethnic identity

Clothing can also be an expression of the wearer's ethnic identity. In China, each minority group has its own traditional ethnic clothing which is bound up with ethnic culture and worn by members of the group to mark their ethnic identity. Take the ethnic costumes of the Miao people as an example. The silver crown and a matching pleated skirt worn by Miao women express the Miao people's worship of the sun and ox as the crown glitters from the center of the sun between the ox horns and the folds of the skirt symbolize sunrays. Another unique costume of the Miao people, "hundred birds blouse" on which is embroidered a dragon with a bird head, is said to narrate a tale of the Miao people. The bird head symbolizes Ji Yu that carried the ancestor of the Miao people to heaven to be granted crop seeds by god when a severe famine happened. As a matter of fact, many Miao garments and accessories are related to certain tales that are central to the origin and history of the Miao people.

2.3　Clothing and gender

The association of clothing with gender is probably as old as the civilized history of mankind. There are tacit dressing codes for men and women and a transgression of them may constitute a violation of gender conventions. In literature, it is not rare to see a character dress as the opposite sex to switch his/her gender identity. In *The Merchant of Venice*, Portia borrows a judge's garment from her brother Doctor Bellario and disguises as a judge to administer the case between Antonio and Shylock. Zhu Yingtai, the female protagonist in *The Butterfly Lovers* (《梁山伯与祝英台》) disguises as a young male scholar by wearing a male scholar's garment and falls in love with Liang Shanbo. Examples like these indicate that clothing is an important marker of one's gender identity and that gender, a social and cultural construct, can be transgressed by switching the gender-based dressing codes.

2.4　Clothing and class

Clothing is also a conspicuous marker of the wearer's class and social status. People are often judged and treated by what they wear. *The Million Pound Note*, a satirical novella by Mark Twain reveals the association between clothing and class. When the protagonist Henry goes into an upscale clothing store in shabby clothes, he is sized by the snobbish clerks as a poor man and receives a cold reception. When he produces the hundred bank note, however, the clerks change their attitude immediately and serve him ingratiatingly. The association between clothing and class was also expressed by Du Fu in "Satire on Fair Ladies" (《丽人行》). The poet described the exceedingly luxurious and extravagant garments of rich beauties in Chang'an.

> Embroidered with peacocks and unicorns in gold, /Their dress in rich silks shines so bright when spring is old. /What do they wear on the head? /Emerald pendant leaves hang down in silver thread./What do you see from behind? / How nice-fitting are their waistbands with pearls combined.
>
> 绣罗衣裳照暮春,蹙金孔雀银麒麟。头上何所有? 翠微匐叶垂鬓唇。背后何所见? 珠压腰衱稳称身。[1]

By highlighting the lavish clothing of the rich beauties, Du Fu criticized their extravagant and dissipated lifestyle.

2.5 Clothing and profession

Speaking of the relationship between clothing and profession, we will probably think of uniforms and their wearers—military uniforms for soldiers, white gowns for doctors, and school uniforms for students. The clothes people wear are indicative of their professions. In "Kung I-Chi" (《孔乙己》), Lu Xun satirized Kung I-Chi's pedantry by insinuating the disjunction between his self-purported profession and his pecuniary condition. "Kung was the only long-gowned customer to drink his wine standing."[2](孔乙己是站着喝酒而穿长衫的唯一的人。) A long gown in ancient China indicated the wearer's identity as a scholar who, required by his scholarly demeanor and dignity would sit to leisurely sip the wine. Kung I-Chi, however, due to his dire poverty had to drink the wine standing and on credit, yet still wearing a long gown to express his adherence to the outdated identity of a traditional scholar. Similarly, fans of *Harry Potter* will not fail to note that Harry wears a black robe to show his wizard identity.

3. TCC Translation as an Activity of Cross-Cultural Negotiation

Since clothing is inseparable from culture, TCC translation is a typical form of

---

① 杜甫:《杜甫诗选》,许渊冲译,石家庄:河北人民出版社,2006 年,第 15 页。

② Yang, Hsien-yi & Gladys Yang, trans. *Selected Stories of Lu Hsun*. New York and London: W. W. Norton & Company, 2003, p. 20.

cross-cultural negotiation. In Chapter 2 of this book，we've known that the fundamental idea of cultural translation is that translation is a process of cross-cultural communication which requires the negotiation between SL culture and TL culture. According to Hermans，translation is "both an intellectual category and a cultural practice."[1] Li Manhong argues that as a subsystem embedded in the social，political，economic，and cultural context，translation becomes a manipulative power within the system.[2] When a translation activity takes place，two systems of culture will encounter and a process of negotiation ensues. Ji Xianlin holds the view that a culture，after migrating to a foreign land，usually undergoes a process of adaptation which often means adjustment to the local culture. As TCC is bound up with Chinese culture，the English translation of TCC involves the encounter and negotiation between Chinese culture and Western culture. A capable translator should be a successful mediator between Chinese and American cultures who can render Chinese TCC texts into readable English versions while retaining Chinese culture as much as possible.

4. The Cultural Elements Affecting TCC Translation

TCC translation，as we've analyzed，is a process of cross-cultural negotiation，then what are the major cultural elements affecting TCC translation? Zhang Huiqin and Xu Jun，by making a comparative analysis of Yang Xianyi's and David Hawks' translations of the descriptions of characters' attires in *A Dream of Red Mansions*(《红楼梦》)，contend that mindset，sociocultural background，values，social psychology，and geohistorical tradition are some of the major cultural elements that affect TCC translation.[3]

4.1　Mindset

A translator's mindset can affect his/her approach to translation. For example，Hawks' translation of the sentence "只见头上皆是素白银器，身上月白缎袄，青缎披风，白绫素裙" from Chapter 68 of *A Dream of Red Mansions* was affected by his Western mindset. He assumed that English readers are unfamiliar with the cultural association of the white color in China，so he explained the symbolic meaning of white and

---

[1]　Hermans，Theo. *Translation in Systems: Descriptive and Systemic Approaches Explained*. Manchester：St. Jerome Publishing，1999，p. 141.

[2]　李满红：《布迪厄与翻译社会学的理论建构》，《中国翻译》2007 年第 5 期，第 9 页。

[3]　张慧琴，徐珺：《文化语境视角下的〈红楼梦〉服饰文化汉英翻译探索》，《山东外语教学》2013 年第 5 期，第 98-101 页。

translated the sentence as: "She was dressed in half-mourning, with hair-ornaments of silver and white and a spencer of some black material with a silver thread in it over the palest of pale blue gowns. Underneath the gown she was wearing a plain white satin skirt." [①] Besides explaining the associative meaning of white, Hawks also added other expressions like "black material with a silver thread in it" and "the palest of pale gowns." He was obviously informing English readers of Chinese culture pertaining to clothing through translation. In contrast, Yang Xianyi who was probably influenced by his Chinese mindset, came up with a much simpler translation of the sentence: "Second Sister Yu saw that Hsi-feng had nothing but silver trinkets in her hair and was wearing a blue satin jacket, black satin cape and white silk skirt." [②]

4.2　Sociocultural background

Another factor affecting TCC translation is the sociocultural background of TCC as many TCC items have their origins in certain sociocultural contexts. For instance, the 翡翠撒花洋绉裙 worn by Wang Xifeng（王熙凤）in Chapter 3 of *A Dream of Red Mansions* was translated differently by Yang Xianyi and Hawks due to their different understandings of the term 洋绉. Some scholars argue that 洋绉 derives its name from the imitation of Japanese patterns and colors in silk garments that are of a domestic origin while others contend that 洋绉 refers to silk of top quality as any precious article during the reign of Emperor Daoguang（道光）, be it imported or domestic, was denominated by the character 洋. Yang translated the garment as "kingfisher-blue crepe patterned with flowers" probably because he opted for the former meaning of 洋绉 and deemed it unnecessary to translate the character 洋; whereas Hawks decided on the latter and put it as "imported silk crepe embroidered with flowers" to highlight its rarity and foreign origin. [③]

4.3　Values

Values can also affect translators' treatment of TCC texts. As values are rich in connotations and can be defined from various perspectives like economy, culture, and mathematics, we limit our discussion of the influence of values on translation in terms

---

① Hawks, David, trans. *The Story of the Stone* (Vol. 3). Shanghai: Shanghai Foreign Language Education Press, 2014, p. 417.

② Yang, Xianyi & Gladys Yang, trans. *A Dream of Red Mansions* (Vol. 2). Beijing: Foreign Languages Press, 1994, p. 473.

③ Yang, Xianyi & Gladys Yang, trans. *A Dream of Red Mansions* (Vol. 1). Beijing: Foreign Languages Press, 1994, p. 38; Hawks, David, trans. *The Story of the Stone* (Vol. 1). New York: Penguin Books, 1973, p. 91.

of economy and culture. 石青银鼠褂 worn by Wang Xifeng, for instance，was translated as "turquoise cape lined with white squirrel" by Yang Xianyi and "jacket lined with ermine" by Hawks.① Hawks' translation is probably affected by his value that ermine is more expensive than squirrel. Compared with Hawks' translation which can be justified，Yang's translation is more faithful to the original text. Another example concerns the translation of 紫羯绒褂 worn by Wang Xifeng. Yang and Hawks put it as "purple woolen gown" and "purplish woolen gabardine" respectively.② Yang's translation may mislead English readers to believe that the gown is made of wool，which actually is not. On the other hand，Hawks' translation reveals the influence of British culture，as gabardine is a British garment originating in southern Britain in the 19th century. Neither Yang's nor Hawks' translation，according to Zhang Huiqin and Xu Jun is faithful to the original text. They propose a new translation—"purple precious fur or wethers."③

4.4 Social psychology

Social psychology studies the psychological activities of individuals or groups in a social context. Humans are "social animals" and their reading expectations are conditioned by social context. For average English readers，they expect to read translations that are concise and smooth as pointed out by Venuti. Redundant translation resulted from the translator's personal style or act of adding cultural information unnecessarily or immoderately may incur the readers' aversion. For example，in his translation of "只见头上皆是素白银器，身上月白缎袄，青缎披风，白绫素裙"，Hawks added a few expressions like "half-mourning" and "the palest of pale，" which ignore the target readers' reading expectations and may prove to be an act of painting the lily.

4.5 Geohistorical tradition

The formation of TCC tradition goes through a process of cultural interaction and integration. Chinese readers are familiar with the story of 胡服骑射 which tells King

---

① Yang，Xianyi & Gladys Yang，trans. *A Dream of Red Mansions* （Vo. 1）. Beijing：Foreign Languages Press，1994，p. 38；Hawks，David，trans. *The Story of the Stone* （Vol. 1）. New York：Penguin Books，1973，p. 91.

② Yang，Xianyi & Gladys Yang，trans. *A Dream of Red Mansions* （Vol. 2）. Beijing：Foreign Languages Press，1994，p. 152；Hawks，David，trans. *The Story of the Stone* （Vol. 2）. Shanghai：Shanghai Foreign Language Education Press，2014，p. 631.

③ 张慧琴，徐珺:《文化语境视角下的〈红楼梦〉服饰文化汉英翻译探索》,《山东外语教学》2013 年第 5 期,第 100 页。

Wuling of Zhao's daring reformation of promoting Hu costumes among soldiers to improve the combative power of the Zhao army. And portraits，paintings，sculptures，historical records，and literature all reveal that the clothing of the Tang dynasty was heavily influenced by the clothing of the Hu people. Likewise，the garments of the Qing dynasty were essentially based on the traditional clothing of the Manchu people. In Chapter 6 of *A Dream of Red Mansions*，the 紫貂昭君套 worn by Wang Xifeng also implies the relationship between clothing and geohistory. 昭君套 derives its name from Wang Zhaojun who supposedly wore a hood when she was sent to marry the leader of the Huns for peace and the hood thereafter was referred to as 昭君套. However，neither Yang nor Hawks mentioned "昭君" in their translations，failing to reproduce the geohistorical factor in the original text. Given this，Zhang Huiqin and Xu Jun tentatively come up with a retranslation of the garment—"the dark sable Zhao Jun styled hood" to reconstruct the geohistorical context of it. [1]

5. The Strategies, Methods, and Skills of TCC Translation

As we've discussed，TCC translation is a process of cross-cultural negotiation that involves the mediation between SL culture and TL culture，and between fidelity and readability. In other words，translators should translate TCC texts in such a way as to make them understandable to English readers and retain their original cultural elements as much as possible. Sometimes when there is irreconciliation between readability and fidelity，translators have to balance between them and make their own choices. Let's illustrate this with Yang's and Hawks' translations of 袄，a major garment in TCC. Yang translated it as "jacket." Although "jacket" is a faithful linguistic transference of 袄，the connotations of "jacket" and 袄 are different. The former refers to a short coat with long sleeves and the latter denotes a garment with unique Chinese characteristics. By translating 袄 into "jacket，" the original cultural connotation of 袄 is lost. Hawks' translation of it as "dress" also results in the loss of the cultural uniqueness of 袄. It's clear that both Yang's and Hawks' translations of 袄 are understandable for English readers，but the original cultural association of 袄 is left unreproduced. The translation of 袄 as "Chinese *ao*"，according to Zhang Huiqin and Xu Jun may be a better negotiation between Chinese and Western cultures. [2] Translators can use free translation， addition， omission， loan translation，

---

① 张慧琴,徐珺:《文化语境视角下的〈红楼梦〉服饰文化汉英翻译探索》,《山东外语教学》2013 年第 5 期,第 100 页。

② 张慧琴,徐珺:《〈红楼梦〉服饰文化英译策略探索》,《中国翻译》2014 年第 2 期,第 113 页。

transliteration，and translation with illustration to negotiate between cultures in TCC translation.

5.1　Free translation

Free translation，also known as sense-for-sense translation，is "a type of translation in which more attention is paid to producing a naturally reading TT than to preserving the ST wording intact."[①] Free translation does not necessarily mean that translators can do violence to the ST on the pretext of "free." It is free in the sense that translators can break loose from the ST structure or literal meaning and reproduce the real meaning of ST in smooth TL. Free translation is probably the most frequently used method in TCC translation. It consists of understanding and expressing. Translators first make a close reading of the original TCC texts to thoroughly grasp their meanings and then express them in English in a faithful and readable way. Take the translation of the sentence from *The Scholars*(《儒林外史》) "周进看那人时，头戴方巾，身穿宝蓝缎直裰，脚下粉底皂靴" by Yang Xianyi and Gladys Yang as an example. The Yang couple interpreted Wang Hui's apparel in terms of its color，material，style，and social function，and then expressed it in English："He was wearing a scholar's cap, a sapphire-blue gown and black slippers with white soles."[②] This is a typical case of free translation. The translators understood the meanings of 方巾，宝蓝缎直裰，and 粉底皂靴 perfectly well and expressed them in readable English faithfully. Translators who fail to understand these items and use literal translation may translate them as "square kerchief," "sapphire-blue straight gown," and "black slippers with pink soles" which are mistranslations，as 方巾 is a typical headwear for traditional Confucian scholars，"gown" is indeed straight，and 粉底皂靴 have white soles，not pink ones. English translations of descriptions of characters' attires in Chinese classics indicate that free translation is probably the most important and most frequently used method in TCC translation.

5.2　Addition

For some culture-specific terms，translators often use the skill of addition to add cultural information to facilitate readers' understanding. One frequently cited example is the English translation of 班门弄斧—to show off one's proficiency with the ax

---

① Shuttleworth, Mark &. Moira Cowie. *Dictionary of Translation Studies*. London and New York：Routledge，2014，p. 62.

② 吴敬梓:《儒林外史》，杨宪益，戴乃迭译，长沙：湖南人民出版社；北京：外文出版社，1999 年，第 45 页。

before Lu Ban，the master carpenter，in which the identity of Lu Ban is added to help readers figure out the meaning. This is a useful method of introducing SL culture to TL culture and is frequently adopted by translators in TCC translation. For example，in their translation of "应天府尹大人戴着幞头，穿着蟒袍，行过了礼，立起身来，把两把遮阳遮着脸"（"[T]he mayor of Nanjing in sacrificial headdress and serpent-embroidered robe bows，stands up and hides his face behind two umbrellas"）①，the Yang couple added the word "sacrificial" to denote the occasion for the headdress，not only indicating the scene of the story，but also telling readers that the headdress was worn by officials for formal and serious occasions like funerals. Besides，the translation，by interacting with the narration of the novel，can contextualize the cultural implications of 幞头. The translation of 凤冠 can serve as another example. According to Zhang Huiqin and Xu Jun，the cultural connotation of 凤冠 will be lost in the literal translation "phoenix crown" or "phoenix coronet" and the method of addition can be used to substantiate its cultural connotation. Therefore，凤冠 can be translated as "phoenix cornet for a woman of noble rank" or "a headwear for a lady or bride."②

Though an effective way to introduce TCC culture into English，addition should not be used unnecessarily and immoderately，otherwise redundancy or pedantry may ensue. A case in point is Hawks' translation of "只见头上皆是素白银器，身上月白缎袄，青缎披风，白绫素裙" in which he made the unnecessary additions of "black material with a silver thread in it" and "the palest of pale gowns." "Half-mourning" is an acceptable addition as English readers may not be familiar with the cultural association of white in Chinese.

5.3 Omission

Opposite to addition，omission is a process in which some information of the source text is left untranslated either because the information is untranslatable or because the translator deems it's unnecessary to translate it. Hervey and Higgins regard translation as a process "fraught with compromise,"③ and omission is a form of compromise. In TCC translation，omission is not infrequently used because translators believe literal translation of the descriptions of exquisite clothes would slow down the

---

① 吴敬梓：《儒林外史》，杨宪益，戴乃迭译，长沙：湖南人民出版社；北京：外文出版社，1999 年，第 1008 - 1009 页。

② 张慧琴，徐珺：《全球化视域下的服饰文化翻译研究从"头"谈起》，《中国翻译》2012 年第 3 期，第 111 页。

③ Hervey, Sándor & Ian Higgins. *Thinking Translation: A Course in Translation Method: French to English.* London：Routledge，1992，p. 34

pace of narration and not make much sense to English readers. For instance, Egerton Clement omitted several descriptions of the supporting characters' attires in his translation of *The Golden Lotus* (《金瓶梅》). In Chapter 24, the author Lanling Xiaoxiaosheng（兰陵笑笑生）offered a relatively detailed descriptions of the characters' attires:

> 正月十六,合家欢乐饮酒。正面围着石崇锦帐围屏,挂着三盏珠子吊灯,两边摆列着许多妙戏桌灯。西门庆与吴月娘居上坐,其余李娇儿、孟玉楼、潘金莲、李瓶儿、孙雪娥、西门大姐都在两边列坐。都穿着锦绣衣裳,白绫袄儿,蓝裙子。惟有吴月娘穿着大红遍地通袖袍儿,貂鼠皮袄,下面百花裙,头上珠翠堆盈,凤钗半卸。春梅、玉箫、迎春、兰香一般儿四个家乐,在傍撮筝歌板,弹唱灯词。①

Clement omitted the descriptions of setting and attires and translated the quoted excerpt as follows:

> On the sixteenth day of the first month the whole household assembled, with Ximen Qing and Wu Yueniang in the place of honor, and the other ladies all beautifully dressed. The four maids who acted as the musicians of the family played and sang many songs about the lanterns. ②

In his translation, Clement left out the setting and translates the characters' garments simply as "beautifully dressed." Though the method of omission can be justified, we have to point out that it should be cautiously used as it can be an indication of the translator's incompetence.

5.4　Loan translation

Loan translation refers to the process or method in which expressions from TL are loaned to replace expressions in SL. The loaned expressions sometimes are also called equivalents. For instance, "train," "orange," and "trousers" are the English equivalents of 火车, 橙子, and 裤子 respectively. For the translation of non-culture-specific terms, loan translation proves an effective method, but for the translation of culture-loaded terms, loan translation is usually a makeshift one as the equivalents and their counterparts usually possess different cultural connotations. Anyway, loan

---

① 　兰陵笑笑生:《金瓶梅词话》(上册),延边:延边大学出版社,1999 年,第 182 页。
② 　Clement, Egerton, trans. *The Golden Lotus* (Volume I). Hong Kong: Tuttle Publishing, 2011, p. 316.

translation is still used in TCC translation. Take the translation of 簪子 as an example. It is usually translated as "pin" or "hairpin," but the connotations of "pin" and 簪子 are different. The former is usually made of steel and used for fastening objects or materials together, such as hair, necktie, cuff, and lapel; whereas 簪子 is made of various materials like wood, bamboo, jade, ceramic, bone, gold, silver, and copper, and chiefly used for fastening the hair.

5.5 Transliteration

Transliteration, according to Catford, is a process in which "SL graphological units are replaced by TL graphological units." It involves three steps: 1) SL letters are replaced by SL phonological units; 2) The SL phonological units are translated into TL phonological units; and 3) The TL phonological units are converted into TL letters. [1] Transliteration is an important way of introducing TCC items into another culture. For example, the English words "cheongsam" and "satin" are transliterations of the Chinese expressions 长衫 and 泉州 respectively. 长衫 used to be worn by both men and women but later specifically referred to a straight, close-fitting, silk dress with a high neck and slit skirt worn by women, and 泉州 was called "Zaitun" or "Tsinkiang" in the past where silk was exported to the outside world. Transliteration can retain the cultural connotations of the original terms but may obstruct understanding, so it is usually used in TCC translation when the garment is a major TCC item and is well-known to target readers. And annotations are usually provided to help readers understand the transliterated terms. The aforementioned term 袄, a major TCC item worn by political leaders in 2001 APEC meeting in Shanghai can be transliterated as "Chinese *ao*" with the annotation—"an upper garment with linings, a fur upper garment, or a cotton wadded jacket in traditional Chinese clothing." It needs to be pointed out that transliteration is not a major method of TCC translation as many TCC items are too culture-unique and the profuse use of transliteration may make the translation unreadable.

5.6 Translation with illustration

For average English readers, the translations of TCC can be difficult to understand however vivid the descriptions are. To make the translations accessible to target readers, translators can resort to illustration which can provide a powerful visual aid to help concretize the descriptions. According to Gérard Genette, picture is

---

[1] Catford, J. C. *A Linguistic Theory of Translation*. Oxford: Oxford University Press, 1965, p. 66.

an important form of paratext which can help readers gain insight into the text. [1] Some illustrated versions of *A Dream of Red Mansions* provide illustrations of the characters' attires, which can help readers get a direct impression of them. For example, an illustration of Wang Xifeng's attire can interact with the verbal description of it and readers can compare their mental picture derived from verbal description with the illustration.

A Short Summary

In this chapter, we've discussed the aesthetic tradition and translation of TCC. The aesthetic tradition of TCC emphasizes ethics, naturalness, and the balance between completeness and variety. TCC plays a role in maintaining social order, draws inspiration from nature, and uses various items to cover and decorate the body. Clothing is an outward expression of one's identity, such as his/her cultural identity, ethnicity, gender, class, and profession. As clothing is an important aspect of Chinese culture, TCC translation is a form of cross-cultural activity in which SL culture and TL culture are negotiated and factors like mindset, sociocultural background, values, social psychology, and geohistorical tradition can affect TCC translation. Translators can use free translation, addition, omission, loan translation, transliteration, and translation with illustration in the translation of TCC.

Reviewing Questions

1. What are the aesthetic features of TCC?

2. What is the relationship between clothing and the wearer's identity?

3. How do you understand TCC translation as a form of cross-cultural negotiation?

4. What are some of the cultural factors affecting TCC translation?

5. What are some of the methods and skills used in TCC translation?

---

[1] Genette, Gérard. *Paratexts: Thresholds of Interpretation*. Trans. Jane Lewin. Cambridge: Cambridge University Press, 1997, pp. 1 - 2.

Chapter 4

Translation of Chinese Cuisine

 Objectives

➢ Understand the features of Chinese cuisine

➢ Understand the relationship between food and cultural identity

➢ Understand the challenges of Chinese cuisine translation

➢ Be able to translate the names of representative Chinese dishes

➢ Be able to translate simple texts on Chinese cuisine into proper English

➢ Be able to use *Skopos* Theory in Chinese cuisine translation

1. Introduction to Chinese Cuisine

Chinese cuisine has a long history. In *Tao Te Ching*（《道德经》），Lao Zi compares the running of a state to cooking，saying that "running a large kingdom is indeed like cooking small fish"（治大国若烹小鲜）.① And Confucius expresses his views on food and cooking in *Confucian Analects*："He did not dislike to have his rice finely cleaned，nor to have his minced meat cut quite small（食不厌精，脍不厌细）."② The history of Chinese cuisine is also a history of cultural communication. From pre-historical period to the present day，Chinese cuisine has developed over several thousand years and many kinds of food have been introduced into China as different cultures and peoples interact and mingle with each other. Currently，Chinese cuisine，with its long history，intricate cooking methods，and vast array of dishes is regarded as one of the world's largest kingdoms of cuisine，the other two being French cuisine and Turkish cuisine.

Chinese national cuisine emphasizes the qualities of color，flavor，taste，shape，and meaning. A fine national dish is supposed to possess all the five qualities. Take "fried mandarin fish in squirrel shape"（松鼠鳜鱼）as an example. An expertly cooked fried mandarin fish in squirrel shape is tangerine-red in color，fresh-fragrant in flavor，sweet sour in taste，and squirrel-like in shape. It implies the meaning of "more than enough for each year"（年年有余）and "a fish leaping over the dragon gate"（鱼跃龙门，meaning passing competitive examinations）. To prepare high-quality dishes，attention has to be paid to the major elements of cooking—ingredients，cutting technique，heat control，and flavor. Viewers of the popular documentary *A Bite of China*（《舌尖上的中国》）will not fail to recognize the meticulous efforts of cooks who are almost fastidious with the four cooking elements to make sure the "end products" are of the finest quality.

Depending on its origin，flavor，and cooking methods，Chinese cuisine is classified into eight major regional culinary traditions，namely，Anhui cuisine，Fujian cuisine，Guangdong cuisine，Hunan cuisine，Jiangsu cuisine，Shandong cuisine，Sichuan cuisine，and Zhejiang cuisine. Each regional cuisine has its own tradition and representative dishes. Let's briefly introduce each of the eight major culinary

---

① Waley，Arthur. *The Way and Its Power: A Study of the Tao Te Ching and Its Place in Chinese Thought*. New York: Grove Press，Inc.，1958，p. 215.

② Legge，James，trans. *The Chinese Classics: Confucian Analects*，*The Great Learning*，*and The Doctrine of the Mean*. Hong Kong: Hong Kong University Press，1960，p. 232. Confucius expresses many of his views on cooking and eating in Chapter 10 of *Confucian Analects*.

traditions.

1.1　Anhui cuisine

Speaking of Anhui cuisine, we may probably think of "chop suey"（炒杂碎）, a dish related with Li Hongzhang, a native of Anhui and prominent statesman of the Qing dynasty. As Anhui neighbors Jiangsu, Anhui cuisine shares resemblance with Jiangsu cuisine, but it emphasizes more on the use of local herbs and vegetables instead of seafood. "Huizhou stinky mandarin fish"（徽州臭鳜鱼）, "Huizhou chafing dish" （徽州一品锅）, and "Bagongshan tofu"（八公山豆腐）are some of the notable Anhui dishes.

1.2　Fujian cuisine

Fujian cuisine is derived from the cooking style of Fujian. It has a light, soft, tender, and flavorful texture and is known for its emphasis on the umami taste and preserving the original flavor of the main ingredients. The most well-known dish of Fujian cuisine is probably "Buddha jumps over the wall"（佛跳墙）. The dish is prepared by stewing many precious ingredients together like abalone, shark fin, sea cucumber, and Shaoxing wine.

1.3　Guangdong cuisine

Guangdong cuisine, also called Cantonese cuisine, is probably the most well-known cuisine in Chinatown as many early Guangdong immigrants bring the dishes of their hometown to the ethnic enclave. Due to Guangdong's closeness to the sea and the daring spirit of Cantonese, many imported foods and almost all possible edible meats are used in Cantonese cuisine. Cooking methods like steaming, frying, steaming, and braising are employed in preparing Cantonese food which is characterized by a balanced flavor. The representative dishes of Cantonese cuisine include "braised abalone"（焖鲍鱼）, "roasted suckling pig"（烤乳猪）, "roasted squab"（烤乳鸽）, "Cantonese seafood soup"（海皇羹）, etc.

1.4　Hunan cuisine

Hunan cuisine is characterized by a spicy flavor, fresh aroma, and deep color. It relies on the cooking methods of frying, roasting, braising, stewing, and smoking. Some can distinguish the spiciness of Hunan food from that of Sichuan food, believing that Hunan cuisine is dry hot while Sichuan cuisine is numbing hot. "Steamed fish head with diced hot red peppers"（剁椒鱼头）, "steamed multiple preserved hams"（腊味合蒸）, and "Chairman Mao's red braised pork"（毛氏红烧肉）are some of the renowned Hunan dishes.

1.5　Jiangsu cuisine

Jiangsu cuisine，derived from the native cooking styles of Huai'an，Yangzhou，Suzhou，and Nanjing，is known for its soft texture，strict selection of ingredients according to seasons，emphasis on using soup to improve flavor，and attention to the matching color and shape of each dish. Many of the dishes recorded in *A Dream of Red Mansions* belong to Jiangsu cuisine. "Braised pork balls in brown sauce"（红烧狮子头），"boiled duck with salt"（盐水鸭），and "fried mandarin fish in squirrel shape"（松鼠鳜鱼）are some of the typical dishes of Jiangsu cuisine.

1.6　Shandong cuisine

Shandong cuisine is probably the most influential culinary tradition in China. Most modern schools of cuisine in northern China—Beijing，Tianjin，Henan，Hebei，Shanxi，Nei Mongol，and Northeast China are all branches of Shandong cuisine and some household dishes in the vast area we call northern China are also prepared in simplified Shandong methods. Shandong cuisine is characterized by saltiness，umami，exquisite technique at preparing soups，and attention to dining etiquette. "Braised intestines in brown sauce"（九转大肠），"fried carp with sweet and sour sauce"（糖醋鲤鱼），and "fried fish slices with distilled grain sauce"（漕溜鱼片）are some of the representative dishes of Shandong cuisine.

1.7　Sichuan cuisine

Sichuan cuisine is well-known for its spiciness and pungency resulting from the profuse use of hot pepper and garlic. Ginger，sesame paste，and peanuts are also liberally used in Sichuan cuisine. We can make a long list of representative dishes of Sichuan cuisine，such as "hotpot"（火锅），"kung pao chicken"（宫保鸡丁），"mapo tofu"（麻婆豆腐），"twice-cooked pork slices with hot sauce"（回锅肉），and "stir-fried diced chicken with green pepper"（辣子鸡）.

1.8　Zhejiang cuisine

Zhejiang cuisine is noted for its fresh and soft flavor with a mellow fragrance. Its typical features include particularity with ingredients，expert cooking methods，emphasis on the original flavor of ingredients，and exquisite preparation process. "West Lake fish in vinegar gravy"（西湖醋鱼），"braised Dongpo pork"（东坡肉），and "stewed spring bamboo shoots"（油焖春笋）are among the well-known dishes of Zhejiang cuisine.

We need to know that within each culinary tradition，there are sub-culinary traditions and local dishes that are representative of local culture and customs. We associate "braised chicken"（扒鸡）with Dezhou，"vegetable pancakes"（菜煎饼）with Linyi，and "mutton soup"（羊汤）with Heze. The association of a dish with its locality is sometimes so powerful that it influences our perception of people. If someone is from south Jiangsu，we stereotypically perceive him/her as a lover of sweet food and if someone is a native of Guangzhou，we may subconsciously believe that he/she often patronizes a steamed vermicelli roll stall for breakfast.

We also need to note that culinary tradition is influenced by local produces and geographical locations. For example，as Fujian is a major producer of fresh bamboo shoots，bamboo shoots are profusely used in Fujian cuisine to enhance the flavor. Likewise，as Xinyang borders Anhui，the staple food there is rice whereas in other cities of Henan，it is flour. From our discussion，we can find that food is not merely something that sustains life，it is also an important aspect of culture and reflects our identity.

2. Food and Cultural Identity

Food nurtures life and reflects one's cultural identity. Li Yiji（郦食其），a counselor of Liu Bang（刘邦），argued that "to the people，food is heaven"（而民以食为天）. And in English，there is the saying that you are what you eat. Food keeps life going and a proper diet is key to health. It is also a marker of cultural identity. People from the same region will find a shared cultural identity in the food they eat. For example，Sichuan people would find spicy food like hotpot a sticker of their regional cultural identity and Northeasterners would feel the cultural kinship brought by typical Northeastern dishcs like "fried potato，green pepper，and eggplant"（地三鲜），"double-cooked pork slices or fried pork in scoop"（锅包肉），and "stewed chicken with mushroom"（小鸡炖蘑菇）.

Food is also an important means of maintaining the cultural identity of diasporic people. In his memoir *Black Dog of Fate*，Armenian American author Peter Balakian argues that food "was a complex cultural emblem，an encoded script that embodied the long history and collective memory of our Near Eastern culture."[①] Overseas Chinese also regard food as a way of expressing their cultural identity. Chinese American authors，particularly female authors，employ culinary narrative or imagery to

---

① Dalessio，William R. *Are We What We Eat？—Food and Identity in Late Twentieth-Century American Ethnic Literature*. Amherst：Cambria Press，2012，p. 1.

represent the characters' cultural identity. Some characters stick to a Chinese diet to demonstrate their loyalty to Chinese culture. In *Mona in the Promised Land* by Gish Jen, the titular character Mona demonstrates her Chinese identity by telling her Jewish friends' mother that she eats "authentic" Chinese food at home while in *Typical American*, another book by Gish Jen, the protagonist Ralph tries to sever all ties with his cultural past by devouring American food.

Here we encounter a major issue in a cross-cultural context. Can people eat authentic Chinese food in foreign countries? Possibly, but more often than not, "authentic Chinese food" in American cultural context is a pseudo concept as Chinese food is usually adapted to suit local taste and culture. According to Appiah, as different peoples move across national borders, different cultures will inevitably clash, interact, and merge with each other.[①] As an important aspect of Chinese culture, Chinese food in Chinatown is also localized and mixes with American cuisine. Dalessio convincingly argues that the purported "authentic" Chinese food eaten by Mona at home is "Americanized versions of Chinese food, similar to the dishes prepared and eaten by her friends' mother."[②] And "kung pao chicken" in San Francisco Chinatown is likely to be different from its Sichuan counterpart. The same phenomenon occurs in an intra-cultural context. For example, when the spicy cuisine of Sichuan migrates to south Jiangsu, it is usually adapted to satisfy the local people's sweet tongues. Obviously, food is an embodiment of culture and a reflection of cultural identity. The translation of cuisine is a typical cross-cultural activity.

3. The Challenges of Chinese Cuisine Translation

The translation of Chinese cuisine can be a daunting task. Novice translators may find the dish names highly figurative and the descriptions of cuisine too refined. Failure to cope with these challenges may result in mistranslation or superfluous translation.

3.1 Figurative dish names

The names of some Chinese dishes are highly figurative and culturally codified. They rely on people's association and imagination or involve historical figures and their anecdotes. It is difficult to know the ingredients and cooking methods by simply

---

① Appiah, Kwane A. *Cosmopolitanism*. New York and London: W. W. Norton, 2007.
② Dalessio, William R. *Are We What We Eat? —Food and Identity in Late Twentieth-Century American Ethnic Literature*. Amherst: Cambria Press, 2012, p. 6.

looking at the names. Translators who don't bother to check the origins of such dish names may come up with mistranslations. For example，蚂蚁上树，a popular dish in Sichuan and Chongqing，derives its name from the shapes of ingredients as sautéed vermicelli with minced pork resembling tree-climbing ants. In Xuzhou and north Anhui，there is a famous main dish called 霸王别姬. The name not only figuratively reveals the main ingredients—turtle and chicken as 王八 and 姬 are homophones of "turtle" and "chicken," but also alludes to the tragic love story of Xiang Yu and Yu Ji who after being defeated by Liu Bang，committed suicide. Novice translators may take dish names literally and produce Chinglish translations. For example，"husband and wife's lung slice," "roasted lion head," and "rolling donkey" are mistranslations of 夫妻肺片，红烧狮子头，and 驴打滚 respectively.

Let's get off the subject for a while to differentiate Chinglish from China English. Chinglish is defined by Pinkham as "that misshapen, hybrid language that is neither English nor Chinese but that might be described as 'English with Chinese characteristics.'"[1] The Chinglish examples analyzed by Pinkham are not extreme ones like "take notice of safe"（注意安全），"bake the cellphone"（烘手机），and "people mountain people sea"（人山人海）. Users of Chinglish usually create a Chinese-style syntax with English words but misuse the rules and conventions of "Standard English." Chinglish is not always grammatically incorrect，but it is unacceptable and should be avoided. Unlike Chinglish which misses the mark in its imitation of "Standard English," China English，based on "Standard English," uses lexis and discourses related with Chinese culture.[2] For example，"dragon boat," "Mid-Autumn Festival," and "red envelop" are China English expressions. They are bound up with Chinese culture and generally accepted.

3.2　Decorative or refined language style

Another challenge of Chinese cuisine translation concerns the language used in describing dishes and the culture behind them. Authors or compilers of publicity materials on Chinese cuisine tend to load their writings with references to history，customs，anecdotes，and poetry，making the language highly decorative and culturally codified. For example，"Culture，the Soul of Huaiyang Cuisine" by Ding Jiemin is soaked with Chinese culture and studded with quotations：

文化是淮扬菜的根，淮扬菜的传承和发展一直和文化密不可分。作为中国四大

---

① 平卡姆，姜桂华：《中式英语之鉴》，北京：外语教学与研究出版社，1998 年，第 1 页。

② Eaves, Meagan. "English, Chinglish or China English?" *English Today* 27（2011）：64 - 70.

传统菜系之一的淮扬菜,历史悠久,早在夏代"淮夷百鱼"已是贡品。隋唐时期,
京杭大运河开通,时人或登舟南下,或驱马北上,一时商贾云集,淮扬菜也随着南
客北旅传播九州。有关淮扬菜的文献记载和野史轶事,不胜枚举:西汉汉赋大师
枚乘写过一篇著名的辞赋《七发》,里面有一段吴客劝楚太子品尝天下美食的文
字:"雏牛之腴,菜以笋蒲;肥狗之和,冒以山肤。楚苗之食,安胡之饭,搏之不解,
一啜而散。于是使伊尹煎熬,易牙调和,熊蹯之臑,勺药之酱,薄耆之炙,鲜鲤之
脍,秋黄之苏,白露之茹。兰英之酒,酌以涤口。山梁之餐,豢豹之胎。小饭大
歡,如汤沃雪。此亦天下之至美也。"这篇文字中涉及的佳肴有:笋蒲配小牛腹
腴,石耳狗肉羹,炖熊掌,五味调和的酱,烤兽脊肉薄片,鲤鱼脍,烹野鸡,烹豹胎,
烹秋蔬等等,这些均是淮扬菜的精品。①

The various dish names in the quoted passage and the excerpt of prose poem by Mei Sheng can pose a challenge for novice translators, but the message underlying the refined language is simple and clear: Huaiyang cuisine has a long history, rich cultural tradition, and many exquisite dishes. Senior translators may seek theoretical support from *skopos* theory and convey the key message of the excerpt, which we will discuss later.

4. The Methods of Chinese Cuisine Translation

Transliteration and free translation are often used in translating Chinese cuisine.

4.1 Transliteration

As the names of some Chinese dishes are culture-loaded, transliteration is frequently used in translating them into English, such as "kung pao chicken," "mapo tofu," and "chow mein" (炒面). Transliteration of dish names is usually used when the dishes are well-known to target readers and/or when free translation of them is difficult or undesirable. Take "chop suey" (炒杂碎) as an example. It is a famous dish in Chinatown and many foreigners go to Chinatown to have a taste of it. If we use free translation and list the assorted ingredients and cooking methods of the dish, the result might be undesirable, if not disastrous. Transliteration utilizes the power of convention and is sometimes used in combination with annotation. If some dishes are transliterated, we need to make people agree or know that the transliterated names signify the specific dishes or juxtapose transliteration with annotation. For example,

① 丁解民:《文化是淮扬菜的魂》,《淮扬美食传奇》,万相龙,主编,哈尔滨:黑龙江人民出版社,2006 年,
第 1 页。

麻婆豆腐 is transliterated as "mapo tofu" and an annotation of it—"stewed tofu with minced pork in pepper sauce" is added to help express the ingredients and cooking method of the dish.

4.2　Free translation

Compared with transliteration，free translation is more often used in translating Chinese dish names to reduce obstacles to cross-cultural communication. As free translation often involves the process of re-expressing the source text in idiomatic target language，translators can break loose from the phonetics，lexis，syntax，and structure of the original text so long as the meaning of the original text is faithfully reproduced. As for dish names，the major information concerns ingredients and cooking method，so a free translation of dish name often focuses on presenting the key ingredients and cooking method of the dish. For example，"braised pork ball in brown sauce，" a free translation of 红烧狮子头，reveals the key ingredients—pork and brown sauce and the major cooking method—braising. And the ingredients and major cooking method of 咸水鸭，a well-known local dish of Nanjing，is indicated by the freely translated name "boiled duck with salt. " For free translation of dish names to be successful，translators need to check the recipes if the ingredients and major cooking methods are not stated in the dish names. ①

5. The Application of *Skopos* Theory in Chinese Cuisine Translation

Skopos theory was initially proposed by German scholar Hans J. Vermeer in the late 1970s and gained wide academic attention in 1984 when *Towards a General Theory of Translational Action: Skopos Theory Explained* was published. The fundamental tenet of *skopos* theory，as indicated by the Greek word *skopos*，meaning aim or purpose，is that the purpose of translation justifies its process. According to Reiß and Vermeer，three assumptions constitute the groundwork behind the general theory of translational action：1）A translational action is a function of its *skopos*；2）A translational action is an offer of information produced in a target culture and language about an offer of information produced in a source culture and language；and 3）The target information offer is represented as a transfer which simulates a source

---

① The English translations of some Chinese dish names are inconsistent and not standardized. For example，清蒸鲈鱼 is translated as "steamed perch with scallion and black beans，" "steamed perch with mixed sauce，" or "steamed sea bass. " These translations reflect the differences in major ingredients and accessories.

information offer.① It is clear that Reiß and Vermeer advocate a functional approach to translation. For translators, the paramount criterion guiding their decisions is the *skopos* and their translation actions can be justified so long as the intended purpose is achieved.

To make translation more congruent with translation process, Reiß and Vermeer classify texts into three types based on their functions—informative texts, expressive texts, and operative texts. The chief function of an informative text is to pass information and in a typical operative text, the author "wants the information offer to convey persuasively organized content in order to encourage the recipient to act in accordance with the intentions of the text sender (or of the commissioner)."② Introductory or descriptive texts on Chinese cuisine, recipes excluded, usually are amalgamations of informative texts and operative texts. They carry the dual aims of conveying information, such as dish names, ingredients, and cooking methods and persuading the readers to have a try.

Let's go back to the excerpt from "Culture, the Soul of Huaiyang Cuisine." In this excerpt, the author not only tells readers the history and specialties of Huaiyang cuisine, but also takes advantage of the appellative function of language by quoting from classic to make the reader's mouth watery and heart itchy. Reiß and Vermeer argue that "the function of the target text or any of its parts" can be "intentionally changed in order to produce a target text appropriate for a specific purpose or use."③ For average English readers, the specific historical development of Huaiyang cuisine is not their primary concern, nor do they care much about the dietary therapy prescribed in "Seven Elicitations" (《七发》). A re-expression of the key information contained in the excerpt will suffice, so the excerpt can be converted into a short informative text.

◈ A Short Summary

In this chapter, we've introduced Chinese cuisine and discussed its translation. Chinese cuisine emphasizes the qualities of color, flavor, taste, shape, meaning and the elements of ingredients, cutting technique, heat control, and flavor. There are

---

① Reiß, Katharina & Hans J. Vermeer. *Towards a General Theory of Translational Action: Skopos Theory Explained*. Trans. Christiane Nord. London and New York: Routledge, 2014, p. 94.

② Reiß, Katharina & Hans J. Vermeer. *Towards a General Theory of Translational Action: Skopos Theory Explained*. Trans. Christiane Nord. London and New York: Routledge, 2014, p. 182.

③ Reiß, Katharina & Hans J. Vermeer. *Towards a General Theory of Translational Action: Skopos Theory Explained*. Trans. Christiane Nord. London and New York: Routledge, 2014, p. 190.

eight major traditions of Chinese cuisine and each of them possesses distinctive features in terms of ingredient selection, cooking method, and preparation process. Chinese cuisine is rooted in Chinese culture and the translation of it is a cross-cultural activity. Some dish names, as culture-loaded terms, are highly figurative and the language used in introducing Chinese cuisine is sometimes too refined, creating difficulties for translation. To cope with these difficulties, translators can use transliteration and free translation. Some dish names can be transliterated and others can be rendered into English by presenting the main ingredients and cooking methods. Based on *skopos* theory, texts on Chinese cuisine, be it informative, operative, or a hybridity of the two, can be converted and condensed into shorter informative texts so long as the key information is reproduced.

◇ Reviewing Questions

1. What are the qualities, elements, and major traditions of Chinese cuisine?

2. What are the main characteristics and representative dishes of each culinary tradition?

3. What is the relationship between food and cultural identity?

4. What are the challenges of Chinese cuisine translation?

5. What are the methods used in Chinese cuisine translation?

6. What is *skopos* theory and its application in Chinese cuisine translation?

Chapter 5

Translation of Traditional Chinese Architecture

 Objectives

➢ Understand the basic features of traditional Chinese architecture（TCA）

➢ Understand the relationship between TCA and Chinese culture

➢ Understand the challenges of translating TCA terminology

➢ Grasp the principles，methods，and skills of translating TCA terminology and texts

➢ Be able to introduce TCA to English readers

1. The Basic Features of TCA

Shelter is a life necessity and an important aspect of culture. Archaeological discoveries reveal that Chinese architecture formed its unique system as early as the 15th century BC when the people of the Shang dynasty had built cities and houses. For the next over 3,500 years, the system has been maintained and perfected, and its influence has reached Japan, Korea, Vietnam, Myanmar, etc. Currently, Chinese architecture is acclaimed as one of the world's greatest architectural systems and many ancient Chinese constructions, such as the Palace Museum, Shenyang Imperial Palace, the Potala Palace, and Classical Gardens of Suzhou enjoy great prestige in the world. Then, what are the basic features of traditional Chinese architecture (TCA)? According to Liang Sicheng, TCA possesses nine basic features. [①]

1.1 Composition of a single construction

A single traditional Chinese construction typically consists of three parts—the groundwork, the room, and the roof. Take an average room as an example. The groundwork is constructed by laying bricks or slabs on rammed earth to withstand the weight. It serves as the foundation of the construction. The middle part is the main structure and upon the main structure is the slope roof which usually adopts the shape of bird's wing for the purpose of aesthetics and rainwater drainage.

1.2 Layout

A typical traditional Chinese house is usually made up of several rooms and auxiliary constructions, such as a winding corridor, wing rooms, and a hall way. The rooms and auxiliaries are constructed around a courtyard in a bilaterally symmetric way along the axis and the major rooms are designed to face the south for maximum exposure to sunlight. This layout principle is also adopted in urban planning. The courtyard, usually paved with bricks or pebbles, are planted with trees, flowers, and grass and serve as an outer living room for daily activities.

1.3 Structure

Unlike modern buildings that use steel-concrete composite structure, traditional Chinese buildings rely on timber structure. A typical timber structure consists of two pillars and over two layers of crossbeams and different timber structures are connected

---

① 梁思成:《拙匠随笔》,北京:北京出版社,2016 年,第 91－97 页。

by square columns and purlins. Walls are also erected between pillars to part the space and the weight of the house falls upon the timber structure. Such a structural design meets the requirements of structural mechanics and are quite sturdy and durable. Luoxingdun, a construction consisting of a pagoda, a temple, and a memorial archway that was built over 1,000 years ago in Poyang Lake lies beneath the water most of the time and resurfaces in winter when the water level drops, attesting to the sturdiness and durability of traditional Chinese constructions.

1.4   Brackets

In TCA, a system of brackets is usually inserted between the top of a column and a crossbeam to reduce the shearing force at the joint of the column and crossbeam. Usually, a *dou* （斗）, or bracket set is used to strengthen the tenon of two crossbeams and an arched timber structure is placed upon the bracket set, forming a bracket system, which is profusely applied in timber and masonry structures. As a distinctive feature of TCA and specimen of craftsmanship, bracket system exerts its influence on Chinese culture. We use 丁一卯二 to describe accuracy and 斗榫合缝 to acknowledge superb artisanship.

1.5   Purlin raising

As the crossbeams of a timber structure are multi-layered with the upper layer shorter than the lower one, the wooden piers between two layers gradually increase in height. This is referred to as purlin raising, which results in the incremental slope of roof from the overhang to the ridge.

1.6   Roof

Roof occupies a special place in TCA. Chinese architectural system regards the roof as an important aesthetic element and talented artisans give full play to their intelligence and ability in utilizing the decorative function of roof to the maximum. To capture the magnificence of a traditional construction, writers always eulogize the elaborate roof with highly decorated and figurative language. Du Mu's description of the E Pang Palace is a typical example:

At each five steps there stood a storeyed building, and at each ten steps, there stood a hall, with corridors winding like waving silk, and the projecting eaves turning high up like birds' bills. Each of the structures possessed its vantage of ground; but they were all ingeniously interlocked together, or one set against another. Some were domed, and others were curved. The courts were like so many cells in the beehive; and of the lofty eave-drippings who can tell how many millions they were. （五步一楼，十步一阁；廊腰缦回，檐牙高啄；各抱地势，钩心斗角。盘盘焉，囷囷焉，蜂房水涡，矗不知其几千万落。）①

In his portrayal of the palace, Du Mu paid special attention to the exquisiteness and diversity of roofs, likening them to birds' bills and pointing out their various shapes.

1.7 Color and colored drawings

TCA is bold in using color and colored drawings. The pillars, gates, windowpanes, and walls are usually painted red as the color red is associated with fortune, happiness, and good luck in Chinese culture. The dominant hue of the Forbidden City is red and the Chinese phrase "vermillion gate" （朱门） has become a symbol of rich and powerful families as indicated by the poetic lines: "The mansion burst with wine and meat; /The poor die frozen on the street." （朱门酒肉臭，路有冻死骨）②

Besides the bold use of color, colored drawings are also created to decorate various parts of the timber structures, stone pillars, and other components of traditional Chinese constructions as attested to by the Chinese idiom "carved beams and painted rafters" （雕栏画栋） and the poetic line by Li Yu: "Carved balustrades and marble steps must still be there, /But rosy faces cannot be as fair." （雕栏玉砌应犹在，只是朱颜改）. ③ The well-known story of Shen Zhuliang, popularly known as Ye Gong also has something to do with colored drawings. To show his admiration of dragons, Ye Gong painted or carved vivid and ferocious-looking dragons on every possible part of his house. However, when a real dragon descended to pay him a tribute, the dragon-adorer was scared out of his wits. Though the satirical story is usually used to express "professed love of what one actually fears," it nevertheless indicates the popularity of colored drawings in TCA.

1.8 Artistic treatment of component junctions

The artistic treatment of component junctions is another prominent feature of TCA. In traditional Chinese constructions, the junctions are usually processed according to their appearances and shapes to bring out their decorative effects. For example, the beam head is often molded to resemble a grasshopper's head and the

---

① These lines are translated by Pan Zhengying （潘正英）.
② 许渊冲译：《杜甫诗选》，石家庄：河北人民出版社，2006年，第18-19页。
③ 许渊冲选译：《许渊冲译唐宋词一百首》，北京：中译出版社，2021年，第41页。

lower end of the lever is processed in the shape of chrysanthemum. As a matter of fact, almost every conceivable part of a traditional Chinese construction, such as the door, the windowpane, the door knocker, and the tiles are painted or carved with patterns for aesthetic purposes. Such treatment reflects the aesthetic orientation of TCA.

1.9　Building materials

The uniqueness of TCA is also embodied in building materials. As we have mentioned in Section 1.7 of this chapter, architects and artisans of TCA are bold in using color and colored patterns. They also maximize the decorative potential of colored glazed bricks and tiles by carving patterns on timber, slabs, and wall bricks. According to archaeologists, simple patterns had been carved on bricks as early as the Shang dynasty and in the Qin and Han dynasties, the technique of baking bricks and tiles had attained such a height that the later generations use the expression 秦砖汉瓦 to show the glory of architectural ornament of the two dynasties.

The nine features and the accompanying techniques of TCA are abided by architects and artisans and well accepted by the people. Liang Sicheng believes that they form the "grammar" of TCA as various architectural components are arranged and joined together to form a solid construction according to architectural principles, just like words are strung together to form a neat sentence on the basis of grammatical rules. [1] Though there are basic rules of TCA "grammar," architects and artisans can make adaptations to them and exercise their personal gift much in the same way as writers give play to their individual talent and make innovations to the literary tradition.

2.　The Relationship Between TCA and Chinese Culture

The primary function of housing is for shelter, but as it interacts with inhabitants and the larger sociocultural context, it grows to be an organic part of Chinese culture and reflects the philosophical thoughts and aesthetic values of Chinese people. The site, layout, and landscape design of TCA reflect the traditional thought of harmony between man and nature and Confucian ethical relations. For example, Xianyang Palace of the Qin dynasty was constructed in imitation of the Celestial Palace as the emperor was believed to be son of heaven. The architects situated the palace on a site that resembled the astrological location of Ziwei Palace where the celestial emperor

---

① 梁思成:《拙匠随笔》,北京:北京出版社,2016 年,第 97 页。

supposedly lived and designed the gates and interior palaces accordingly[1], reflecting a primitive perception of the universe and the traditional thought of unity between man and nature. TCA is also influenced by Confucian ideas, particularly the hierarchical ethical relations of Confucianism. In a traditional house, the rooms are assigned to family members according to their ethical status. The typical practice is that the main room is allocated to the elders while the wing rooms are dwelled by the younger ones. According to Wang Guowei, quadrangle dwelling is the ideal family residence in ancient China as it can sustain family ties and maintain ethical relations. [2] It's clear that traditional Chinese houses reflect people's inclination to be close with nature and embody the influence of Confucian ethics.

Traditional Chinese architecture also indicates people's aesthetic taste. Tang Xiaoxiang discusses the aesthetics of folk houses, believing that the beauty of a typical folk house lies in its model, conception, and surroundings. [3] As China is a vast multi-ethnic country, there are many ethnic and local style houses with various unique models that are unseen in other parts of the world, such as the Haka round houses, stilted buildings, earthen buildings, and cave dwellings, all of which reflect the geographical conditions of different localities and the aesthetic inclinations of different peoples. Conceptual beauty of folk houses usually relies on the symbolic and associative meanings of structural components, language, and patterns.

Let's take Cangpo, a historic village in Zhejiang as an example. The layout of the village alludes to the "four treasures of the Chinese study." The plane of the village is rectangular, symbolizing paper. The pond in the south of the village and the slab on the bank are symbols of inkstone and inkstick. And an east-west running street named Bi Jie (笔街), literally meaning "brush street" and the mountain opposite to it, if viewed far, looks like a brush resting on the holder. The villagers' aesthetic taste and love of knowledge are symbolically expressed by the layout of the village.

The conceptual beauty of a folk house is also coded in decorative patterns as people often resort to the associative and symbolic meanings of animals, plants, and homonymous characters to express their wishes for wealth, health, and good fortune. For instance, the pattern of "two mandarin ducks tumbling merrily about in the water"（鸳鸯戏水）is pasted or carved on windowpanes to symbolize an affectionate couple and the pattern of "carps jumping over the dragon gate"（鱼跃龙门）is etched on the door heads of private schools and Confucian temples to express scholars' wish of

---

① 孙星衍:《三辅黄图》,庄逵吉校,上海:商务印书馆,1936 年,第 3 页。

② 王国维:《王国维手定观林堂集》,黄爱梅点校,杭州:浙江教育出版社,2014 年,第 56 - 57 页。

③ 唐孝祥:《传统民居建筑审美的三个维度》,《南方建筑》2009 年第 6 期,第 82 - 85 页。

passing the imperial examination.

Surroundings are another aspect that embodies the beauty of traditional Chinese folk houses. Many celebrated ancient towns and villages like Zhouzhuang in Suzhou and Hongcun in Huangshan blend with the natural surroundings and are known for their breathtaking beauty. The appellation "ancient village" itself can evoke a picturesque scene of running rivers, stone bridges, mossed alleys, and bamboo groves in the mind of Chinese readers.

From the above introduction and analysis, we know that TCA has its distinctive features and is an indispensable aspect of Chinese culture that codifies the philosophical views and aesthetic tastes of the Chinese people. The translation of TCA, like the translation of Chinese clothing and cuisine, is a typical cross-cultural activity that demands the negotiation between SL culture and TL culture.

3. The Challenges of TCA Translation

The challenges of TCA translation are multifarious. From a lexical perspective, TCA, as a highly specialized field, contains a large number of terms that are culturally unique and have no proper English equivalents. For instance, 泥道栱, 瓜子栱, and 令栱, which are architectural terms coined in the Song dynasty and recorded in the earliest TCA classic *Yingzao Fashi* (《营造法式》, literally meaning methods of construction) cannot be replaced by English words without losing their original meanings. From a stylistic perspective, TCA texts, particularly those for a tourism or publicity purpose, tend to use highly decorative and figurative language, as is the case with publicity materials on Chinese cuisine. Chinese readers are probably familiar with "Classical Gardens of Suzhou" by Ye Shengtao which abounds with elaborate sentences describing the beauty of classical gardens. These sentences, if they are to be reproduced faithfully and stylistically, would prove a daunting task for translators. The difficulty of TCA translation also lies in the lack of translation corpus. Unlike the translation of ancient Chinese philosophical classics and poetry which has a large body of translated texts to refer to, the English translations of TCA texts are meager and even *Yingzao Fashi*, the most well-known Chinese architectural classic by Northern Song architect Li Jie remains to be translated. Translators venturing into TCA translation are likely to feel lonely but rewarding as they are farming a land that has not been well cultivated by predecessors. Now, let's analyze these challenges and discuss some of the feasible solutions.

3.1 Terminology

As we have mentioned，TCA has its own set of terms that can pose a challenge to translators，because the terms are sometimes inconsistent and puzzling. The same architectural components，for example，are referred to by different names in different parts of China. Eave tiles in south China are called 滴水 while in north China，they are referred to as 瓦当. And 美人靠，a long wooden armchair in Anhui style architecture is accorded the appellation "吴王靠" in Suzhou. These inconsistencies need to be resolved through standardization，otherwise confusion will arise and the translation of TCA and its international dissemination will be hampered.

Like Chinese dish names，TCA terms are oftentimes figurative and readers will probably be at a loss by focusing on the literal meanings. Who would understand the meanings of 雀替，惹草，and 吻兽 except people engaged in TCA? These terms require translators either to be familiar with TCA or do some research to ascertain their references. A literal translation of these terms without proper explanations is likely to create trouble for cross-cultural understanding.

The translation of TCA terminology is also challenging in that translators do not have many parallel texts to refer to. A review reveals that translation activities in the field of TCA are scarce and that very few TCA texts have been put into English. [①] The earliest English text on TCA is *A Pictorial History of Chinese Architecture* (《图像中国建筑史》)，a Chinese-English bilingual book written by Liang Sicheng and the translations of TCA texts have remained scarce. In 1988，British scholar Alison Hardie published her translation of *The Craft of Gardens: The Classic Chinese Text on Garden Design* (《园冶》)，a book on garden-making by the Ming dynasty architect Ji Cheng (计成). Shanghai Jiaotong University Press has published a series of translated books on TCA in the south of the lower reaches of the Yangtze River，such as *Canal Towns South of the Yangtze* (《江南水乡》) by Lin Feng，*Folk Houses South of the Yangtze* (《江南民居》) by Ding Junqing and *Wood Construction South of the Yangtze* (《江南木构》) by Liu Jie. And authoritative dictionaries of TCA terminology are yet to be published.

3.2 Stylistics

Another challenge of TCA translation concerns stylistics. Some tourism or publicity TCA texts are evocative texts and use elaborate and figurative language

---

① 李家坤,李硕,任淼:《以建筑典籍翻译为局限性补偿路径的近五年典籍英译现状分析》,《沈阳建筑大学学报》(社会科学版)2021年第1期,第83页。

which may daunt even seasoned translators. It is true that a good translation should reproduce both the meaning and style of the source text, or as Fu Lei argued, a good translation should resemble the spirituality of the original,[①] yet for most translators, this is a high standard to meet and they often have to choose between the reproduction of meaning and the reproduction of style. In Chapter 4 of this book, we've discussed *Skopos* Theory which holds that the purpose of translation justifies its process. As the main purpose of tourism or publicity TCA texts is to persuade readers and pass information, translators usually focus on the reproduction of meaning.

4. Principles of TCA Translation

The principles and methods of translation are influenced by text type and translation purpose. As for TCA texts, they can be divided into technical ones and evocative ones with the former focusing on theorizing and explaining techniques to professionals and the latter aiming to provide average readers with basic TCA knowledge. In this book, we limit our discussion to the translation of evocative TCA texts, particularly those for tourism and publicity purposes. The translation of TCA publicity texts can be guided by the principles of communication-friendliness, conciseness and clarity.

4.1   Communication-friendliness

The purpose of translating tourism and publicity TCA texts is to familiarize foreign readers with the basic features and cultural connotations of TCA. To attain this purpose, translators often regard communication as a priority and translate the texts in such a way as to reduce difficulties in cross-cultural communication. In other words, they should keep the target readers in mind and translate or even rewrite the text in a way that is understandable and friendly to foreign readers so that they can gain insights into Chinese culture through TCA.

4.2   Conciseness and clarity

The principle of conciseness and clarity is also based on the purpose of smooth cross-cultural communication, as a redundant translation will do nothing but obscure the meaning of source text and hinder communication. As we've explained in the previous section, average foreign readers usually are not interested in the specific techniques of TCA. What they hope for is oftentimes a concise and clear introduction

---

① 傅雷:《重译本序》,巴尔扎克:《高老头》,傅雷译,武汉:长江文艺出版社,2018年,第3页。

to TCA. For these readers, they are likely to be frustrated or even exasperated by an elaborate translation studded with jargons and highly refined expressions. A concise and clear translation may prove to be a better option.

5. Methods and Skills of TCA Translation

To meet the TCA translation principles of communication-friendliness, conciseness and clarity, translators usually resort to the methods and skills of loan translation, transliteration plus annotation, free translation, translation plus illustration, addition, and omission.

5.1 Loan translation

Loan translation, also referred to as *calque* in French, is a form of direct translation in which expressions from SL are borrowed to replace the SL terms.[1] Some TCA terms, though originating in Chinese cultural context, refer to the same or identical architectural components that are given different English names. This might remind us of the conventionality of language which is well illustrated by Shakespeare's famous line in *Romeo and Juliet*: "A rose by any other name would smell as sweet."[2] Rose is called 玫瑰 in Chinese, but it refers to the same flower and is equally fragrant. Likewise, some architectural terms, though different in names and/or materials actually refer to the same things. This is the foundation for loan translation. For example, 梁 and 柱 are also important architectural components in Western architecture which are named "beam" and "column" respectively. This is loan translation. We can illustrate loan translation with another example. As we've discussed, patterns are profusely used in TCA for decoration and there are two major methods of carving them—阳刻 and 阴刻 which can be substituted by the English words "relief" and "intaglio" respectively. Since many architectural components are identical or the same in Chinese and Western architectures, loan translation is an important method in rendering TCA terminology into English.

5.2 Transliteration plus annotation

Transliteration plus annotation is another method used in translating TCA terms, particularly terms that are culturally unique and without English equivalents.

---

[1] Shuttleworth, Mark & Moira Cowie. *Dictionary of Translation Studies*. London and New York: Routledge, 2014, p. 18.

[2] Shakespeare, William. *Romeo and Juliet*. Irvine: Saddleback Educational Publishing, 2003, p. 30.

Transliteration can help preserve the cultural connotations of TCA terms，but may create problem for understanding，which can be compensated by providing annotations to the transliterated terms. This method largely takes advantage of the conventionality of language as it first offers a verbal sign of the transliterated term and then specifies its meaning and connotation through annotation. Some key TCA terms are rendered into English this way. For example，斗拱 and 木踬 are first put into *dougong* and *muzhi* according to their pronunciations and then annotations are offered to clarify their meanings (*dougong*—interlocking wooden bracket set；*muzhi*—a wooden piece between the column and the plinth to prevent the columns from moisture，corrosion，and earthquake). The general practice of adding annotations to translated TCA terms is to state the materials，functions，and features of TCA terms in plain language so as to help target readers better make sense of the meanings. [1]

5.3   Free translation

Free translation is also used in translating TCA terms into English. Take two key TCA terms 间 and 进 as an example. The former means the measurement of width and length between beams in TCA and the latter refers to the measurement of residence depth as in the expression 三进院落. These two terms in tourism or publicity materials can be freely translated as "beams of width or length" and "courtyard" respectively. Similarly，terms describing the types and shapes of roofs can also be freely translated as the cases with 重檐庑殿顶 and 单檐歇山顶 which can be put into "a double-eave hopped roof" and "a hipped gable roof with single eave."[2]

5.4   Translation plus illustration

Illustration can provide a powerful visual aid in helping readers understand TCA terms. As we've mentioned in the previous chapter，illustration and language can be collaborative in the production of meaning. Some TCA terms，even if they are put into English，are still abstract or confusing for foreign readers. In this case，translators can use illustration to help them grasp the translated terms through visualization. For example，we can offer an illustration of a hipped gable roof with double eaves（重檐歇山顶）to help readers understand the term. In addition to offering a visual aid for understanding，illustration can also make the translated text

---

①　方梅,赵进,纵兆荣:《旅游文本中的中国古建筑术语英译研究》,《浙江工业大学学报》(社会科学版) 2014 年第 4 期,第 477 页。

②　方梅,赵进,纵兆荣:《旅游文本中的中国古建筑术语英译研究》,《浙江工业大学学报》(社会科学版) 2014 年第 4 期,第 478 页。

vivid and appealing.

5.5 Addition

Some TCA terms are figurative and a literal translation of them may cause target readers to misunderstand their real meanings. For example，梭柱，月梁，and 马头墙 are commonly seen components in TCA which derive their names from imitations of the shapes of shuttle，moon，and horse head respectively. If they are translated as "shuttle column," "moon beam," and "horse head wall" respectively, English readers are likely to be baffled. To solve this problem，translators can resort to addition，adding the word "like" or "shape" to clarify their real meanings. The three terms can be translated as "shuttle-like column," "crescent moon-shaped beam," and "horse head-shaped wall." Similar to TCA components，some traditional Chinese constructions are also given figurative names whose literal meanings can obscure the constructions they refer to. For example，a small gallery bridge in Zhuozheng Garden (拙政园，literally meaning "humble administrator's garden") is figuratively named 小飞虹，as it not only resembles the shape of a rainbow but also alludes to the associative meanings of it. If it is translated as "Little Flying Rainbow," foreign readers are probably at a loss as to the reference of the English title，so addition can be used to remove the ambiguity and retranslate 小飞虹 as "the Little Flying Rainbow-Like Bridge."

5.6 Omission

Omission is often used in translating tourism or publicity TCA materials which tend to use highly decorative language. The refined language，though meeting Chinese readers' aesthetic taste and demonstrating the author's literary prowess，can create substantial difficulty for translators. Reproduction of the original style is not always necessary from the perspective of *skopos* theory as foreign readers' primary concern is the meaning of the source text. Experienced translators are usually skilled users of omission and focus on the reproduction of meaning. For example，when translating TCA publicity materials that are studded with quotations and four-character Chinese expressions，translators might simply summarize the key meaning of these quotations and expressions and re-express them in plain English. For instance，translators can use omission in putting the following paragraph into English.

拙政园的布局主题是以水为中心，池水面积约占总面积五分之三，主要建筑物十之八九皆临水而筑。文征明《拙政园记》："郡城东北界娄、齐门之间，居多隙地，有积水亘其中，稍加治，环以林木。"据此可以知道是利用原来地形而设计的，与明末计成《园冶》中《相地》一节所说"高方欲就亭台,低凹可开池沼……"的因地制宜方法相符合。故该园以水为主,实有其道理在。在苏州不但此园如此,阔街头巷的网师园,水占全园面积达五分之四,平门的五亩园亦池沼逶迤,望之弥然,莫不利用原来的地形加以浚治的。①

In this paragraph, the author Chen Congzhou not only quotes from TCA classics but also uses quite a few four-character Chinese expressions to explain the principle of taking advantage of the existing typography in making gardens. If the material is aimed at English average readers intending to get a general idea of Suzhou Gardens, translators can use omission and re-express its meaning in plain English as follows:

> The layout of the Humble Administrator's Garden centers around water. With over three fifth of the garden's area covered by water, most of the major constructions are built along the water. According to "Record of the Humble Administrator's Garden" by Wen Zhengming, the garden was made by adjusting to the local typography where there was a large area of lowland covered by water. The same principle was explained by Ji Cheng in *The Craft of Gardens* that pavilions should be built on highlands while lowlands were suitable for digging ponds, so the prominence of water in the Humble Administrator's Garden is well justified. The same principle also explains the prominence of water in other Suzhou Gardens as well, such as Wangshi Garden at Kuojietou Alley where the water coverage reaches eighty percent and Wumu Garden at Ping Gate in which several small ponds were linked together to form a vast water surface. All of these gardens are created by taking advantage of the existing typography.

In the English translation, the quotations from Wen Zhengming and Ji Cheng are partially omitted and rewritten, and the four-character expressions 池沼逶迤 and 望之弥然 are rendered into simple and plain English. Though the literariness of the original text is compromised, its primary meaning is faithfully and concisely reproduced.

　　Translators engaged in TCA translation often use these methods and skills jointly and flexibly to produce readable texts.

---

① 　陈从周:《苏州园林》,上海:同济大学出版社,2018年,第24页。

A Short Summary

In this chapter, we've discussed the features and translation of TCA. According to Liang Sicheng, TCA possesses unique features in layout, structure, roof, building materials, etc. which distinguish it from other architectural systems and reflect the aesthetic taste and philosophical views of Chinese people. Translation of non-technical TCA texts, particularly those for tourism and publicity purposes, is essentially a cross-cultural activity, but TCA terminology and the highly decorative language of non-technical TCA texts pose a challenge to translators. To meet these challenges and come up with communication-friendly and concise translations, translators can adopt the methods and skills of loan translation, transliteration plus annotation, free translation, translation plus illustration, addition, and omission.

Reviewing Questions

1. What are the basic features of TCA according to Liang Sicheng?

2. What is the relationship between TCA and Chinese culture?

3. What are the challenges of TCA translation?

4. What are the principles of TCA translation?

5. What are the commonly used methods and skills in TCA translation?

Chapter 6

Translation of Chinese Relics

 Objectives

➢ Understand the relationship between relics and culture

➢ Understand the difficulties of translating Chinese relics

➢ Know about the common types of mistranslations of Chinese relics and their causes

➢ Grasp the principles of translating Chinese relics

➢ Grasp the strategies, methods, and skills of translating Chinese relics

➢ Be able to translate major Chinese relics and simple texts on Chinese relics into proper English

1. The Relationship Between Relics and Culture

Relics, as objects surviving from earlier times, are usually of historical or sentimental interests and regarded as familial, local or national treasures. They can reveal a lot about the ways of living of different historical periods and possess great historical, cultural, artistic, technological, and educational values.

First, relics are tangible historical documents through which we can enrich our knowledge and deepen our understanding of history, particularly history that is not well-recorded. For example, the existence of the Xia dynasty once was arguable as the historical record of Xia is largely mythical, but archaeological discoveries and unearthed relics show that the Xia dynasty indeed existed between approximately 2,070 BC to 1,600 BC. [1] Relics can also prove or disprove written history. *Shih Chi*, or *Records of the Historian* records the use of mercury in Qin Shi Huang Mausoleum and the burning of E Pang Palace. Archaeological relics confirm the presence of mercury in the tomb but refute the record that the palace was burned by Xiang Yu. It is certain that our knowledge of history will be further enriched with new archaeological discoveries and unearthed relics.

Second, relics can also tell us about the various aspects of cultures of different periods. Take Mawangdui Han Dynasty Tomb, a great archaeological discovery, as an example. The various unearthed relics, such as costumes, seals, lacquerware, pottery, silk manuscripts, musical instruments, and medical books reveal a lot about the clothing, food, handicraft, music, painting, and medicine of the Han dynasty. The culture of our early ancestors is also known through the relics they left. The tools made of bone unearthed in 1973 at Hemudu Village in Yuyao, Zhejiang show that our ancestors began to use bone to make tools over 7000 years ago, [2] which is a mark of civilization.

Third, some relics are works of art and possess great artistic values. Several dynasties leave relics that are of unparallel artistic values and are regarded as national treasures. Houmuwu Ding of Shang, terracotta warriors of Qin, jade clothes sewn with gold wire of Han, tricolor-glazed pottery of Tang, celadon of Song, and Xuande incense burners of Ming are highly acclaimed for their artistic values. They demonstrate the aesthetic tastes and consummate craftsmanship of these historical periods.

---

[1] 邹衡:《关于探讨夏文化的几个问题》,《文物》1979 年第 3 期,第 64 - 69 页。
[2] 朱筱新:《文物与历史》,北京:东方出版社,1999 年,第 9 页。

Fourth, relics can also show the technological aspect of culture. Relics of metalware and workshops, for example, indicate the progress of metallurgical technology in ancient China. Zhu Xiaoxin argues that according to relics, the method of charcoal reduction had been used in the Warring States period to forge bronzeware and blacksmiths in the Han dynasties had been able to produce malleable hard iron and decarburized steel.[1] These relics and the technology behind them not only demonstrate the technological feats of ancient China, but also prove a source of inspiration and confidence for future generations of Chinese.

Fifth, relics also serve educational functions, especially in helping people learn about history, build national pride, increase cultural confidence, and enhance cultural identification. In museums and exhibitions, we can see visitors gazing at relics which present the uninterrupted history of China in a visible way. By viewing these relics, people are likely to be impressed by the splendid culture and long history of China and feel proud of being members of the Chinese nation. Besides, these relics also constitute an important medium of cultural memory through which we construct and preserve our cultural identity.[2]

2. The Difficulties of Translating Chinese Relics

Unlike other aspects of Chinese culture which we can encounter in daily life, relics are far removed from our daily existence and give us a sense of mysteriousness and unfamiliarity. Most people derive their limited and superficial knowledge of Chinese relics mainly from the screen and exhibitions, and for translators who do not specialize in translating Chinese relics, their knowledge of Chinese relics may not be richer than that of average people, so the first difficulty of translating Chinese relics lies in the lack of background knowledge. Usually, the translation of relics' names needs to present their shapes, materials, colors, basic features, functions, and craftsmanship. For example, "Elephant-Shaped Vessel" indicates the shape and function of 象尊, "Bronze Tripod" reveals the material and shape of 三脚鼎, and "Red Pottery Dish with White Patterns" indicates the color, material, function, and basic feature of 白衣红陶盘. To produce faithful and readable translations, translators need to acquaint themselves with the background knowledge of relics.

Another difficulty of translating Chinese relics concerns cultural differences. As

---

① 朱筱新:《文物与历史》,北京:东方出版社,1999 年,第 170 - 172 页。

② Assmann, Jan. *Cultural Memory and Early Civilization: Writing, Remembrance, and Political Imagination.* Cambridge: Cambridge University Press, 2011, p. 6.

Chinese relics are closely associated with the historical and cultural contexts from which they are dated, the translation of them usually involves a process of cultural negotiation in which translators have to mediate between cultures and translate the relics in a way that is understandable to the target readers. Take the translation of 胡人牵骆驼俑 and 三彩天王俑 as an example. The former, if simply translated as "Foreign Figure Leading a Camel, Tang Dynasty" will be unfriendly to average English readers as they often have no idea of the period of the Tang dynasty, so "618 AD to 907AD", the time period of Tang, is better provided to compensate readers' lack of historical knowledge. And the latter, if translated as "Tri-Colored Heavenly King", may mislead the target readers to perceive the relic as a figurine of a deity dwelling in the heaven, which actually is a guardian of tombs, so it should be translated as "Tri-Colored Tomb Guardian King."[①]

3. The Common Types of Mistranslations of Chinese Relics and Their Causes

Visitors to Chinese museums who are good at English would probably be amused, shocked, or even abhorred by the mistranslations of Chinese relics, which can be generally classified into five types—spelling mistakes, grammar mistakes, misinterpretations, loss of key information, and inconsistency. Let's exemplify and analyze them one by one.

3.1　Spelling mistakes

Not a few translations of Chinese relics contain spelling mistakes. For example, "pottery" is misspelt as "potery" or "poetry," "ink slab" as "ink salad" or "ink slad," and "utensil" as "untensil" or "untensed." Spelling mistakes like these can be easily noticed by careful readers and are usually caused by carelessness and poor professional ethics of the translator. They can be avoided by adopting a rigorous attitude towards translation and double checking the draft.

3.2　Grammar mistakes

Grammar mistakes can often be seen in translations of Chinese relics. For example, both the expression "use of polish stoneware" and the sentence "How people bury in Shijiahe Culture" contain grammar mistakes. The former should be corrected as "use of polished stoneware" and the latter should be corrected as "How people were buried in Shijiahe Culture." Carelessness is probably the primary cause of grammar

---

① 　林文涛：《文物翻译的规范化探析》，《四川文物》2013 年第 4 期，第 87 页。

mistakes, but the translators' language incompetence and poor machine translation may also be held accountable.

3.3　Misinterpretations

Unlike spelling mistakes and grammar mistakes, misinterpretations are not easily discernable. For example, readers tend to take translations like "kettle"（釜）and "polychrome tureen"（彩陶碗）for granted and do not bother to examine whether they are appropriate. A close examination of them in relation to the Chinese relics reveals that they actually misrepresent the relics. 釜, a larger round container for cooking over a fire is usually called "cauldron," not "kettle" which usually refers to a container with a lid, handle, and a spout that is used for boiling water. Similarly, 彩陶碗, as a food holder used in ancient China, more resembles a bowl in shape and is better translated as "painted pottery bowl." Misinterpretations often result from translators' unfamiliarity with the relics and translators can do some research and search the pictures of relics so as to represent them as accurately as possible in the target language.

3.4　Loss of key information

Some translations of Chinese relics fail to reproduce the cultural connotations of relics and result in the losses of key information. For example, the five pottery granaries collected by National Museum of China—"白米万石"陶仓, "大豆万石"陶仓, "麻万石"陶仓, "大麦万石"陶仓, and "黍粟万石"陶仓 are simply translated as "Pottery Polished Rice Granary," "Pottery Soybean Granary," "Pottery Hempseed Granary," "Pottery Barley Granary," and "Pottery Millet Granary." Though achieving functional equivalence, these translations do not capture the wish for harvest and abundance implied by the Chinese names, which indicates an unsuccessful cultural negotiation on the part of translators.[1] This inadequacy can be redressed by adding annotation to the translation. For instance, we can add a note to "Pottery Polished Rice Granary" in brackets: "Pottery Polished Rice Granary"（literally meaning "granary holding tens of thousands of kilos of rice," it expresses people's wish for harvest and abundance）. If translators rely too heavily on functional equivalence and overlook the reproduction of cultural connotations in translating Chinese relics, the introduction of Chinese culture to the outside world would be hampered.

---

① 朱安博,杨艺:《国家博物馆文物翻译实证研究》,《中国科技翻译》2017 年第 3 期,第 46 页。

3.5 Inconsistency

Inconsistency is another major problem in the translation of Chinese relics. An empirical study of the English translations of various relics in National Museum of China reveals that quite a few terms are translated inconsistently. Let's illustrate this with the translations of 桶形，壶，and 钟. 筒形陶罐 is translated as "Barrel-like Pottery Jar" while 筒形彩陶器 is translated as "Painted Cylindrical Pottery Vessel"；船形彩陶壶 is translated as "Boat-shaped Painted Pottery Jar" while 朱绘兽耳陶壶 is translated as "Painted Pottery *Hu*（vessel）with Animal-shaped Ears"；and 陶钟 is translated as "Pottery Bell" while 青铜钟 is translated as "Bronze *Zhong*"（percussion instrument）.[①] These inconsistencies can cause confusion and are probably caused by translators' carelessness or poor collaboration of translators. They can be avoided by standardizing the translations of relic terms.

4. The Principles of Translating Chinese Relics

As a form of cross-cultural activity，translation of Chinese relics usually follows the principles of faithfulness，readability，and nationality.

4.1 Faithfulness

Faithfulness is highly prized by Lu Xun who prioritizes faithfulness over smoothness. For translation of Chinese relics，the importance of faithfulness can never be overemphasized，as a faithful English reproduction of Chinese relics is the first as well as the most important step in introducing them to the outside world and unfaithful translations will mislead readers. The English translation of 紫砂 as "violet sand earthenware," "purple clay pottery," "red ware," or "purple earthenware"，for example，is unfaithful in that neither "earthenware" nor "pottery" can evoke the image of 紫砂 in the mind of English readers. A transliteration of it as "Zisha" would suffice.

4.2 Readability

Translation of Chinese relics should also be made readable for foreign readers by clearing possible obstacles to understanding. "Bronze Container with Openwork Animal Design,"though a faithful translation of the Chinese relic 镂空兽纹青铜奁，may cause English readers to speculate its function. The translation can be improved

---

① 朱安博，杨艺：《国家博物馆文物翻译实证研究》，《中国科技翻译》2017 年第 3 期，第 45－46 页。

by adding its function—"Bronze Dressing Container with Openwork Animal Design." Translation of Chinese relics, as we have discussed, is a form of cross-cultural communication. Translators need to take the differences between source culture and receptor culture into consideration and eliminate possible barriers to understanding.

4.3　Nationality

One purpose of translating Chinese relics is to introduce Chinese culture to the foreign world and overreliance on the strategy of domestication may erase the unique cultural connotations of relics. Therefore, a good translation should strike a balance between readability and nationality, which is usually achieved by adopting the method of free translation plus annotation or transliteration plus annotation. For example, 青瓷花尊 is rendered into "Celadon Vessel with Lotus Pattern (used for holding wine and water, for decoration, or for religious rituals)" by using free translation plus annotation. 编钟 is transliterated as *Bianzhong* and the annotation "bell set chime" is added to clarify its meaning. By retaining Chinese cultural elements of the relics in translation, translators can help disseminating Chinese culture in the foreign world.

5.　The Methods of Translating Chinese Relics

Guided by the principles of faithfulness, readability, and nationality, translators usually use free translation, transliteration, and half transliteration to translate Chinese relics into English.

5.1　Free translation

The activity of translation, as we know, consists of two steps—understanding and expressing. The translator first makes a thorough understanding of the source text and then expresses it in the target language in a faithful and readable way. The same process applies to the translation of Chinese relics as well. The translator first needs to understand the relics in terms of their materials, shapes, colors, functions, and cultural backgrounds and then puts them into readable English. In this process, the structures of the names of Chinese relics are usually disrupted and rearranged in English. For example, 交错三角彩纹陶壶 is understood as a painted pottery jar with triangular pattern and translated as "Painted Pottery Jar with Interlocking Triangle Design" and 观星望月气功镜 is translated as "Mirror with Patterns of Astronomical Observation and *Qigong* (a body-building method)" based on the translator's interpretation of it. Free translation can avoid awkwardness and mistranslations caused by word-for-word translation, but sometimes may fall short of retaining the cultural connotations of the relics. And transliteration can be used to compensate this inadequacy.

5.2 Transliteration

Transliteration，as we have discussed in the translation of traditional Chinese clothing，is an important method of preserving the cultural connotations of culture-specific terms and introducing new terms into the target language. As is often the case，transliteration is usually used to put core culture-loaded terms into English，such as 仁，道，and 袄 and overuse of it may impede understanding. Regarding Chinese relics，some key terms like 紫砂 and 鼎 are transliterated as "Zisha" and "Ding." Other terms like 钟 and 卣 are also transliterated but their transliterations are not well accepted. Zhu Anbo and Yang Yi point out that transliteration is overused in translating Chinese relics and that it is a major cause of inconsistency in relics translation. [①]

5.3 Half-transliteration

Half-transliteration，as indicated by its name，refers to the method in which one half of the term is translated (usually freely) while the other half is transliterated as in "tung oil" (桐油). In the translation of Chinese relics，the characters denoting the genres，particularly the prominent genres of relics are sometimes transliterated while the descriptors of the relics are freely translated. Let's exemplify it with the translation of 兽耳青铜壶. The genre of the relic 壶 is transliterated while 兽耳青铜，descriptor of the relic's shape and material is freely translated，so we have the half-transliterated term "Bronze Hu (wine vessel) with Animal-shaped Handles." It can be noted that in the English translation of 兽耳青铜壶，the transliterated term "Hu" is explained by adding an annotation in the parentheses，revealing that transliteration and half-transliteration are often used in combination with annotation to help clarify the meanings of transliterated terms.

◇ A Short Summary

In this chapter，we've analyzed the relationship between relics and culture and discussed the translation of Chinese relics. Relics are specimens of the ways of living of past times and possess significant historical，cultural，artistic，technological，and

---

① 朱安博，杨艺：《国家博物馆文物翻译实证研究》，《中国科技翻译》2017 年第 3 期，第 46 页。

educational values. The English translation of Chinese relics can be challenging in that translators usually need to research the relics in terms of their materials, shapes, colors, patterns, functions, histories, cultural backgrounds, etc. and translate them in a way that is faithful to the originals and readable to English readers. Failure to meet these challenges may result in mistranslations. As a form of cross-cultural activity, translation of Chinese relics is guided by the principles of faithfulness, readability, and nationality and translators often use the methods of free translation, transliteration, and half-transliteration in translating Chinese relics.

Reviewing Questions

1. What are the functions of Chinese relics?

2. What are the challenges of translating Chinese relics into English?

3. What are the common types of mistranslations of Chinese relics and their causes?

4. What are the principles of translating Chinese relics?

5. What are the commonly used methods of translating Chinese relics?

Chapter 7

Translation of Traditional Chinese Medicine

 Objectives

➢ Understand the significance and history of traditional Chinese medicine (TCM) translation

➢ Understand the characteristics of TCM translation

➢ Understand the difficulties of TCM translation

➢ Understand the principles of TCM translation

➢ Grasp the methods of TCM translation

➢ Understand the relationship between nomenclature and standardization

➢ Be able to put simple TCM texts into proper English

1. The Significance of TCM Translation

The biblical story of the Tower of Babel is often quoted to explain the origin of translation. Li Zhaoguo, a Chinese scholar dedicated to the translation of TCM, draws inspiration from *The Yellow Emperor's Classic of Internal Medicine* and explains the origin and significance of TCM translation by fictionalizing a dialogue between the Yellow Emperor and his senior ministers—Qibo and Leigong in a modern context. In the dialogue titled "Bring Peace to All the Countries in the World", the triad, using the aliases of Mingshi, Didi, and Xiangji respectively, discuss the importance of introducing TCM to the West, the history of cross-cultural communication through translation, the challenges of putting TCM into Western languages, and the necessity of seeking TCM translation talents. As the abridged version of the dialogue is well translated, we'll quote the translation here at length. [①]

Huangdi was sitting in the palace in the Heaven. Qibo and Leigong, his senior ministers, were standing on either side in attendance.

Huangdi said: "I have established this system of medicine for people all over the world, not just for the Chinese nation. I hope that it can be disseminated and practiced over the world."

Qibo said: "The medicine that Your Majesty have established is indispensable to the life of the people, so it should be disseminated to all the world and serve for peoples from different countries. Since the publication of *Huangdi Neijing*, Chinese medicine was spread to Korea, Japan, Viet Nam and northern areas of China. It has made great contributions to the prosperity and development of these countries."

Huangdi said: "The languages spoken in these countries and areas are different from the Chinese language. How was the Chinese medicine disseminated to these places?"

Qibo answered: "At that time medicine and written language in these countries and areas were not established yet. These countries sent students and

---

① Three things need to be clarified. First, the identity of the translator is yet to be ascertained and we don't know for sure whether it is translated by Li Zhaoguo himself or someone else. Whoever the translator is, his good translation is acknowledged. Second, in the abridged version, the names of Huangdi, Qibo, and Leigong are used instead of the alias. Third, readers interested in the original text can refer to the original text. 李照国：《中医英语翻译技巧问难》，上海：第二军医大学出版社，2009 年，第 1 - 4 页。

scholars to China to acquire the Chinese language and study Chinese medicine. After mastering Chinese medicine and returning to their countries, they practiced and taught Chinese medicine through the media of Chinese characters. That is why today Chinese characters still can be found in Japanese written language. Korea and Viet Nam also write Chinese and practiced Confucianism."

Huangdi said: "Korea, Japan, and Viet Nam are all the countries within the circle of Confucian civilization. The dissemination of Chinese medicine in these countries is certainly not very difficult. What I am always worrying about is the countries in the West. The Western countries are quite different from China in language and customs. What shall we do to disseminate Chinese medicine to these countries?"

Qibo answered: "It is true that the Western languages are totally different from the Chinese language. That is why there are many errors in the current translation of Chinese medicine into Western languages."

Huangdi said: "Medicine is closely related to the life of people. One small mistake may lead to a great disaster. But Western languages are so different from the Chinese language. How can we translate Chinese medicine into Western languages then?"

Qibo answered: "It can only be done by those who have a good command of both Western languages and Chinese medicine."

Huangdi asked: "Where can we find such erudite scholars to undertake such a difficult task?"

Qibo answered: "China now is stable and peaceful. The government pays much attention to education. Qualified translators can certainly be found in this country with such a great ancient civilization. Your Majesty may send an official from the Heaven to the world of man to look for such qualified translators."

Huangdi said: "Good suggestion! Where's Leigong?"

Leigong kowtowed and answered: "I am ready to follow Your Majesty's edict."

The gist of the dialogue is explicit. The translation of TCM is a meritorious deed as it can help people recuperate from illness and maintain health, yet it is quite challenging as English and Chinese differ from each other considerably and mistranslation can lead to disasters, so translators with bilingual proficiency and a good command of TCM is highly sought after.

2. History of TCM Translation

The fictional dialogue between the Yellow Emperor and his ministers has made a reference to the history of TCM translation. As an important component of cross-cultural communication，the translation of TCM into Western languages probably dates back to *The Journals of Matteo Ricci* in which TCM was briefly and peripherally introduced.[①] The first English book on TCM is *A Treatise of the Gout* which was written by an East Indian Company clerk and published in London in 1676. Lan Fengli divides the nearly 350-year history of English translation of TCM into five stages which we will briefly discuss as follows.[②]

2.1　The first stage（1676—1854）

In this stage，the major translated TCM work was the aforementioned *A Treatise of the Gout*. It was retranslated from Dutch into English and offered a brief introduction to acupuncture，TCM history，herbs，and sphygmology. Though an introductory book，*A Treatise of the Gout* helped coin some of the major TCM terms like acupuncture and moxibustion which were later standardized and are still used in the present day.

2.2　The second stage（1855—1949）

In this stage，some TCM classics were translated into English.《洗冤录集》，a forensic work authored by Song Ci of the Southern Song dynasty was translated into English—*Hsi Yüan Lu* or *Instructions to Coroners* by Herbert Allen Giles in 1873 and retranslated by Brian E. McKnight as *The Washing Away of Wrongs: Forensic Medicine in Thirteenth-century China* in 1981. *The Yellow Emperor's Classic of Internal Medicine* and *Compendium of Materia Medica* （《本草纲目》），another two TCM classics were also translated into several English versions. In addition to the

---

① The book was edited by Nicolas Trigault and narrates Ricci's experiences in China. The original English title is *Concerning the Christian Expedition to China Undertaken by the Society of Jesus, from the Journals of Fr. Matteo Ricci of the Same Society. Five Books Dedicated to our Holy Lord Paul V in Which the Customs, Laws, and Principles of the Chinese Kingdom and the Most Difficult First Beginnings of the New Church There Are Described Accurately and with Great Fidelity, Authored by Fr. Nicolas Trigault, Belgian, of the Same Society.* The Chinese version of the books was published in 2010. 利玛窦,金尼阁:《利玛窦中国札记》,何高济,王遵仲,李申译,北京:中华书局,2010 年。

② 兰凤利:《中医英译的历史回顾》,《中华医史杂志》2008 年第 1 期,第 28 - 32 页。

English translation of TCM classics，Wang Jimin and Wu Liande integrated translating with rewriting and composed *History of Chinese Medicine*，an important book for English readers studying Chinese medicine.

2.3   The third stage（1950—1971）

The most notable achievement in this period was the *Science and Civilization in China* series authored by Joseph Needham. Consisting of seven volumes，the series offer a comprehensive and systematic introduction to and analysis of various branches of natural sciences in China. Book VI of Volume VI *Medicine* is devoted to Chinese medicine，including medicine in Chinese culture，hygiene and preventive medicine，qualifying examinations，the origins of immunology，and forensic medicine. [1]

2.4   The fourth stage（1972—1991）

The visit of Richard Nixon to China in 1972 rekindled the interest in TCM. Acupuncture，herbal medicine，massage，*qigong*，dietary therapy，and medial classics began to be introduced into the U.S. To promote TCM in the West，journals like *The American Journal of Chinese Medicine* and *American Journal of Acupuncture* were founded，books like *Medicine in China: A History of Pharmaceutics*，*Medicine in China: A History of Ideas*，and *Chinese Medicine: The Web That Has No Weaver* were published，and TCM classics，most notably *Nan-Ching: The Classic of Difficult Issues* （《难经》）were translated into English. It's also notable that in this period efforts were made to standardize the terms of TCM，particularly those of acupuncture，such as *Standard Acupuncture Nomenclature* issued by WHO，which plays an indispensable role in the standardization and spread of TCM.

2.5   The fifth stage（after 1992）

As more TCM classics like *The Divine Farmer's Materia Medica: A Translation of the Shen Nong Ben Cao* （《神农本草经》），*Treatise on Febrile Diseases Caused by Cold* （《伤寒论》），*Synopsis of Prescriptions of the Golden Chamber* （《金匮要略》）and *Pulse Diagnosis* （《濒湖脉学》）were translated into English，and medical communication between China the West deepened，TCM translation reached a peak in this period. In 2007，FDA acknowledged TCM as a holistic medicine with a complete set of theories and practices in *Draft Guidance for Industry on Complementary and Alternative Medicine Products and Their Regulation by the Food and Drug Administration* and later

---

[1]　Needham，Joseph. *Science and Civilization in China*，*Volume 6: Biological and Biological Technology Part VI: Medicine*. Cambridge：Cambridge University Press，2004.

WHO promulgated *WHO International Standard Terminologies on Traditional Medicine in the Western Pacific Region*, accelerating the process of standardization and international dissemination of TCM.

From the survey of TCM translation, we can find that English publications on TCM chiefly consist of introductory books, textbooks, and translated TCM classics and that standardization of TCM terms is of paramount importance in the translation and dissemination of TCM.

3. Difficulties of TCM Translation

Since TCM is associated with Chinese culture, especially traditional Chinese philosophy, and TCM translation is a form of cross-cultural activity, there are some typical difficulties in putting TCM terms and texts into English, such as lack of philosophical context, lack of equivalents, misunderstanding, and polysemy.

3.1 Lack of philosophical context

TCM translation is a systematic task. To help English readers understand TCM, we have to recreate the cultural and philosophical foundation of it, since the lack of it would substantially hinder the spread and acceptance of TCM. In translation, this difficulty is usually solved by offering explanations and annotations. For example, in her translation of *The Yellow Emperor's Classic of Internal Medicine*, Ilza Veith devotes an entire chapter to explaining the philosophical foundations of TCM, namely, *Tao*, *Yin* and *Yang*, the five elements, the system of numbers, and the celestial stems. [①]

3.2 Lack of equivalents

As indigenous Chinese medicine, TCM has a system of nomenclature that has no equivalent in English. For example, key terms like 经脉, 五脏, and 六腑 are unique to TCM and have no English counterparts. One possible solution is the formulation and promulgation of TCM nomenclature standard to standardize the translations of major TCM terms. For instance, *Basic Theory Nomenclature of Traditional Chinese Medicine* (GB/T 20348—2006) drafted by Liaoning University of Traditional Chinese Medicine was jointly issued by General Administration of Quality Supervision, Inspection and Quarantine and Standardization Administration as a national standard, which can

---

① Veith, Ilza, trans. *The Yellow Emperor's Classic of Internal Medicine*. Oakland: University of California Press, 2016, pp. 9 - 24.

greatly facilitate the translation and dissemination of TCM.

3.3　Misunderstanding

Some TCM terms are figurative or euphemistic，such as 带下医，失笑散，and 色诊，which shouldn't be translated literally. As good and accurate translation of TCM nomenclature is the basis of standardization，translators should check the real meanings of TCM terms to make sure that they are translated in an accurate and reader-friendly way.

3.4　Polysemy

In TCM，there are some polysemic terms whose meanings depend on collocations and contexts. Take 虚 as an example. It means weakness or debility in 体虚 and deficiency or asthenia in 脾虚. One feasible way of dealing with polysemy in TCM translation is to clarify its meaning in specific collocation and context by consulting authoritative reference books or TCM nomenclature standard.

4. Principles of TCM Translation

Some scholars argue that text types can influence the criteria，strategy，approach，and method of translation. Based on Bühler and Jakobson's classification of language functions，Newmark classifies texts into three broad categories—literary，institutional，and scientific and discusses the translation of each of them. [1] TCM texts，though sometimes using figurative language and exhibiting a considerable degree of literariness，are predominately technical ones whose main function is to express information. [2] According to Newmark，translators of technical texts should regard faithful reproduction of information as top priority and "translate or transfer，if not，account for everything，every word，every figure，letter，every punctuation mark."[3] As for TCM translation，it is unnecessary，if not impossible to recreate the classical or archaic style of some original texts. Nida and Taber contend that the style of language is historical and that what we call archaic today is not necessarily so in the past；therefore，they propose the concept of dynamic equivalence and advocate translators

---

[1]　Newmark, Peter. *A Textbook of Translation*. Hemel Hempstead：Prentice Hall，1988，p. 44.

[2]　李照国,刘希和:《论中医翻译的原则》,《中国翻译》1991 年第 3 期,第 41 页。

[3]　Newmark, Peter. *A Textbook of Translation*. Hemel Hempstead：Prentice Hall，1988，p. 156.

to keep target readers in mind. [①] Based on the features of TCM texts and the purpose of TCM translation, Li Zhaoguo suggests the following principles for the English translation of TCM.

4.1 Natural principle

TCM and Western medicine, as two independent medicines rooted in their respective cultures, often use different terms for same things. For example, 寸白虫 and "taeniasis," 痨瘵 and "tuberculosis," 疳积 and "malnutrition," 筋疝 and "varicocele," 囟填 and "hydrocephalus," each pair refers to the same disease or symptom. In translating these TCM terms, we can use the extant English names since coining new terms may cause confusion. This is also a way to seek common ground in translation.

4.2 National principle

While seeking common ground as required by the principle of naturalness, translators also need to reserve differences, i.e., to retain the unique cultural elements of TCM. The most central terms of TCM like 阴, 阳, 气, 表, 里, 虚, and 实 are deeply rooted in traditional Chinese culture and have no proper equivalents in English. If we substitute them with makeshift English equivalents, their rich connotations will be compromised and the theoretical foundation of TCM will be corrupted. For TCM terms that are unique to Chinese culture and do not exist in the West, transliteration is often used to render them into English. For example, *WHO International Standard Terminologies on Traditional Medicine in the Western Pacific Region* transliterates 阴, 阳, 气 as *yin*, *yang*, and *qi* respectively and terms containing these key concepts are put into English by combining transliteration with free translation, such as 阳中之阴 (*yang* within *yin*), 阴阳互根 (mutual rooting of *yin* and *yang*), 阴阳消长 (waxing and waning of *yin* and *yang*), 先天之气 (innate *qi*), 真气 (genuine *qi*), and 元气 (source *qi*). [②]

4.3 Back-translation principle

Shuttleworth and Cowie define back-translation as a "process in which a text which has been translated into a given language is retranslated into SL." The

---

① Nida, Eugene & Charles R. Taber. *The Theory and Practice of Translation*. Leiden: E. J. Brill, 1982, pp. 7 - 8.

② World Health Organization. *WHO International Standard Terminologies on Traditional Medicine in the Western Pacific Region*. Geneva: World Health Organization, 2007, pp. 13 - 14, 18 - 19.

procedure of back-translation is used for the purpose of illustrating the differences between SL and TL or "comparing specific syntactic, morphological or lexical features from two or more languages."[①] Concerning TCM translation, the principle of back-translation demands that the English translations of TCM terms resemble the structures of original terms so that a two-way transmission of information can be achieved. For instance, 活络止痛, 肝气不足, and 湿热 are translated as "activating collaterals to relieve pain," "insufficiency of liver-*qi*," and "damp-heat" respectively. The English translations share similarities with the originals in meanings and syntactic structures and show a high degree of back-translatability.

4.4   Prescriptive principle

TCM translation is essentially a process of standardization. Translators dedicated to the cause of TCM translation usually need to utilize the prescriptive and conventional property of language to specify the meanings and connotations of TCM terms. The communicative function of language or any other system of signs largely depends on the convention or prescription of its rules of usage. Once these prescribed rules are accepted and observed by all the users, the communicative function of language can be realized. It's the same case with TCM translation. Translators need to specify the meanings and connotations of TCM terms and standardize them through standards and reference books, which is exactly what has been done and is being done in TCM translation. For example, some argue that 辨证施治 shouldn't be translated into "treatment based on syndrome differentiation" as "syndrome" and 症 have different connotations, but translators settle the dispute by prescribing that the word "syndrome" in "treatment based on syndrome differentiation" specifically refers to the TCM term 症. Similarly, WHO's standardization of TCM terminology also draws support from the prescriptive and conventional property of language.

5. Methods of TCM Translation

Guided by the aforementioned principles, translators often use loan translation, literal translation, free translation, transliteration, and transliteration plus free translation in putting TCM texts into English.

---

① Shuttleworth, Mark & Moira Cowie. *Dictionary of Translation Studies*. London and New York: Routledge, 2014, pp. 14 – 15.

5.1 Loan translation

As we've discussed in Section 3 of this chapter，TCM and Western medicine are rooted in different cultural traditions and many TCM terms lack proper English equivalents. For example，心，肝，脾，肾，and 肺，collectively referred to as 五脏 (five *zang*-organs)，are unique TCM terms that don't correspond to the anatomical terms of "heart," "liver," "spleen," "kidney," and "lung," but translators still loan these terms and specify their connotations in TCM，as new coinages may lead to confusion. In addition to anatomical terms，disease names and treatment methods are also loaned. Table 1 lists some of the disease names and treatment methods and their loaned English expressions.

Table 1　Some Loaned English Expressions of TCM Disease Names and Treatment Methods

Chinese	English	Chinese	English
心悸	palpitation	放血	bloodletting
便秘	constipation	正骨	reduction
呃逆	hiccup	止血	hemostasis
遗尿	enuresis	止痛	analgesia
黄疸	jaundice	止泻	antidiarrhea
白喉	diphtheria	按摩疗法	massotherapy
纳呆	indigestion	驱虫	anthelmintic treatment

5.2 Literal translation

Literal translation，as opposed to free translation，has been an important notion at the heart of translation controversies for many centuries. In this section，we use literal translation in a narrower sense，delimiting it as a method of translation that takes word-for-word translation as its starting point，although because of the necessity of conforming to TL grammar，the final TL text may also display group-group or clause-clause equivalence.① Literal translation is widely applied in translating technical texts and is also frequently used in TCM translation. Besides，the principle of back-translation as we've discussed in Section 4.3 is largely observed through literal

---

① Catford，John C. *A Linguistic Theory of Translation*. London：Oxford University Press，1965，p. 25.

translation. Many TCM terms are literally translated into English，such as 木生火 (wood generating fire)，and 抑木扶土 (inhibiting wood to strengthen earth). In Table 2，we list some TCM terms and their literal translations.

Table 2 Some TCM Terms and Their Literal Translations

Chinese	English	Chinese	English
母子关系	mother-child relation	藏而不泄	storage without excretion
金克木	metal restricting wood	阴阳失调	imbalance between *yin* and *yang*
脾主运化	The spleen controls transportation and transformation.	脾失健运	failure of the spleen to transport normally
肝藏血	The liver stores blood.	胃失和降	failure of the stomach *qi* to descend
肾藏精	The kidney stores essence.	风热腰痛	lumbago due to wind-heat

5.3 Free translation

We've pointed out that TCM texts are primarily technical ones and that back-translation and literal translation are two major methods in putting TCM terms into English，yet some TCM terms，because of their cultural uniqueness，are rendered into English through free translation. For example，气门，气功，数脉 are freely translated into "energy gate，" "breathing exercise，" and "rapid pulse" respectively. [1] If they were literally put into "air gate，" "air exercise，" and "counting pulse，" misunderstandings might arise.

5.4 Transliteration

Transliteration is often used to render culturally specific terms into TL. TCM terms that are unique to Chinese culture are often transliterated as we've discussed in Section 4.2 of this chapter. Some herbs，as local products of China that do not exist in English-speaking countries，are also transliterated，such as 猫眼草（*maoyancao*），虎刺 （*huci*），and 蛇床子（*shechuangzi*）. The Latin names of the transliterated herbs are also provided to facilitate understanding. [2]

5.5 Transliteration plus free translation

Regarding TCM translation，transliteration and free translation are often used in combination to render TCM terms with transliterated character(s) into TL，which

---

① 孙秀芳,赵维庚:《中医词汇的直译、意译和音译》,《外语学刊》1990 年第 5 期,第 62 页。

② 孙秀芳,赵维庚:《中医词汇的直译、意译和音译》,《外语学刊》1990 年第 5 期,第 62 页。

we've mentioned in Section 4. 2 of this chapter. For example，translators jointly use transliteration and free translation to put TCM terms containing 阴，阳 and 气 into English，such as 阴阳平衡 and 元气.

6. Standardization of TCM Nomenclature

The internationalization of TCM largely depends on the standardization of nomenclature. To establish TCM as an internationally recognized discipline，the terminology，theories，and practices of TCM must be defined. As terminology is the starting point for theory construction and practice instruction，the central issue of internationalizing TCM lies in standardizing TCM nomenclature. According to Newmark，technical translation "is primarily distinguished from other forms of translation by terminology，although terminology usually only makes up about 5%—10% of a text."[1] As a discipline with a high degree of professionalism，TCM contains a large terminology and the translation of it is the basis for the internationalization of TCM.

The standardization of TCM nomenclature undergoes a long process. Initially，the English translations of TCM terms were inconsistent and a same term might possess several translations. For example，牛皮癣 can be translated as "psoriasis" or "oxhide lichen." The lack of consistency and standardization in nomenclature translation impedes the international dissemination of TCM. The problem can be addressed by compiling dictionaries and formulating standards on TCM nomenclature. For example，scholars like Nigel Wiseman，Paul U. Unschuld，Giovanni Maciocia，Xie Zhufan，Li Zhaoguo，and Wang Yongyan have compiled reference books of TCM lexicon. Associations like WHO and Translation Society of China Association of Chinese Medicine also engage in the standardization of TCM terminology. These efforts can greatly contribute to the standardization of TCM terminology and the international dissemination of TCM.

◆ A Short Summary

In this chapter，we've discussed TCM translation from six aspects—its significance，history，principles，difficulties，methods，and standardization of TCM nomenclature. Starting from the 17th century，TCM translation has developed over

---

① Newmark，Peter. *A Textbook of Translation*. Hemel Hempstead：Prentice Hall，1988，p. 151.

300 years and the theoretical foundation, terminology, prescriptions, and practice methods of TCM were introduced to the West. Due to cultural differences, translators often encounter some typical difficulties in TCM translation—lack of philosophical context, lack of equivalents, misunderstanding of TCM terms, and polysemy. Guided by natural principle, national principle, back-translation principle, and prescriptive principle, translators often use loan translation, literal translation, free translation, transliteration, and transliteration plus free translation in putting TCT terms and texts into English. To help promote the international dissemination of TCM, reference books and standards are written to standardize TCM nomenclature.

◆ Reviewing Questions

1. What is the significance of TCM translation?

2. What is the historical development of TCM translation?

3. What are the difficulties of TCM translation?

4. What are the principles of TCM translation?

5. What are the methods of TCM translation?

6. Why is the standardization of TCM nomenclature central to TCM translation?

7. How can we standardize TCM nomenclature?

Chapter 8

Translation of Traditional Chinese Festivals

 Objectives

➢ Understand the relationship between traditional Chinese festivals and Chinese culture

➢ Understand the difficulties of translating traditional Chinese festivals

➢ Grasp the methods of translating traditional Chinese festivals

➢ Be able to translate texts on traditional Chinese festivals into proper English

1. The Relationship Between Traditional Chinese Festivals and Chinese Culture

The American Heritage Dictionary defines festival as an "occasion for feasting or celebration, especially a day or time of religious significance that recurs at regular intervals."[①] This definition is obviously made from a Western perspective as many Western festivals, such as Christmas, Easter, and Halloween are indeed closely related with Christianity, but China is a secular country, and traditional Chinese festivals are usually celebrated for non-religious purposes. Religious or secular, festivals are inseparable from culture and traditional Chinese festivals have their roots in various aspects of Chinese culture like myth, legends, astronomy, and lunar calendar and reflect Chinese people's way of living and their wish for love, family reunion, and harvest. For example, the Qixi Festival originates from the legend of the Cowherd and the Weaving Maid who meet only once a year when magpies fly together to form a bridge over the Milky Way and expresses people's wish for love and reunion. And the Mid-Autumn Festival, another major traditional Chinese festival, expresses people's wish for abundance and family reunion.

2. Introduction to Major Traditional Chinese Festivals

In this section, we'll briefly introduce some major traditional Chinese festivals in terms of their dates, customs, significances, origins, and literary representations.

2.1 The Spring Festival

Of all the traditional Chinese festivals, the Spring Festival is probably the most important and most well-known one. Starting with the first day of the new year and ending on the 15th day of the lunar calendar, the Spring Festival is a time for family reunion and thanksgiving and the common customs of it include pasting couplets, enjoying family reunion dinner, staying up late on New Year's Eve, handing out red envelopes, and paying New Year's calls. Nowadays, these customs are adapted to suit the new way of living. For example, red envelops are often sent electronically and personal calls are sometimes replaced by phone calls or WeChat messages.

It's difficult to trace the origin of Spring Festival accurately. Many people tend to believe that the Chinese character 年 originally refers to a monster that devours people

---

① Soukhanov, Anne H. et al. *The American Heritage Dictionary of the English Language* (3rd edition). Boston: Houghton Mifflin Company, 1996, p. 2717.

before the new year. The monster was alleged to have a huge mouth and could swallow many people with one bite. When people were desperately horrified，an immortal disguising as an old man confronted the monster and persuaded it to eat evil beasts on the earth. The monster consented and started to prey on beasts in the wilderness，but people still pasted red couplets to ward off the monster 年 in case it returned and the custom was passed down from generation to generation. The original meaning of 过年，literally meaning "surviving the monster 年" gradually transformed into that of observing the new year.

There are many poems on the Spring Festival and "The Lunar New Year's Day" (《元日》) by Wang Anshi is probably the most famous one. "With cracker's cracking noise the old year passed away；/The vernal breeze brings us warm wine and warm spring day. /The rising sun sheds light on doors of each household，/New peachwood charm is put up to replace the old." (爆竹声中一岁除,春风送暖入屠苏。千户万户瞳瞳日,总把新桃换旧符。)① The poem visualizes New Year's celebration and expresses people's wish for freshness and gaiety.

2.2　The Lantern Festival

The Lantern Festival falls on the 15th day of the first lunar month and is believed to be established by Emperor Wen of the Western Han dynasty. In ancient China，the festival provided an opportunity for young men and women to meet and interact with each other through lantern shows，but the romantic significance of the festival gradually faded. "Tune：Green Jade Cup，Lantern Festival"(《青玉案·元夕》)，a *ci* poem by Xin Qiji is said to tell a romantic encounter during the lantern festival："But in the crowd once and again/I look for her in vain. /When all at once I turn my head，/I find her there where lantern light is dimly shed." (众里寻他千百度,蓦然回首,那人却在,灯火阑珊处。)② Major customs of the Lantern Festival include viewing lanterns，guessing lantern riddles，performing dragon lantern dances，and eating *yuanxiao*.

2.3　Tomb Sweeping Day

Tomb Sweeping Day is observed on April fourth or fifth to commemorate and pay respect to one's deceased ancestors by visiting and cleaning their grave sites. In addition to visiting cemeteries，people also go for walks in the countryside，plant willows，or fly kites.

The festival is based on the Cold Food Festival which is related to the story of Jie

---

① 许渊冲,许明译:《许渊冲译千家诗》,北京:中译出版社,2021 年,第 14 - 15 页。
② 许渊冲选译:《许渊冲译唐宋词一百首》,北京:中译出版社,2021 年,第 202 - 203 页。

Zitui who was a loyal minister to Chong Er of the State of Jin. During a civil war，Prince Chong Er and Jie fled and lived in exile for 19 years. During their exile，Jie prepared broth out of his own flesh and offered it to his royal highness. When Chong Er ascended the throne，he rewarded those who once helped him，but forgot Jie Zitui. Jie Zitui refused to claim repay for his loyalty and lived alone in the mountains. When Chong Er heard about it，he was ashamed of his oversight and sought for Jie. As the conditions were harsh and Jie was nowhere to be found，Chong Er set fire to the mountain upon the suggestion of his officials，but Jie Zitui still didn't come out. When the fire was out，Jie was found dead with his mother on his back. He was under a willow tree and a letter written in blood was found in a hole in the tree. The letter read：

> Giving meat and heart to my lord，hoping my lord will always be upright. An invisible ghost under a willow is better than a loyal minister beside my lord. If my lord has a place in his heart for me，please make self-reflection when remembering me. I have a clear conscience in the nether world，being pure and bright in my offices year after year.

To commemorate Jie's death，Chong Er created the Cold Food Festival and ordered that no fire be set on this day and that only cold food be eaten. One year later，Chong Er went back to the willow tree to hold a memorial ceremony and found the willow tree was in bloom again. The willow was named "Pure Bright White" and the Cold Food Festival became known as "Pure Brightness Festival."

The most well-known poem about Tomb Sweeping Day is probably Du Mu's "The Mourning Day for the Dead" (《清明》) which depicts people's heavy-heartedness on the festival.

> On the day of mourning for the dead it's raining hard，/My heart is broken on my way to the graveyard. /Where can I find a wine-shop to drown my sad hours? /A cowherd points to a cot amid apricot flowers.
> 清明时节雨纷纷，路上行人欲断魂。借问酒家何处有？牧童遥指杏花村。[1]

2.4　Dragon Boat Festival

Dragon Boat Festival，also called Double Fifth Festival，is celebrated on the fifth

---

[1]　许渊冲译：《汉英对照：唐诗一百五十首》，西安：陕西人民出版社，1984 年，第 128 页。

day of the fifth lunar month to commemorate the death of Qu Yuan, a great Chinese poet known for his patriotism and contributions to classical poetry. However, some people believe that the festival has a much earlier origin. Prior to Qu Yuan's time, the fifth lunar month was known to ancient Chinese as the "month of poison" when people would easily get sick and epidemics spread, so people in ancient times regarded it as an important time to prevent diseases and keep evil spirits away and Dragon Boat Festival was originally regarded as a festival for people to ceremonially ward off diseases and poisonous insects, which was attested to by the practices of drinking realgar wine and wearing perfume pouches. Nowadays, Dragon Boat Festival is usually celebrated by eating glutinous rice dumplings, participating in or viewing dragon boat races, hanging Chinese mugwort or calamus, drinking realgar wine, and wearing perfume pouches.

2.5　Mid-Autumn Festival

Mid-Autumn Festival, also referred to as the Moon Festival or Mooncake Festival, falls on the 15th day of the eighth month of the lunar calendar. It was derived from the custom of worshiping the moon in autumn to thank it for the harvest, and in the long process of cultural development, the festival has been infused with people's wishes for family reunion, health, and happiness. Celebrations of the festival include enjoying a dinner with family, eating mooncakes, and viewing the moon.

The origin of Mid-Autumn Festival is associated with the legend of Chang'e. Hou Yi, the husband of Chang'e, was rewarded with an elixir by the Queen Mother for his heroic deed of shooting down nine of the ten suns. He did not drink it straight away and asked Chang'e to keep it for him. However, on mid-autumn day when Hou Yi was out hunting, someone tried to force Chang'e to hand over the elixir. Chang'e swallowed the elixir instead and flew all the way to the moon where she looked down on her beloved husband on earth. Hou Yi was distressed and made sacrifices to Chang'e with cakes and fruits. Along with the legend, the custom of eating mooncakes and worshipping the moon has been passed down from generation to generation.

The most famous poem associated with Mid-Autumn Festival is probably "Tune: Prelude to the Melody of Water" (《水调歌头 · 明月几时有》) by Su Shi in which the poet expresses his wish for reunion and good health:

Men have sorrow and joy, they part or meet again;/The moon may be bright or dim, she may wax or wane./There has been nothing perfect since olden days./So let us wish that man/Live as long as he can!/Though miles apart, we'll share the beauty she displays. ”

人有悲欢离合，月有阴晴圆缺，此事古难全。但愿人长久，千里共婵娟。①

3. The Difficulties of Translating Traditional Chinese Festivals

The challenge of translating traditional Chinese festivals lies in negotiation between SL culture and TL culture，which often involves successful translation of culture-specific terms. “The source-language word may express a concept which is totally unknown in the target culture. The concept in question may be abstract or concrete；it may relate to a religious belief，a social custom or a type of food. Such concepts are often referred to as ‘culture-specific.’”② From our introduction to traditional Chinese festivals，we know that traditional Chinese festivals are deeply rooted in Chinese culture and each festival carries with it a set of culture-specific words，phrases，and expressions. Take the Spring Festival as an example. Expressions like 春联，年夜饭，守岁，拜年，and 红包 are all unique to Chinese culture. In addition to culture-loaded expressions，the customs of traditional Chinese festivals are also culture-specific. They constitute another challenge for translators as they have to explain them in English to help target readers make sense of them and get the cultural connotations of the festivals. For example，the custom of eating mooncakes and gazing the moon is based on the culturally symbolic meanings of the moon—love，reunion，and homesickness，which needs to be rendered into English to help readers understand the custom and cultural significance of the festival.

4. The Methods of Translating Traditional Chinese Festivals

To make the translation of traditional Chinese festivals a successful cross-cultural negotiation，translators often use the methods of transliteration，transliteration plus annotation，literal translation，literal translation plus annotation，and free translation.

4.1 Transliteration

In the previous chapters of this book，we've mentioned transliteration several

---

① 许渊冲译：《苏轼诗词选》，石家庄：河北人民出版社，2006 年，第 58 - 59 页。

② Baker，Mona. *In Other Words: A Coursebook on Translation* (3rd edition). London and New York：Routledge，2018，p. 19.

times. It is a commonly used method in translating Chinese culture-specific words into English, but there are three unwritten principles for its usage: 1) the culture-specific words are often core terms of Chinese culture; 2) the culture-specific words are well-known to target readers; and 3) literal or free translation of culture-specific words will substantially compromise their cultural connotations. The names of some major traditional Chinese festivals, such as Qingming Festival, Qixi Festival, and Zhongyuan Festival are transliterated. It needs to be pointed out is that transliteration should be used in a cautious and moderate manner, as overuse of it may make the translation unreadable and impede cross-cultural communication.

4.2   Transliteration plus annotation

Transliteration and annotation are usually used in combination to help persevere the cultural connotations of culture-loaded words on the one hand and clarify their meanings on the other hand, thus striking a balance between fidelity and readability. Transliteration of culture-loaded words, particularly those that are not that well-known to target readers, can create trouble in understanding, so explanations are provided to promote communication. As we have mentioned, each major traditional Chinese festival carries with it a set of culture-specific words which, once transliterated, should be explained to help foreign readers understand them. For example, the Spring Festival has a culture-specific lexicon, such as 饺子, 财神 and 红包 which can be rendered into English by using transliteration plus annotation: *Jiaozi* (Chinese dumpling consisting of a thinly rolled piece of dough which contains either meat or a vegetable filling, is one of the most popular and most commonly eaten dishes in China and East Asia); *Caishen* (The deity of wealth, widely believed to bestow on his devotees the riches carried about by his attendants); and *Hongbao* (Red-colored envelope containing money which is commonly given to child or unmarried adult during the Chinese New Year celebration). However, there is a limitation to the method of transliteration plus annotation—annotations may slow down and even jar reading.

4.3   Literal Translation

Some major traditional Chinese festivals and culture-loaded expressions are translated into English in a literal way. For example, 清明节 and 寒食节 can be literally translated as "Pure Brightness Festival" and "Cold Food Festival" respectively.

4.4　Literal translation plus annotation

Literal translations of Chinese festivals sometimes don't make much sense to target readers and annotations are usually added to facilitate understanding. For example, the literal translation of 冬至 as "Winter Solstice" is inadequate as it sounds like an objective calendar term rather than a festival. Therefore, an annotation can be provided to clarify its meaning: Winter Solstice, *Dongzhi* in Chinese, occurring each year around December 22, is an important festival for Chinese and its celebrations include worshipping the Heaven and ancestors and eating dumplings.

4.5　Free translation

Free translation, as indicated by the examples we've discussed in the previous chapters, is a method of translation that focuses on the production of a readable SL text instead of keeping the syntactic structure of the SL text intact. Seen from a linguistic perspective, a freely translated text is "made on a higher level than is necessary to convey the content unchanged while observing the target text norms."① Yang Xianyi and Gladys Yang mainly use free translation in putting the scene of preparing New Year's sacrifice in "The New Year's Sacrifice" (《祝福》) into English.

> 杀鸡,宰鹅,买猪肉,用心细细的洗,女人的臂膊都在水里浸得通红,有的还带着绞丝银镯子。煮熟之后,横七竖八的插些筷子在这类东西上,可就称为"福礼"了……②

They kill chickens and geese and buy pork, scouring and scrubbing until all the women's arms turn red in the water. Some of them still wear twisted silver bracelets. After the meat is cooked some chopsticks are thrust into it at random, and this is called the "offering."③

Yang Xianyi and Gladys Yang broke away from the wording of the original text and expressed it in smooth English.

Usually, translators of traditional Chinese festivals make use of all the five methods to make successful negotiations between SL culture and TL culture and come

---

① Shuttleworth, Mark & Moira Cowie. *Dictionary of Translation Studies*. London and New York: Routledge, 2017, p. 62.
② 鲁迅:《鲁迅全集(第二卷)》,北京:人民文学出版社,2005 年,第 5 - 6 页。
③ Lu, Xun. *Selected Stories of Lu Hsun*. Trans. Yang, Hsien-yi & Gladys Yang. New York and London: W. W. Norton & Company, 2003, p. 126.

up with translations that are both culturally faithful and readable.

A Short Summary

In this chapter, we've briefly discussed the relationship between traditional Chinese festivals and Chinese culture, introduced some major traditional Chinese festivals, and discussed their English translation in terms of difficulties and methods. As traditional Chinese festivals are rooted in Chinese culture, the English translation of them is essentially a form of cross-cultural activity that involves the translation of culture-loaded terms and cultural significance of festivals. To produce translations that are both faithful to the original texts and readable for target readers, translators often make use of transliteration, transliteration plus annotation, literal translation, literal translation plus annotation, and free translation.

Reviewing Questions

1. What is the relationship between traditional Chinese festivals and Chinese culture?

2. What are the challenges of translating traditional Chinese festivals?

3. What are the commonly used methods of translating traditional Chinese festivals?

Chapter 9

Translation of Traditional Chinese Thoughts and Philosophies

 Objectives

➤ Understand the important schools of traditional Chinese thoughts and philosophies and their introduction to the English world

➤ Grasp the strategies and methods of translating traditional Chinese thoughts and philosophies

➤ Be able to put the core concepts of Confucianism into proper English

➤ Be able to put the core concepts of Taoism into proper English

➤ Be able to put the core concepts of Buddhism into proper English

➤ Be able to maintain patriotism in introducing traditional Chinese thoughts and philosophies to the English world

1. Introduction to Traditional Chinese Thoughts and Philosophies

It is beyond the scope of this book to discuss all the schools of traditional Chinese thoughts and philosophies. To make our discussion manageable，we focus on Confucianism，Taoism，and Buddhism，which，after over a thousand years of interaction and intermingling，converged in the Sui and Tang dynasties and constituted the core of traditional Chinese culture. After integration，they are sometimes collectively referred to as traditional Chinese philosophy，which coexists with Western and Indian philosophies as one of the three philosophy systems in the world. It has shaped，is shaping，and will continue to shape every aspect of our life，especially our values，customs，and way of thinking，playing an irreplaceable role in binding the Chinese people together as a nation and marking diasporic Chinese as "descendants of the dragon." The translation of traditional Chinese thoughts and philosophies can help spread Chinese culture to foreign land and promote mutual learning between cultures. In this chapter，we first introduce Confucianism，Taoism，and Buddhism and then discuss their translation.

2. Translation of Confucianism

This section offers an overview of Confucianism and discusses its English translation.

2.1 Overview of Confucianism

Confucianism is such an important school of traditional Chinese thoughts and philosophies that it is sometimes used synonymously with Chinese culture，though in an unjustified way. As a school of thought represented by Confucius and Mencius，Confucianism began to take definite shape during the Spring and Autumn Period and enjoyed thriving development during the Warring States Period when a hundred schools of thoughts contended. Taking the teachings of Confucius as its core of thought and regarding the words and deeds of Confucius as its highest code，Confucianism had been continually developed by scholars over the years and became the orthodox school of philosophy in the Western Han dynasty when Emperor Wudi banned all schools of thoughts except Confucianism. It has ever since served as the ideological foundation of the feudal rule throughout the dynasties in China. It advocates benevolence，righteousness，propriety，wisdom，sincerity，and the doctrine of the golden mean and values the ethical relations of men which are summarized in the three cardinal guides—ruler guides subject, father guides son, and husband guides wife and five constant virtues—benevolence, righteousness, propriety, wisdom, and sincerity. The golden mean advocates impartiality, reconciliation, and compromise in one's approach to people or matters. Though not without its benefits, Confucianism in feudal China constricted people's mind and impeded China's process to modernization. During the May Fourth Movement, intellectuals represented by Hu Shi attacked traditional Confucian ideas and introduced Western science and democracy into China. Nowadays, we are reexamining and making innovations to Confucianism, particularly in terms of its value in contemporary China.

The influence of Confucianism has extended beyond national borders. Besides Japan, South Korea, North Korea, Singapore, and Viet Nam which are believed to fall within the circle of Confucian civilization, Western countries like the US also receive influence from Confucianism. In 1738, Franklin published a series of articles entitled "Morals from Confucius" in *Pennsylvania Gazette*, in which he expounded Confucius' way of attaining virtues and governing the people. The 13 virtues listed in *Autobiography* and his way of attaining them are in accordance with Confucian ethics. In a letter to George Whitefield, Franklin recommended Confucius' way of governing the people: If we preach the great people to live "a good and exemplary life, wonderful changes will follow in the manners of the lower ranks." He further explained:

> On this principle, Confucius, the famous Eastern reformer, proceeded. When he saw his country sunk in vice, and wickedness of all kinds triumphant, he applied himself first to the grandness; and having, by his doctrine, won them to the cause of virtue, the commons followed in multitudes. ①

In cultivating his personal and public virtues, Franklin drew inspiration from Confucian ethics, exhibiting the influence of Confucianism overseas, which was largely due to the introduction of Confucian classics to the Western world through translation.

2.2　Translation of Confucianism

Prior to Franklin's *Gazette* articles, Confucianism had been introduced to the West through translation and the earliest translation of *The Analects of Confucius* is

---

① Franklin, Benjamin. *The Works of Benjamin Franklin*. New York and London: G. P. Putnam's Sons, 1904, p. 267.

supposedly the Latin version *Confucius Sinarum Philosophus*，*sive*，*Scientia Sinensis Latine Exposita* published in Paris in 1687. The English version titled *The Morals of Confucius* appeared in 1691，but it was only a summary of the Latin version. Later，the Confucian classics were retranslated several times and the translations of James Legge and Arthur Waley enjoyed a large readership in the West.

Most translators of Confucian classics adopt the method of free translation. They get rid of the wording and structure of the original text and re-express its meaning in the target language based on their understandings. Let's take the translation of the Confucian concept 仁 as an example. James Legge translated it as "virtue，" "virtuous，" or "perfect virtue" as in the following analects.

Fine words and an insinuating appearance are seldom associated with true virtue. (巧言令色，鲜矣仁。)①

The wise find pleasure in water；the virtuous find pleasure in hills. The wise are joyful；the virtuous are long-lived. (智者乐水，仁者乐山，智者动，仁者静，智者乐，仁者寿)②

To subdue one's self and return to propriety，is perfect virtue. (克己复礼为仁。)③

Burton Watson put it as "humaneness" or "humane." His translations of the same three analects are as follows.

Clever words and a pleasing countenance—little humaneness there!④

The wise delight in water；the humane delight in mountains. The wise move；the humane are still. The wise are happy；the humane live long. ⑤

To master the self and return to ritual is to be humane. ⑥

---

① Legge，James，trans. *The Chinese Classics: Confucian Analects*，*The Great Learning*，*and The Doctrine of the Mean*. Hong Kong：Hong University Press，1960，p. 139.

② Legge，James，trans. *The Chinese Classics: Confucian Analects*，*The Great Learning*，*and The Doctrine of the Mean*. Hong Kong：Hong University Press，1960，p. 192.

③ Legge，James，trans. *The Chinese Classics: Confucian Analects*，*The Great Learning*，*and The Doctrine of the Mean*. Hong Kong：Hong University Press，1960，p. 250.

④ Watson，Burton，trans. *The Analects of Confucius*. New York：Columbia University Press，2007，p. 16.

⑤ Watson，Burton，trans. *The Analects of Confucius*. New York：Columbia University Press，2007，p. 45.

⑥ Watson，Burton，trans. *The Analects of Confucius*. New York：Columbia University Press，2007，p. 80.

仁 was also translated as "the Good" or "Goodness" by Arthur Waley, "moral life" or "moral character" by Gu Hongming, and "benevolence" by Liu Dianjue. All the translators resort to the method of free translation and express their understandings of 仁 in English.

Free translation of Confucianism receives harsh criticism from cultural nationalists and supporters of foreignization. They postulate that Confucian classics are canonical writings with normative and cohesive power that play a pivotal role in binding the Chinese community. As a form of domestication, free translation would reduce the rich cultural connotations of Confucian ideas and subjugate Chinese culture to Anglo-American centrism. They propose transliteration as a countermeasure and advocate the transliteration of key Confucian terms, for example, 仁 as *ren*. This approach, as we've discussed, may impede reading. In translating Confucian concepts, transliteration is often used with annotation. Translators first put the concepts into Chinese *pinyin* and then provide English annotations in terms of their connotations. For instance, "Key Concepts in Chinese Thoughts and Culture," a database launched by Foreign Language Teaching and Research Press puts 仁 into *ren* and provides the following annotation:

> The basic meaning of the term is love for others. Its extended meaning refers to the state of harmony among people, and the unity of all things under heaven. *Ren* (仁) constitutes the foundation and basis for moral behavior. It is also a consciousness that corresponds to the norms of moral behavior. Roughly put, *ren* has the following three implications: 1) compassion or conscience; 2) virtue of respect built upon the relationship between fathers and sons and among brothers; and 3) the unity of all things under heaven. Confucianism holds *ren* as the highest moral principle. *Ren* is taken as love in the order of first showing filial piety to one's parents and elder brothers, and then extending love and care to other members of the family, and eventually to everyone else under heaven. [1]

This approach, a compromise between foreignization and domestication, can preserve the connotations of Confucian terms and make the translations readable. However, with many long annotations, the translated texts might not be able to offer a pleasant reading experience.

Domestication and free translation still predominate in the translation of Confucian classics. Table 3 lists the generally accepted translations of some Confucian terms.

---

[1] https://shuyuku. chinesethought. cn/shuyuinfo. aspx? shuyu_id=593.

Table 3　Generally Accepted Translations of Some Confucian Terms

Chinse	English	Chinese	English
四书五经	the Four Books and the Five Classics	《春秋》	*The Spring and Autumn Annals*
《大学》	*The Great Learning*	仁	benevolence
《中庸》	*The Doctrine of the Mean*	义	righteousness
《论语》	*The Analects of Confucius*	礼	propriety
《孟子》	*The Works of Mencius*	智	wisdom
《诗经》	*The Book of Poetry*	信	sincerity
《尚书》	*The Book of History*	忠	loyalty
《礼记》	*The Book of Rites*	孝	filial piety
《易经》	*The Book of Changes*	悌	love and respect one's elder brother

3. Translation of Taoism

This section offers an overview of Taoism and discusses its English translation.

3.1　Overview of Taoism

Taoism，also translated as Daoism，is an indigenous school of thought in China. Some regard it as a religion. In *Culture of the Taoism*，Liu Tao defines it as "an indigenous religion of China originating from the belief in immortals and alchemy."[1] Foreigners also tend to regard Taoism as a religion and think that "Daoism is undoubtedly the most incompletely known and most poorly understood" religion among the world.[2] As a school of thought，Daoism originates from the ideas of Lao Zi and Zhuang Zi. Adherents of Daoism believe that *Dao* is the course，the principle，the essence，and the standard of all things，to which all people must abide by. They advocate governance through non-action and promote the belief that people should live a simple life，neither striving for wealth，nor fame or power which will bring nothing but worry and trouble.

The school of Taoism transformed into Huang Lao Theory in the late Warring States Period by absorbing ideas from Confucianism，the Mohist school，and others. It became the official ideology of the Western Han dynasty and was promoted by the rulers to help the nation recuperate from desolation caused by years of war through non-interference. During the Eastern Han dynasty，as the Yellow Emperor and Lao

---

① Liu，Tao. *Culture of the Taoism*. Hefei：Huangshan Publishing House，2013，p. 1.

② Kohn，Livia. *Daoism Handbook*. Leiden：Brill，2000，p. xi.

Zi were deified, the Huang Lao Theory was mystified, prefiguring the establishment of Taoism as a religion. In the process of development, Taoism drew extensively from "the Taoist school, the divination mystics (*Chen Wei*, divination combined with mystical Confucian philosophy), theories of *Yin Yang* and the Five Elements, the mythical and immortal practice of alchemy, primitive religion, witchcraft, and many others."[①]

3.2　The influence of Taoism

The influence of Taoism on Chinese culture is extensive and profound. As for fiction, all novels or short stories featuring ghosts, spirits, and other supernatural elements draw inspiration from Daoism—*The Classic of Mountains and Seas* (《山海经》), *In Search of the Supernatural: The Written Record* (《搜神记》), *Flowers in the Mirror* (《镜花缘》), *Investiture of the Gods* (《封神演义》), *Strange Tales from a Chinese Studio* (《聊斋志异》), to name a few of them. Poetry is also influenced by Taoism, such as Guo Pu's poetry on mythical excursions (《游仙诗十四首》), Li Bai's "A Poem for Climbing Mount Tai" (《登泰山诗》) and "Tianmu Mountain Ascended in a Dream" (《梦游天姥吟留别》).[②] In addition to literature, the influence of Taoism is also found in arts, music, martial arts, and tourism.

Taoism goes beyond national borders and finds believers in the West. William Somerset Maugham went to China in 1919 and published several works about China. In *The Painted Veil*, Maugham quoted from Taoism several times and expressed his understanding of *Tao*:

It is the Way and the Waygoer. It is the eternal road along which walk all beings, but no being made it, for itself is being. It is everything and nothing. From it all things spring, all things conform to it, and to it at last all things return. It is a square without angles, a sound which ears cannot hear, and an image without form. It is a vast net and though its meshes are as wide as the sea it lets nothing through. It is the sanctuary where all things find refuge. It is nowhere, but without looking out of the window you may see it. Desire not to desire, it teaches, and leave all things to take their course. He that humbles himself shall be preserved entire. He that bends shall be made straight. Failure is the foundation of success and success is the lurking-place of failure; but who can tell when the turning point will come? He who strives after tenderness can

---

① Liu, Tao. *Culture of the Taoism*. Hefei: Huangshan Publishing House, 2013, p. 1.
② Liu, Tao. *Culture of the Taoism*. Hefei: Huangshan Publishing House, 2013, pp. 144 – 170.

become even as a little child. Gentleness brings victory to him who attacks and safety to him who defends. Mighty is he who conquers himself. [1]

In the above excerpt, Maugham uses a lot of antithetical sentences to explain the idea of Dao, highlighting its quintessential characteristics of mysteriousness, non-action, and conversion.

Chinese American writers also bring Taoism into their writing. In *The Woman Warrior*, Maxine Hong Kingston devotes a whole chapter to the protagonist's experience of learning martial arts on the mountain and Taoist elements are omnipresent in the chapter. [2]

Apart from its influence on serious literature, Taoism is also an inexhaustible source of inspiration for Western pop culture. Martial arts have become a cultural icon of China and Chinese viewers will not fail to recognize the presence of Taoism in the blockbuster *Kung Fu Panda*.

3.3 Translation of Taoism

The translation of Taoism also chiefly relies on domestication and free translation, but the key term 道 is either transliterated as "*Dao*"/"*Tao*" or freely translated as "the Way." For example, James Legge put 道可道非常道 as "The Tao that can be trodden is not the enduring and unchanging *Tao*"[3] and Arthur Waley translated it as "The Way that can be told of is not the Unvarying Way."[4] Except 道, other Taoist terms are put into English mainly through free translation as Table 4 shows.

Table 4　Some Generally Accepted Translations of Taoist Terms

Chinse	English	Chinese	English
《道德经》	*Tao Te Ching*	四御	the Four Royalties
《太平经》	*The Scripture on Great Peace*	三官	the Three Officials
《正统道藏》	*Orthodox Treasury of Taoist Scriptures*	四象	the Four Symbols
《太上感应篇》	*Tract of the Most Exalted on Action and Response*	八仙	the Eight Immortals

---

① Maugham, William Somerset. *The Painted Veil*. London: Vintage, 2001, p. 170.

② Kingston, Maxine Hong. *The Woman Warrior, China Men, Tripmaster Monkey, Hawai'i One Summer and Other Writings*. New York: Library of America, 2022, pp. 20 - 50.

③ Legge, James, trans. *The Tao Te Ching*. Auckland: The Floating Press, 2008, p. 8.

④ Waley, Arthur. *The Way and Its Power: A Study of the Tao Te Ching and Its Place in Chinese Thought*. New York: Grove Press, 1994, p. 141.

（**Continued**）

Chinse	English	Chinese	English
五斗米道	the Way of the Five Pecks of Rice	门神	door gods
太平道	the Way of the Great Peace	关圣帝君	Saintly Emperor Guan
柔弱不争	non-contentious suppleness	碧霞元君	Azure Cloud Prime Goddess
性命双修	dual cultivation of innate nature and physical life	画符	painted charms
神仙方士	immortality wizards and alchemists	念咒	incantation chanting
全真七子	the Seven Masters of the All True Taoism	扶乩	sciomancy
三清	the Three Pure Gods/ the Three Clarities/Purities	仙道	the way of immortality

It is obvious that domestication and free translation predominate the translation of Taoist terms. Before winding up this section，we'd like to mention that in translating tourism publicity materials，translators may encounter texts that are related with Taoism since some tourist attractions are Taoist architectures. For example，in the introduction to a Taoist temple，there is the sentence "主殿供奉有三清,即手握珍珠的玉清、怀抱宇宙的上清和手持羽扇的太清." The difficulty of translating sentences like this lies in putting the Taoist terms into proper English. If we know the generally accepted translations of Taoist terms，it would not be difficult to put them into proper English. We can use inversion and put the aforementioned Chinese sentence into this： "In the main hall are enshrined the Three Pure Ones—Jade Pure who has a pearl within his fingers，Upper Pure who holds the universe in his arms，and Great Pure who has a feather fan in his hand."

4. Translation of Buddhism

This section offers an overview of Buddhism and discusses its translation.

4.1 Overview of Buddhism

Buddhism in China was supposedly imported from India in the Eastern Han dynasty. In 68，under the edict of Emperor Mingdi，White Horse Temple was constructed to commemorate the transportation of Buddhist scriptures by two eminent Indian monks. It gradually became a sacred place and a cradle of Buddhism. Ever since its introduction into China，Buddhism had enjoyed quick development and attracted a lot of followers. Beginning from Eastern Han dynasty，Buddhist masters like An Shigao（安世高），Zhi Qian（支谦），Shi Daoan（释道安），Kumārajīva（鸠摩罗

什），and Xuan Zang（玄奘）dedicated themselves to the translation of Buddhist scriptures，not only contributing to the development of Buddhism in China，but also enriching translation theory and practice.

In this section，we will discuss Buddhism both as a religion and school of thought. Buddhism "gives a central role to the doctrine of karma." "The 'four noble truths' of Buddhism state that all existence is suffering，that the cause of suffering is desire，that freedom from suffering is nirvana，and that this is attained through the 'eightfold path' of ethical conduct，wisdom，and mental discipline（including meditation）" that specifically refers to right knowledge，right thought，right speech，right behavior，right livelihood，right effort，right mindfulness，and right concentration."[1] There are two major traditions of Buddhism—Theravada and Mahayana. Chinese Buddhism mainly belongs to the tradition of Mahayana but also draws elements from Theravada.

4.2 The cultural legacy of Buddhism

Though a foreign religion in origin，Buddhism is localized in China and leaves a rich cultural legacy. Many words in everyday use are of Buddhist origin. For example，槟榔 is transliterated from Indonesian，西瓜 from Jurchen，玻璃，茉莉，and 昙花 from Sanskrit. Actually，many precious stones，trees，plants，and objects derive their names from Buddhist countries and some words originally "coined for Buddhist purposes entered the secular vocabulary with quite a different meaning."[2] Besides，the method of transliteration，developed from Buddhist scripture translation，was profusely used in translating Western ideas，thoughts，science，and technology during the late Qing and early Republic of China. Many familiar Chinese expressions owe their coinage to transliteration such as 罗曼蒂克，transliteration of "romantic," 摩登，transliteration of "modern," and 幽默，transliteration of "humor."

The cultural legacy of Buddhism is also embodied in beliefs，architecture，literature，and pop culture. The notions of karma and after-life are deeply rooted in the Chinese psyche. In Buddhist temples，devotees prostrate themselves before the gods，praying for health and fortune or confessing sins and evil doings. When someone commits evil doings，he/she would be condemned to meet his/her retribution. And if we are indebted to someone else，we would show our gratitude by saying "I would repay your favor even if I toil like beasts of burden next life."

---

[1] Stevenson，Angus. *Oxford Dictionary of English* （3rd edition）. Oxford：Oxford University Press，2010，p. 4204.

[2] Wright，Arthur F. *Buddhism in Chinese History*. Stanford：Stanford University Press，1959，pp. 108 – 109.

Many scenic spots and architectures are related with Buddhism，such as Mo Kao Grotto at Dunhuang，Longmen Grottos，the Potala Palace，Shaolin Temple in Henan，Temple of Great Gratitude in Nanjing，Longhua Temple in Shanghai，Dazu Rock Carvings in Chongqing，and the Wild Goose Pagoda in Xi'an. These are sacred places of Buddhism and attract tens of thousands of visitors each year.

Perhaps the most well-known specimen of Buddhist influence on literature is *Journey to the West*（《西游记》）by Wu Cheng'en. The prototype of the story is Xuan Zang's pilgrimage to India for Buddhist scriptures. In the novel，we have Sakyamuni，Kwan-yin Bodhisattva，and the eighteen Arhats，all of which are figures from Buddhism. Let's digress a little bit. In the novel，Taoist gods and Buddhist figures coexist peacefully and the Jade Emperor，supreme deity of Taoism，even seeks the help of Sakyamuni to bring the Monkey King under control，indicating the coming of Buddhism and Taoism. Other works that exhibit the influence of Buddhism include *The Palace of Eternal Youth*（《长生殿》）by Hong Sheng，*The Romance of West Chamber*（《西厢记》）by Wang Shifu，"The New Year's Sacrifice，" etc.

In pop culture，the influence of Buddhism is also great. The movie *Shaolin Temple*（《少林寺》）（directed by Zhang Xinyan and starring Jet Li）narrates the story of "Little Tiger" who learns martial art in Shaolin Temple to revenge his father and helps Li Shimin out of trouble. The movie was a phenomenal success and garnered a box office of over 160 million yuan in 1982.

4.3   Translation of Buddhism

The translation of Buddhism is much earlier than that of Confucianism and Taoism. As early as the Eastern Han dynasty，Buddhist scriptures like *The Scripture in Forty-two Sections*（《四十二章经》）had been translated into Chinese. In Sui and Tang dynasties，with the arduous efforts of Xuan Zang and other translators，Buddhism translation reached a climax. The translation of Buddhism has such a long and robust tradition that it becomes a special branch of translation studies. There are many notable translators in the history of Buddhism translation，such as An Shigao，Zhi Chen（Lokaksema，支谶），Zhi Qian，Shi Daoan，Kumārajīva，Paramārtha（真谛），Xuan Zang，Yi Jing（义净），and Amoghavajra（不空）. In this section，we only introduce Kumārajīva，Paramārtha，Xuan Zang，and Amoghavajra who are acclaimed as the four masters of Buddhism translation.

4.3.1   Kumārajīva

Kumārajīva was an eminent monk of the Later Qin dynasty（384—417）and renowned translator of Buddhist scriptures. He and his disciples translated over 300 volumes of Buddhist scriptures into Chinese，exerting a great influence on Chinese and world Buddhism. Kumārajīva believed that the sutras contain teachings and deep meanings of the Buddha which should not be compromised in translation. He objected to Zhi Qian's use of refined language and advocated the use of plain language. To better reveal and promote the teachings of the Buddha, Kumārajīva resorted to abridged translation instead of full translation and provided explications to the sutras, trying as he could to present the truth in his translation. Though "not having done full justice to the aesthetic beauty of the source," he nevertheless had "not compromised the true meaning of the sutras."[1] Therefore, on his deathbed, Kumārajīva said: "I have tried in my inadequate way to serve as a translator. If I have not transgressed the truth in my translations, let my tongue not be destroyed in my cremation."[2] When his body turned to ashes, his tongue remained intact.

Kumārajīva left a rich legacy on translation. Later translators who offer explication of the text either in the form of introduction or preface owe their debt to him and advocators of abridged translation and free translation also regard Kumārajīva as one of their precursors.

4.3.2 Paramārtha

Paramārtha was born into a Braham family in India and was well-versed in Buddhist writings. Between 535 and 545, he responded to the call for eminent monks by Emperor Wu of the Southern Liang dynasty and travelled through Cambodia to China with over 200 fascicles of Sanskrit sutras. When his translation project was about to begin, Houjing Rebellion broke out and he was forced to move from place to place. He held to the cause of translating and preaching Buddhist sutras, particularly those of Mahayana during the unsettled times and became a great master of Buddhist doctrine and philosophy. Paramārtha translated and preached on 41 sutras, such as *Theory of Mere Consciousness* (《大乘唯识论》), *A Compendium of the Great Vehicle* (《摄大乘论》), and *A Treatise on the Abhidharma Storehouse* (《俱舍论》).[3]

Paramārtha took a rigorous attitude to sutra translation and emphasized on faithful expression of the sutra's original meaning. He would not set the brush to paper until he had a thorough grasp of the sutra's meaning after deliberation and verification. To ensure a faithful translation, he sometimes chose to sacrifice

---

① Cheung, Martha, P. Y. *An Anthology of Chinese Discourse on Translation Volume One: From Earliest Times to the Buddhist Project*. London and New York: Routledge, 2014, p. 92.

② Cheung, Martha, P. Y. *An Anthology of Chinese Discourse on Translation Volume One: From Earliest Times to the Buddhist Project*. London and New York: Routledge, 2014, p. 109.

③ Cheung, Martha, P. Y. *An Anthology of Chinese Discourse on Translation Volume One: From Earliest Times to the Buddhist Project*. London and New York: Routledge, 2014, p. 127.

smoothness and elegance of the original text, resulting in his half literary and half plain style. And obscurities are not uncommon in his translation. Paramārtha's attitude and approach to translation were inherited and carried forward by his disciples.

4.3.3   Xuan Zang

Xuan Zang, originally named Chen Yi and popularly known as "the Tripitaka-master", came from Henan Province and was an eminent monk in the Tang dynasty. He aspired to devote to Buddhism at an early age and studied Buddhist scriptures eagerly. During his study, Xuan Zang found that the sutras and treaties showed discrepancies in "the underlying principles of Buddhism and the processes and methods for pursuing Buddhist enlightenment."[①] To dispel his doubts and resolve these differences, he journeyed to India to learn Buddhism and fetch scriptures. After finishing his study, Xuan Zang returned to Chang'an and settled down in Hongfu Monastery to translate the collected sutras. He and his team formed a well-organized assembly, set up the translation criteria of faithfulness and plainness, and initiated a standardized translation process. They verified interpretations and doctrinal issues, checked the Sanskrit meanings, standardized terminology, and polished the translations.

Based on his experience, Xuan Zang set down five guidelines for not-translating a term.

"First, if a term partakes of the occult, it is not-translated."[②] According to Xuan Zang, there are many occult terms and incantations in Buddhist sutras that acquire a psychologically deterrent power through generations' repeated chanting. These terms should be transliterated to preserve their original occult flavor and power. For example, 陀罗尼, meaning "mantra" or "magic spell," is a transliteration of the Sanskrit term *dhāraṇi* and 唵嘛呢叭咪吽, meaning "pearl in the lotus flower," is also a transliteration from Sanskrit. This method is also used in the translation of spells in *Harry Potter* by J. K. Rowling. In *Harry Potter and the Sorcerer's Stone*, "Wingardium leviosa," the spell for floating, is transliterated as 羽加迪姆勒维奥萨.

"Second, if a term has multiple meanings, it is not-translated."[③] Many terms in Buddhist sutras are rich in meaning and have no Chinese equivalents. If they are

---

① Cheung, Martha, P. Y. *An Anthology of Chinese Discourse on Translation Volume One: From Earliest Times to the Buddhist Project*. London and New York: Routledge, 2014, p. 156.

② Cheung, Martha, P. Y. *An Anthology of Chinese Discourse on Translation Volume One: From Earliest Times to the Buddhist Project*. London and New York: Routledge, 2014, p. 157.

③ Cheung, Martha, P. Y. *An Anthology of Chinese Discourse on Translation Volume One: From Earliest Times to the Buddhist Project*. London and New York: Routledge, 2014, p. 157.

rendered into existing Chinese phrases or expressions, their original meanings would be partially lost. For example, the Sanskrit term *bhagavat* has six meanings, namely, sovereignty, glory, austerity, name, fortune, and honor. If it is substituted by any one of these words, other meanings will be lost, so it is transliterated as 薄伽梵 to preserve its rich connotations.

"Third, if the object represented by a term does not exist in this part of the world, that term is not-translated."[①] These terms are culture-specific and transliteration is usually used to render them into the target language. For example, the Sanskrit word *jambu* refers to a type of plant that is originally found in South Asian countries and has not been introduced into China when it was translated, so it was rendered into 阎浮 according to its Sanskrit pronunciation. The term 阎浮树 is thus created by combing 阎浮, a transliteration of *jambu* and 树, the Chinese generic term for "tree." Through this way, many foreign terms were introduced into China.

"Fourth, if a past rendering of a term has become established and accepted, the term is not-translated."[②] This is not only to acknowledge the contributions of past translators, but also to avoid unnecessary confusion. For example, the Sanskrit term "*anou puti*," meaning "the Way of the highest correct and all-embracing knowledge/awareness," is not untranslatable, but ever since the time of Kāśyapa-Mātaṅga (迦叶摩腾), an eminent Indian monk of the Eastern Han dynasty, its Sanskrit pronunciation 阿耨菩提 has been kept. Similarly, many transliterated terms like 罗曼蒂克 and 幽默 in the late Qing and early Republic of China are also kept to this day.

"Fifth, if a term elicits positive associations, it is not-translated."[③] One purpose of Buddhism is to elicit mercy, kindness, and awe from people. If the awe-eliciting terms are put into common expressions, their meanings might become lighter and shallower and their religious power might be reduced. Let's illustrate it with the translation of the Sanskrit term *prajñā* which means divine wisdom that can only be attained through physical and mental cultivation. If it is translated as "wisdom," its sense of divinity and authority will be substantially reduced, if not completely lost. Thus, it is transliterated as 般若 to preserve its religious weight and dissociate it from the secular implications of 智慧.

These five guidelines for not-translating a term leave a rich legacy on translation.

① Cheung, Martha, P. Y. *An Anthology of Chinese Discourse on Translation Volume One: From Earliest Times to the Buddhist Project*. London and New York: Routledge, 2014, p. 157.

② Cheung, Martha, P. Y. *An Anthology of Chinese Discourse on Translation Volume One: From Earliest Times to the Buddhist Project*. London and New York: Routledge, 2014, p. 157.

③ Cheung, Martha, P. Y. *An Anthology of Chinese Discourse on Translation Volume One: From Earliest Times to the Buddhist Project*. London and New York: Routledge, 2014, p. 157.

On the one hand, they provide inspiration for terminology translation, and on the other hand, they generate incessant debates on the merits of transliteration as opposed to free translation.

4.3.4 Amoghavajra

Amoghavajra was a master of Esoteric Buddhism and translator of Esoteric Buddhist scriptures. He was born in Java, Indonesia and went to Luoyang in 720. Four years later, he was initiated into monkhood and dedicated to translating and teaching Esoteric Buddhism under the guidance of his master Vajrabodhi（金刚智）. Finding that his master's collection of Esoteric Buddhist scriptures was incomplete, Amoghavajra journeyed to the south of India and obtained a large number of scriptures. Back to China, he engaged himself in translating these scriptures and produced the second largest translation corpus in the Sinitic Buddhist canon.

Unlike Paramārtha and Xuan Zang who prized faithful expression of the sutras' original meanings, Amoghavajra took a comparatively liberal attitude towards scripture translation and incorporated his own teachings into his translations. Due to this approach, his translations were more like adaptations of the original texts. Strickmann thus commented on Amoghavajra's translations:

> Properly speaking, many of these were not translations at all. Instead, they might better be called "adaptations"; essentially, he refurbished Tantric texts that had already been translated into Chinese so as to bring them into line with his own terminology and ritual practice. [1]

Amoghavajra produced a large textual corpus of Esoteric Buddhist scriptures through free translation and played a pivotal role in establishing Esoteric Buddhism in China. [2]

In addition to the four master translators we've introduced here, there are over 200 other recorded translators of Buddhist scriptures in history. Together they devoted to the translation, explication, and promotion of Buddhism in China, ushering in the first major period in the history of translation in China and leaving a rich legacy. Many contested issues in translation like foreignization vs. domestication, literal translation vs. free translation, faithfulness vs. smoothness, were set up by translation of Buddhist sutras and continued well into the present day.

---

[1] Strickmann, Michel. *Chinese Magical Medicine*. Stanford: Stanford University Press, 2002, p. 229.

[2] Goble, Geoffrey C. *Chinese Esoteric Buddhism*. New York: Columbia University Press, 2019, pp. 12 – 13.

A Short Summary

In this chapter, we've elucidated the basic tenets, core concepts, and impact of Confucianism, Taoism, and Buddhism, and then discussed their translation. The translation of Confucian and Taoist classics into foreign languages started from the 17th century and translators usually relied on domestication to produce smooth translations for target readers. The translation of Buddhist sutras from Sanskrit into Chinese has a much longer history and transliteration is an important method in converting Buddhist terminology. It is through translation that Buddhism was introduced into China and interacts with Confucianism and Taoism. After centuries of intermingling, they converge and form the core of traditional Chinese culture.

Reviewing Questions

1. What are the basic ideas of Confucianism?

2. What is the impact of Confucianism on Chinese culture?

3. What are the basic tenets of Taoism?

4. What is the historical development of Taoism as a religion?

5. What is the impact of Taoism on Chinese culture?

6. What are the key ideas of Buddhism?

7. What is the impact of Buddhism on Chinese culture?

8. What are the advantages and disadvantages of domestication in translating Confucian and Taoist classics?

9. What is your understanding of Xuan Zang's five guidelines for not-translating?

10. What is your view of transliteration in the translation of Buddhist sutras?

Chapter 10

Translation of Chinese Classics

 Objectives

➢ Understand the meaning and value of Chinese classics

➢ Know about the translation history of Chinese classics

➢ Grasp the styles and chief contributions of major translators

➢ Be able to use various methods and skills in translating Chinese classics

1. The Meaning and Value of Chinese Classics

The English word "classic" is derived from its Latin predecessor "classicus," meaning "of the highest class." If a work of art is of recognized and established values, we call it a classic. [1] For example, *The Analects of Confucius* is taken as a Confucian classic due to its well-acknowledged, generally-accepted, and time-tested values. Sometimes, the word "classic" is used interchangeably with "canon," but there are differences between them. Any work, whatever field it belongs to, can be referred to as a classic so long as it is typical, excellent, and timeless as a model, but it may not be canonical. Canon, originally meaning "a general law, rule, principle, or criterion by which something is judged," has a strong religious color as shown in the expression "the biblical canon." It is later used to refer to a selected "list of works considered to be permanently established as being of the highest quality." [2] Canon emphasizes judgement and selection. In *The Western Canon*, Harold Bloom assumes the role of arbitrator of Western literature and makes a list of the authors and works that he believes are instrumental in creating and developing the Western literary tradition. Many Western literary classics like *Robinson Crusoe*, *David Copperfield*, *Tess of the D'Urbervilles*, and *The Sound and the Fury* are excluded from the Western canon. [3]

Classics are of great value. First, they are the most important carriers of culture and play an irreplaceable role in creating and preserving national community. Assmann argues that religious and juridical canons are means through which early Egyptians, Greeks, and Jews imagine and build themselves as national communities by following the customs and practices prescribed by these canons. [4] Similarly, Chinese classics carry the collective experience and memory of the Chinese people and shape their national identity. Wherever we are, when we read Chinese classics, we identify ourselves with Chinese culture and find kinship with other Chinese. Second, classics can cultivate our character, enlighten our mind, broaden our horizon, enrich our knowledge, and improve our aesthetic taste. Having stood the test of time, classics

---

[1] Stevenson, Angus. *Oxford Dictionary of English* (3rd edition). Oxford: Oxford University Press, 2010, pp. 5906 – 5907.

[2] Stevenson, Angus. *Oxford Dictionary of English* (3rd edition). Oxford: Oxford University Press, 2010, pp. 4719 – 4720.

[3] Bloom, Harold. *The Western Canon*. New York: Riverhead Books, 1995, pp. 15 – 39.

[4] Assmann, Jan. *Cultural Memory and Early Civilization: Writing, Remembrance, and Political Imagination*. Cambridge: Cambridge University Press, 2011, pp. 261 – 267.

preserve "the best which has been thought and said in the world" and can help us grow into intellectuals. [1] They teach us how to deal with nature, others, and ourselves, how to think critically, and how to act responsibly and reasonably. They can help us enjoy solitude and lift us out of misery and despair.

2. The Translation History of Chinese Classics

The history of English translation of Chinese classics can be traced back to the publication of *The Morals of Confucius* in 1691. Over the past over 300 years, many Chinese classics have been put into English with the continuous arduous work of missionaries, sinologists, and Chinese translators. Scholars tend to divide the translation history of Chinese classics into the following four stages.

2.1   Before the 18th century

English translation of Chinese classics before the 18th century was at its initial stage. During this period, not many English scholars were proficient with classic Chinese and Chinese classics were translated into English via French or secondary sources. For example, *A Description of the Empire of China and Chinese-Tartary* which includes excerpts from *The Books of Songs* and prescriptions from *Compendium of Materia Medica* was translated from the French book *Description Geographique, Historique, Chronologique, Politique, et Physique de L'Empire de la Chine et de la Tartarie Chinoise* (《中华帝国全志》, 1735) by French missionary Jean Baptiste du Halde. And *Hau Kiou Choaan, Or, The Pleasing History* (《好逑传》, 1761) which was edited and published by Thomas Percy was another translated major Chinese classic in this period.

The English translations of Chinese classics during this period were not many and possessed two inadequacies. First, they lacked accuracy and literariness as many of them were not based on the original Chinese texts and the translators were not good at classic Chinese. Second, they were chiefly adapted translations, selected translations, or rewritings instead of complete translations. However, they still marked the intense efforts and pioneering spirit of scholars who were determined to bring Chinese classics to the English world.

2.2   The 19th century

When the door of China was forced open by foreign powers, foreign

---

[1]   Arnold, Matthew. *Culture and Anarchy*. Oxford: Oxford University Press, 2006, p. 5.

missionaries，merchants，and diplomats came in. Some of them mastered the Chinese language and became the main force in introducing Chinese classics to the outside world. John Francis Davis（德庇时，1795—1890），James Legge（理雅各，1815—1897），Herbert Allen Giles（翟理思，1845—1935），Elijah Coleman Bridgman（裨治文，1801—1861），and Samuel Wells Williams（卫三畏，1812—1884）were supposed to be the greatest sinologists in this period and had illustrious careers in translating Chinese classics into English.

2.2.1　John Francis Davis

John Francis Davis came to Guangzhou at the age of 18 and served as the governor of Hong Kong from 1844 to 1848. His translation oeuvre includes *An Heir in His Old Age*（《老生儿》，1817），*Chinese Novels*（《中国小说选》），*Chinese Moral Maxims*（《贤文书》），*The Fortunate Union*（《好逑传》），*The Sorrows of Han*（《汉宫秋》），and *Poeseos Sinicae Commentarii*（《汉文诗解》）. In his translations，Davis adopted the strategy of domestication to reduce heterogeneity of the original texts and used abridgement，supplement，and rewriting to deal with the plot，aiming to produce smooth readings for English readers.

2.2.2　James Legge

James Legge was a prolific translator of Chinese classics. As we have known from the previous chapter，he translated the complete Confucian canon and part of the Taoist canon. The well-known translation work *A Record of Buddhistic Kingdoms*（《法显传》），a pivotal text in Buddhism history，geography，and cross-cultural communication，is also under his name. Legge's translations indicate his meticulous attitude and excellent scholarship. He based his translation upon a systematic study of the original text and combined translation with explication. His translation，known for its faithfulness and accuracy，is highly reputed in the West. The comment from his best Chinese friend Wang Tao（王韬，1828—1897）would suffice to prove Legge's rigorous attitude towards translation and scholarship：

> Dr. Legge，however，did not shrink from difficulties. Concentrating on the study of the *Thirteen Classics*，he threaded together，scrutinized，examined into sources，and analyzed. He maintained his own views and did not simply follow tradition. In his study of the classics，he did not favor any one school or devote himself to any one theory，but he made wide and extensive his studies in order to reach a perfect comprehension ... He translated the *Four Books* and the *Book of History* which，when published and read by Western scholars，were received with admiration for their thoroughness，lucidity，and accuracy and were

accepted by them as authoritative. ①

Legge, acclaimed as a paragon of the early English translators of Chinese classics, remains a source of inspiration for translators and his translations are still widely read and studied.

2.2.3　Herbert Allen Giles

Herbert Allen Giles received a classical education in Latin and Greek, which helped foster his rigorous academic attitude and laid a solid foundation for his future research and translation. In 1867, he passed the examination of British Foreign & Commonwealth Office and served as a translator in various British consulates in China. During his 25 years' sojourn in China, he devoted himself to Sinology and translation of Chinese classics. Giles' scholarship covers a wide range of areas. He edited dictionaries and reference books, wrote on Chinese literature, and described the Chinese people.

Giles started his translation career with the translation of *Three Character Classic* (《三字经》) and *Thousand Character Essay* (《千字文》) which were collected in *Two Chinese Poems*. Though a daunting task, Giles tried his best to put the two Chinese classics into English and offered long explanations and annotations. He also translated *Instructions to Coroners* (《洗冤录》) and his translation was held to be the most influential and authoritative one. His translation of Pu Songling's *Strange Stories from a Chinese Studio* (《聊斋志异》) was well accepted by English readers and republished several times. In 1884, Giles published *Gems of Chinese Literature*, a collection of the English translations of Chinese prose and poetry from the pre-Qin period to late Qing. In addition to these classics, Giles also translated, edited, and published some popular literary works, such as *Quips from a Chinese Jest-Book* and *Chinese Fairy Tales*.

Giles' translations are also noted for their faithfulness, readability, and scholarship. He based his translation on a thorough understanding of the source text and Chinese culture and offered detailed and comprehensive notes and introductions to it, aiming to help English readers better understand the classic and introduce Chinese culture to the West.

2.2.4　Elijah Coleman Bridgman and Samuel Wells Williams

We put Bridgman and Williams together because they were both American

---

① Ride, Lindsay. "Biographical Note." *The Chinese Classics: Confucian Analects, The Great Learning, and The Doctrine of the Mean*. Trans. James Legge. Hong Kong: Hong University Press, 1960, pp. 16 - 17.

missionaries and editors of *The Chinese Repository* (《中国丛报》), a Guangdong-based monthly dedicated to the translation and introduction of Chinese classics. Their translation careers were not as productive as those of James Legge and Herbert Allen Giles. Bridgman introduced, translated, and commented on *Filial Duty* (《孝经》) and Williams retranslated *The Compared Tunic* (《合汗衫》) from French into English. Though their translations were few, their studies on Sinology were very influential, sparking the Western readers' interest in China. [①]

2.2.5　Gu Hongming (1856—1928)

Gu Hongming was among the first Chinese scholars who translated and introduced Chinese classics to the West. Gu, born in Malaysia, was a mixed-blood and received his education at The University of Edinburgh and Leipzig University. Gu was erudite and informed in knowledge both Chinese and Western and was purported to be the first Chinese who excelled in Western science, technology, languages and Sinology. We know Gu Hongming probably from his popular work *The Spirit of the Chinese People* (《中国人的精神》), but he was also fruitful in retranslating part of the Confucian canon.

Gu's determination to retranslate the Confucian canon arose from his dissatisfaction with the existing translations. He harshly criticized Western sinologists for distorting the Chinese classics. His comments on James Legge's translation could illustrate his critical stance:

> The quantity of work done is certainly stupendous, whatever may be thought of the quality. In presence of these huge volumes we feel almost afraid to speak. Nevertheless, it must be confessed that the work does not altogether satisfy us. Mr. Balfour justly remarks that in translating these classics a great deal depends upon the terminology employed by the translator. Now we feel that the terminology employed by Dr. Legge is harsh, crude, inadequate, and in some places, almost unidiomatic. So far for the form. As to the matter, we will not hazard our own opinion, but will let the Rev. Mr. Faber of Canton speak for us. "Dr. Legge's own notes on Mencius," he says, "show that Dr. Legge has not a philosophic understanding of his author." We are certain that Dr. Legge could not have read and translated these works without having in some way tried to conceive and shape to his own mind the teaching of Confucius and his school

① Samuel Wells Williams' *The Middle Kingdom*, for example, is extremely influential in the West. As the first encyclopedia about China in the US, the book offers a systematic introduction to and deep analysis of various aspects of China and remains a canonical text in Sinology.

as a connected whole; yet it is extraordinary that neither in his notes nor in his dissertations has Dr. Legge let slip a single phrase or sentence to show what he conceived the teaching of Confucius really to be, as a philosophic whole. Altogether, therefore, Dr. Legge's judgment on the value of these works cannot by any means be accepted as final, and the translator of the Chinese Classics is yet to come. ①

Gu Hongming retranslated *The Discourses and Sayings of Confucius* (《论语》), *The Conduct of Life*, *or The Universal Order of Confucius* (《中庸》), and *Higher Education* (《大学》). He attempted to be faithful to the original texts and reproduce their styles as well. Gu would first get a thorough understanding of the source text, and then reproduce it in English, both linguistically and stylistically. It is also worth mentioning that Gu adopted a comparative paradigm in his translation. He quoted Western writers like Goethe, Shakespeare, and Arnold to annotate the texts and compare their views with those of Confucius. Though innovative in several ways, Gu's translations were criticized for overusing free translation.

As we can see from the above biographical sketches, the translation of Chinese classics in the 19th century exhibited the following features. First, the number of translated classics increased as more classical texts on traditional Chinese culture and thoughts were put into English, but the translations of literary classics were few. Second, foreign missionaries and sinologists were still the mainstay of classics translation and their Chinese was better than their predecessors', enabling them to produce "first hand" translations of a superior quality. Third, Chinese scholars began to realize their mission in translating classics and began to assume the "translator's burden."

2.3   From the early 20th century to the 1970s

The early 20th century witnessed the unprecedented cultural exchange between China and the West through translation and Chinese classics were translated into English on a larger scale. Many well-known translators produced their acclaimed translations during this period.

2.3.1   Arthur Waley (1889—1966)

A graduate of Cambridge and Oxford, Waley received an elite education on Sinology and took a great interest in putting Chinese classics into English. His well-

---

① 辜鸿铭:《中国人的精神》(英汉双语),秦海霞等译,北京:中国城市出版社,2008 年,第 228 - 230 页。

known translations of Chinese literature include *The Book of Songs*, *A Hundred and Seventy Chinese Poems*, *More Translations from the Chinese*, and *Monkey*. In poetry translation，Waley combined free verse with literal translation lest deliberate use of rhyme spoil the meaning of the original text. Waley's translation of *Monkey* is one of the best English versions. He explicitly stated his approach to translation：

I have aimed at literal translation，not paraphrase ... I have not used rhyme because it is impossible to produce in English rhyme-effects at all similar to those of the original，where the same rhyme sometimes runs through a whole poem. [1]

2.3.2　Lionel Giles（翟林奈，1875—1958）

Lionel Giles was the son of Herbert Allen Giles. Working in the British Library，he carried on the translation cause of his father and put several classics into English— *The Sayings of Lao Tzu*, *Musings of a Chinese Mystic: Selections from the Philosophy of Chuang Tzu*, and *The Art of War*（《孙子兵法》）.

2.3.3　David Hawks（1923—2009）

David Hawks received his education at Oxford and Peking University. He was conversant with Chinese and able to write Chinese verses. His fame as a translator largely rests on his translation works：*Ch'u Tz'ŭ*, *The Songs of the South*（《楚辞》），*A Little Primer of Tu Fu*, and *The Story of the Stone*. Hawks actually translated the first 80 chapters of *The Story of the Stone* and the rest 40 chapters were finished by his son-in-law John Minford. The co-translated work was the first complete English translation of《红楼梦》. Hawks was also an expert on the studies of *The Story of the Stone* and expressed his admiration of the novel cordially：

My one abiding principle has been to translate *everything*—even puns. For although this is，in the sense I have already indicated，an "unfinished" novel，it was written (and rewritten) by a great artist with his very lifeblood. I have therefore assumed that whatever I find in it is there for a purpose and must be dealt with somehow or other. I cannot pretend always to have done so successfully，but if I can convey to the reader even a fraction of the pleasure this

---

[1]　Waley，Arthur，trans. *A Hundred and Seventy Chinese Poems*. New York：Alfred • A • Knopf，1922，pp. 33 - 34.

Chinese novel has given me, I shall not have lived in vain. ①

Love and dedication are really indispensable to the success of a translator!

2.3.4　Angus Charles Graham（葛瑞汉，1919—1991）

Angus Charles Graham was a famous British sinologist and received the Prix Stanislas Julien in 1979, the highest prize in Sinology. His English translations of Chinese classics include *The Book of Lieh-tzu*（《列子》）, *Chuang-tzu: The Seven Inner Chapters and Other Writings from the Book Chuang-tzu*, and *Poems of the West Lake*, a collection of English translations of poems about Hangzhou's scenic spot—the West Lake. Graham's poetry translation was accused by some scholars of lacking faithfulness. "Graham occasionally drops an image and his palette contains only primary colors—for instance, 'blue' is all he can come up with for half a dozen distinct words indicating different degrees of hue and brightness between green and purple—but he has a sure feel for the movement and rhythm of the lines."②

2.3.5　Ezra Pound（1885—1972）

Ezra Pound was a famous American poet and originator of Imagism. He advocated the use of dominant images to express momentary feelings. Chinese poem, as we know, conveys feelings by virtue of imagery and is essentially imagistic. Chinese poetry is an important source of inspiration for Pound's imagist poetry. He was well acquainted with Chinese poetic tradition and translated several Chinese classics into English. *Cathy*, *Shih-ching: The Classic Anthology Defined by Confucius*, and *Confucius: The Unwobbling Pivot / The Great Digest / The Analects* are among some of his major translation works. Pound put more emphasis on cadence, images, and variation than on faithfulness and infused his original interpretation into translation. According to Singh, "Pound sets out to define poetic translation not so much as the literal and verbal equivalent of the text established, as the equation of the emotion behind it."③ In this sense, *Cathy* is more of a recreation than a translation.

2.3.6　Pearl S. Buck（赛珍珠，1892—1973）

Pearl S. Buck grew up in Zhenjiang, China with her missionary father. Her novel

---

① Hawks, David. "Introduction." *The Story of the Stone*. Trans. David Hawks. London: Penguin Books, 1973, p. 46.

② P. W. K. et al. "Review of *Poems of the West Lake: Translations from the Chinese* by A. C. Graham; *Du Mu, Plantains in the Rain: Selected Chinese Poems* by R. F. Burton; and *The Deep Woods' Business: Uncollected Translations from the Chinese* by Arthur Cooper." *Journal of the American Oriental Society* 112 (1992), p. 180.

③ Singh, G. *Ezra Pound as Critic*. New York: St. Martin's Press, 1994, p. 120.

The Good Earth，depicting a Chinese farmer Wang Lung's obsession with land，won the Nobel Prize for Literature in 1938. As a translator，her fame rests on *All Men Are Brothers*，a popular translation of《水浒传》in the English world. The title indicates that Buck adopted domestication in translating the Chinese literary classic since a literal translation of the title would be Water Margin，which，according to Buck，didn't make any sense to English readers，so she borrowed the well-known saying "all within the four seas are his elder and younger brothers"（"四海之内，皆兄弟也"）from *The Analects of Confucius* and made it the title of her translation.① Buck's justification of her title deserves to be quoted at length to illustrate the importance of culture transference in translation：

> The English title is not，of course，a translation of the Chinese title，which is singularly untranslatable. The word SHUI means water；the word HU，margins or borders. The word CHUAN is the equivalent of the English word novel. The juxtaposition of these words in English is so nearly meaningless as to give，in my opinion at least，an unjust impression of the book. I have chosen arbitrarily，therefore，a famous saying of Confucius to be the title in English，a title which in amplitude and in implication expresses the spirit of this band of righteous robbers. ②

2.3.7　Lin Yutang（林语堂，1895—1976）

Lin Yutang is more known as a writer than a translator. Most of his major works are written in English，such as *My Country and My People*（《吾国与吾民》），*Moment in Peking*（《京华烟云》），and *The Art of Living*（《生活的艺术》）. His translations concentrate on Confucian and Taoist classics and ancient Chinese literature. He translated *Six Characters of a Floating World*（《浮生六记》）by the Qing dynasty author Shen Fu to pay homage to the married life of the protagonists Shen Fu and his beloved wife Chen Yun，which "is one of the saddest and yet at the same time 'gayest' lives，the type of gaiety that bears sorrow so well."③

2.3.8　Yang Xianyi and Gladys Yang（杨宪益，1915—2009；戴乃迭，1919—1999）

Yang Xianyi was born in Huai'an and studied at a missionary school and Oxford.

---

① Watson，Burton，trans. *The Analects of Confucius*. New York：Columbia University Press，2007，p. 81.

② Buck，Pearl S. "The Translator's Preface." *All Men Are Brothers*. Trans. Pearl. S. Buck. New York：The George Macy Companies，Inc. ，1948，p. xxi.

③ Lin，Yutang. "Preface." *Six Characters of a Floating World*. Trans. Lin Yutang. Beijing：Foreign Language Teaching and Research Press，1999，p. 22.

During his study at Oxford, he met his future wife Gladys Margaret Tayler who was born in Beijing and held a deep affection for China. They worked for Foreign Languages Press in 1951, beginning their long and fruitful cooperation in translating Chinese works into English. Backed by the Chinese government, Yang and his wife co-translated over 20 works and quite a few of them became classical translations. Let's list some of them: *A Dream of Red Mansions*, *The Scholars*, *Li Sao* (《离骚》), *Selected Tales of the Han*, *Wei and Six Dynasties Periods* (《汉魏六朝小说选》), *Poetry and Prose of the Han*, *Wei and Six Dynasties* (《汉魏六朝诗文选》), *The Palace of Eternal Youth* (《长生殿》), *Selections from Records of the Historian* (《史记选》), *The Travels of Lao Can* (《老残游记》), and *Wandering* (《彷徨》). Gladys Yang also translated some works on her own, such as *Recollections of West Hunan* (《湘西散记》), *Leaden Wings* (《沉重的翅膀》), and *A Small Town Called Hibiscus* (《芙蓉镇》).

2.3.9   Weng Xianliang (翁显良，1924—1983)

Weng Xianliang was born in Hong Kong and worked at Jinan University and Guangdong University of Foreign Studies. He specialized in poetry translation and put over 200 poems into English. 124 of these poems, covering such diverse mini-genres as prose poem, *yuefu* poems, regulated verses, etc., were collected in *An English Translation of Chinese Ancient Poems* (《古诗英译》). Weng rendered the rhymed verses into prose and infused his own emotions into translation. For instance, he translated "忽如一夜春风来，千树万树梨花开" into "Behold! The woods have taken on the look of a pear orchid in full blossom, as if capricious spring, returning in the night, had breathed its magic into this Tatar land."[①] It is obvious that Weng was emotionally charged when translating the poem and projected his own feelings to it. His style, as commented by Xu Yuanchong, belongs to "the school of creation."[②]

As we can see from the biographical sketches, more literary classics were put into English and more Chinese translators embarked on the translation of Chinese classics from the early 20th century to the 1970s. The translation of ancient Chinese poetry reached a climax and influenced American Imagist Movement.

2.4   From the 1980s to the present

Since reform and opening-up, the increasing cultural exchange between China and the West has further spurred the translation of Chinese classics. Well-known English translators of Chinese classics in this period included Howard Goldblatt, John Minford, Julia Lovell, Stephen Owen, Xu Yuanchong, etc.

---

① 翁显良:《古诗英译》,北京:北京出版社,1985 年,第 33 页。
② 许渊冲:《诗词英译漫谈》,《中国翻译》1998 年第 3 期,第 41 页。

2.4.1 Howard Goldblatt（葛浩文，1939— ）

Howard Goldblatt is one of the most prolific translators of Chinese literature. Up till now，he has translated nearly ninety modern and contemporary Chinese literary works into English. Lest a long list of his oeuvre jar our reading，we present some of his major translations in Table 5.

Table 5　Some Major Translations by Howard Goldblatt

Chinse Title	English Title	Author
《尘埃落定》	*Red Poppies*	阿来
《丰乳肥臀》	*Big Breasts and Wide Hips*	莫言
《干校六记》	*Six Chapters from My Life "Downunder"*	杨绛
《河岸》	*The Boat to Redemption*	苏童
《红高粱》	*Red Sorghum*	莫言
《呼兰河传》	*Tales of Hulan River*	萧红
《蛙》	*Frog*	莫言
《狼图腾》	*Wolf Totem*	姜戎
《骆驼祥子》	*Rickshaw Boy*	老舍
《生死场》	*The Field of Life and Death*	萧红
《生死疲劳》	*Life and Death Are Wearing Me Out*	莫言
《檀香刑》	*Sandalwood Death*	莫言
《天堂蒜薹之歌》	*The Garlic Ballads*	莫言
《推拿》	*Massage*	毕飞宇
《温故一九四二》	*Remembering 1942*	刘震云
《一句顶一万句》	*Someone to Talk to*	刘震云

For Goldblatt，translation is rewriting. A successful translator needs to modulate，interpret，and interpolate to make the translated text more accessible to target readers. He relates the taste and expectation of English readers to his perception of Chinese literature as a Westerner. "I'm a translator for an American reader and that reader is very close to my understanding of what literature is and what language is." Goldblatt often abandons the Chinese original and focuses on polishing the translation once he finishes the first draft. He regards this as hard-won experience and offers it to young translators. "What you really need to do is hone your own abilities to read literature in your own language and then put the Chinese into that as closely as possible. "①

2.4.2 John Minford（闵福德，1946— ）

In our introduction to David Hawks, we mentioned Minford who finished the last 40 chapters of *The Story of the Stone*. Minford is a British sinologist and translator. He retranslated *Tao Te Ching*, *I Ching*, *The Art of War*, and *Strange Tales from a Chinese Studio* and collaborated with the Chinese translator Liu Shaoming（刘绍铭）in editing and publishing *Classical Chinese Literature: An Anthology of Translations Volume I: From Antiquity to the Tang Dynasty*（《含英咀华集》）. The scope of the anthology is explicitly stated by Minford and Liu as follows：

This anthology then is a new *Cathy*, pieced together from the work of translators of the past three hundred years. It presents the three-thousand-year-old literary tradition of China, from its very beginnings to the fall of the Manchu dynasty in 1911, seen through a Western tradition of translation and interpretation that itself (as we have seen) stretches back to the last decades of the seventeenth century. ②

The anthology, providing notes to the texts and introductions to the translators and their works, demonstrates fine scholarship and offers foreign readers a panoramic view of ancient Chinese literary classics.

2.4.3 Julia Lovell（蓝诗玲，1975— ）

Julia Lovell belongs to a new generation of British sinologists. She has retranslated some classics like *Monkey King* and *The Real Story of Ah-Q and Other Tales of China: The Complete Fiction of Lu Xun* and put several contemporary Chinese writers' representative works into English, such as *A Dictionary of Maqiao*（《马桥词典》）by Han Shaogong, *Sky Burial*（《天葬》）by Xue Xinran, *I Love Dollars and Other Stories of China*（《我爱美元》）by Zhu Wen, *Lust, Caution*（《色戒》）by Zhang Ailing, and *Serve the People*（《为人民服务》）by Yan Lianke. Lovell expresses her view on literature translation as follows：

---

① Stalling, Jonathan &. Howard Goldblatt. "The Voice of the Translator: An Interview with Howard Goldblatt." *Translation Review* 88 (2014), pp. 9 – 10.

② Minford, John &. Joseph S. M. Lau. "Music from Two Rooms: Editors' Introduction." *Classical Chinese Literature: An Anthology of Translations Volume I: From Antiquity to the Tang Dynasty*. Eds. John Minford and Joseph S. M. Lau. New York: Columbia University Press, Hong Kong: The Chinese University Press, 2000, p. xlix.

Literary translators have two responsibilities：to the original text and to readers of the target language. Whichever languages translators work between，satisfying both constituencies can be difficult，but when working between two literary cultures as remote chronologically and geographically as sixteenth-century China and the twenty-first-century Anglophone world，the challenges are redoubtable. Sometimes，a translator has to sacrifice technical，linguistic fidelity to be true to the overall tone of a text. Wordplays—ubiquitous in *Journey to the West*—are difficult to translate without explanatory footnotes that problematically slow down the delivery of the joke. Where I decided to omit these puns，I sometimes tried to compensate by enhancing the humor of other parts of the narrative or dialogue. In places，therefore，this version might read as a reworking as well as a translation；my hope throughout has been to communicate to contemporary English readers the dynamism，imagination，philosophy，and comedy of the original.[①]

Lovell adheres to the criteria of faithfulness and smoothness，but places the latter over the former as she believes the essence of literary translation lies in the transference of the texture and spirituality of the original work.

2.4.4 Stephen Owen（宇文所安，1946—　）

Stephen Owen，an American sinologist，specializes in the translation and study of ancient Chinese poetry. *The Poetry of the Early Tang*（《初唐诗》），*The Great Age of Chinese Poetry: The High Tang*（《盛唐诗》），and *The Late Tang Chinese Poetry of the Mid-Ninth Century*（*827—860*）（《晚唐：九世纪中叶的中国诗歌 827—860》）are some of his major translations. Owen also edited anthologies of Chinses literature，such as *The Cambridge History of Chinese Literature* and *An Anthology of Chinese Literature* and authored monographs on ancient Chinese poetry，such as *Traditional Chinese Poetry and Poetics*，*Mi-Lou: Poetry and the Labyrinth of Desire*，and *Borrowed Stone*. Owen uses commentary to compensate the loss of meaning in translation. He believes that "there is no best translation，only good explanations" and that "the translations are given not to stand on their own but to work together with the commentaries."[②]

2.4.5 Xu Yuanchong（许渊冲，1921—2021）

Xu Yuanchong，recipient of the 2014 Aurora Borealis Prize for Outstanding

---

① Lovell，Julia. "A Note on the Translation." *Monkey King*. Trans. Julia Lovell. New York：Penguin Books，2021，p. 8.

② Owen，Stephen. *Readings in Chinese Literary Thought*. Cambridge：The Council on East Asian Studies，Harvard University，1992，pp. 16 - 17.

Translation of Literature, was proficient with Chinese, French, and English. He put many ancient Chinese literary classics, particularly Tang, Song, and Yuan verses into both French and English and formed his own theory on verse translation—"Three Beauties Theory," i. e. , beauty in sense, beauty in sound, and beauty in form. Xu summarized his own views on translation as follows:

> From 1978 on, I contributed a number of articles on the art of translation to various journals of foreign languages and literature in Beijing and Shanghai, in which I put forward the following principles.
>
> (1) A verse translation should not only be faithful to the original verse but also as beautiful as the original in sense, sound and form.
>
> (2) Translation may be divided into literal translation and liberal translation. A good literal translation is faithful to the original in sense; a bad one only in form. A good liberal translation can be faithful to the original in spirit; generally speaking, a free translation is faithful in sense.
>
> (3) In prose translation, the translator should make the fullest possible use of the best expressions of the target language, for the original contains the best words in the best order of the source language.
>
> (4) In translating, three methods may be used, that is, equalization, generalization and particularization (or concretization). Equalization includes the concept of dynamic equivalence. Generalization is meant to state in general terms what is particular in the original ...
>
> (5) A literary translation should be readable, enjoyable and delectable (or delightful). If it is not readable, it has not fulfilled the lowest criterion for translation, for it is not true to the original. If it is not enjoyable, it has not fulfilled the medium criterion for it is not a good version. If it is delightful to read, then it has fulfilled the highest criterion for translation and it must be a beautiful version ... [1]

Besides Xu Yuanchong, many other contemporary Chinese translators like Wang Rongpei (汪榕培), Zhang Peiji (张培基), Luo Jingguo (罗经国), etc. , also devote to the English translation of Chinese literary classics.

English translation of Chinese classics from the 1980s to the present exhibits two characteristics. First, translations of literary works, particularly modern and

---

[1] Xu, Yuanchong. *Vanished Springs*. Beijing: Foreign Language Teaching and Research Press, 2011, pp. 127 - 128.

contemporary Chinese literary works constitute a large proportion of all translations. Second，Chinese government begins to back translation of Chinese classics by launching publishing projects and funds，such as Library of Chinese Classics（大中华文库），Panda Books（熊猫丛书），and Chinese Academic Translation Project of National Social Science Fund of China（国家社科基金中华学术外译项目）.

The introduction to the translation history of Chinese classics seems long for this book，but actually it is general and highly condensed，aiming to help readers get a panoramic view of classics translation in China. Scholars studying classics translation usually focus on a particular area of it to make their researches deep and systematic，for example，English translation of ghost fiction in Wei and Jin dynasties，English translation of Yuan drama，English translation of Lu Xun's short stories.

3. Difficulties and Methods of Classics Translation

Since we've mentioned the criteria and strategies of classics translation in our introduction to translators，we'll focus on some of the difficulties and commonly used methods and skills in translating Chinese classics in this section. Classic Chinese is different from vernacular Chinese and possesses some unique linguistic phenomena that deserve special attention in translation. In putting Chinese classics into English，translators are likely to encounter the following difficulties and use specific methods to resolve them.

3.1　Chinese characters/expressions without English equivalents

Classics，usually culture-loaded，contain characters or expressions that are unique to Chinese and have no English counterparts. To cope with this difficulty，translators usually use makeshift English equivalents or transliteration，with or without annotation. Let's exemplify this with the translation of the Taoist term 道. Arthur Waley used the English equivalent "Way" and capitalized the initial letter to differ it from "way" in its common usage，designating it specially for 道 while James Legge and Lin Yutang transliterated it into "*Tao*." Whatever method/skill is used in translating these terms，the translated terms are often contextualized and readers can grasp their meanings by referring to the contexts. If they are isolated from the contexts，annotations are preferably provided to help understand their connotations.

3.2　Polysemes

Polysemous characters in classic Chinese can pose a challenge for translators. They have to scrutinize the original text and even do research to ascertain the meanings of polysemes. A typical case concerns the translation of 知 in "由,海女知之乎? 知之为知之,不知为不知,是知也." James Legge and Gu Hongming translated the first and last 知 differently. Legge understood it as knowledge; whereas Gu decipherd it as understanding. Legge translated the sentence as: "Yu, shall I teach you what knowledge is? When you know a thing, to hold that you know it; and when you do not know a thing, to allow that you do not know it;—this is knowledge."[①] And Gu's translation is: "Shall I teach you what is understanding? To know what it is that you know, and to know what it is that you do not know,—that is understanding."[②]

In dealing with polysemes, translators often consult reference books and the contexts to clarify their meanings. Sometimes, they have to rely on their own understandings and come up with personal interpretations.

3.3　Interchangeable Chinese characters(通假字)

The causes of interchangeable Chinese characters are multifarious and complicated, which we will leave to philologists and linguists and focus our discussion on how to deal with 通假字 in translation. Let's illustrate the translation of interchangeable characters with the character 说 from *The Analects of Confucius*. In the sentence "有朋自远方来,不亦说乎," the character 说 is interchangeable with 悦, meaning "delightful" or "pleasant," so Legge and Watson put the sentence into "Is it not delightful to have friends coming from distant quarters?"[③] and "To have a friend come from a long way off—that's a pleasure, isn't it?"[④] respectively. The character 说 also appears in 成事不说, but here 说 means "speak" and was translated into "speak" and "comment" respectively by Legge and Watson. Legge's translation is: "Things that are done, it is needless to speak about."[⑤] And Watson's translation is: "Completed affairs one does not comment on."[⑥]

① Legge, James, trans. *The Chinese Classics: Confucian Analects*, *The Great Learning*, *and The Doctrine of the Mean*. Hong Kong: Hong University Press, 1960, p. 151.

② 辜鸿铭:《西播〈论语〉回译:辜鸿铭英译〈论语〉详释》,王京涛译注,上海:东方出版中心,2013 年,第31 页。

③ Legge, James, trans. *The Chinese Classics: Confucian Analects*, *The Great Learning*, *and The Doctrine of the Mean*. Hong Kong: Hong University Press, 1960, p. 137.

④ Watson, Burton, trans. *The Analects of Confucius*. New York: Columbia University Press, 2007, p. 16.

⑤ Legge, James, trans. *The Chinese Classics: Confucian Analects*, *The Great Learning*, *and The Doctrine of the Mean: Confucian Analects*, *The Great Learning*, *and The Doctrine of the Mean*. Hong Kong: Hong University Press, 1960, p. 162.

⑥ Watson, Burton, trans. *The Analects of Confucius*. New York: Columbia University Press, 2007, p. 29.

The examples cited above indicate the underlying method for translating interchangeable characters. If the original meaning of a character does not fit the context，we need to consider the interchangeability of a character. For example，in 八月剥枣，a line from *The Book of Songs*，the character 剥 is an interchangeable character of 攴，which means "beat down." Originally，剥 means "peel" as in the expression 剥橘子（peel oranges），but we usually do not peel dates，so the original meaning of 剥 misfits the context and the character interchangeability needs to be considered. Xu Yuanchong got it and accurately translated the line as："In eighth moon down the dates we beat."①

3.4　Passive structures

Classic Chinese abounds with passive structures. Structures with characters 于，见，为，and 被 are often used to express passivity. These structures can be put into English passive voice by using "be + past participle" or converted into English active sentences. Let's illustrate the translation of Chinese passive structures with examples. "劳心者治人，劳力者治于人，" a line from *The Works of Mencius*，uses 于 to express passivity and was translated by James Legge as："Those who labor with their minds govern others；those who labor with their strength are governed by others."② The sentence "吾长见笑于大家" uses 见 to mark passivity and was translated by Wang Rongpei as："I would always be sneered at by those who are well-versed in Tao."③ In "妆成每被秋娘妒，" the passive voice is marked by 被 and the sentence was put into："My beauty was envied by songstresses fair still" by Xu Yuanchong.④ In these examples，the Chinese passive structures are put into English passive sentences，but sometimes，they are also converted into active ones. "暴见于王" was put into："I [Chwang Pao] had an interview with the king" by James Legge.⑤And "吴广素爱人，士卒多为用者" and "不者，若属皆且为所虏" were translated by Burton Watson into "Wu Kuang had always been kind to others and many of the soldiers would do anything for him" and "If you don't，you and all of us will end up as his prisoners" respectively.⑥

① 许渊冲译:《诗经》,北京:海豚出版社,2013 年,第 170 页。
② Legge, James, trans. *The Chinese Classics: The Works of Mencius*. Hong Kong：Hong University Press，1960，pp. 249 – 250.
③ 汪榕培译:《庄子》,长沙:湖南人民出版社,北京:外文出版社,1999 年,第 161 页。
④ 许渊冲译:《许渊冲译唐诗三百首》,北京:中译出版社,2021 年,第 675 页。
⑤ Legge, James, trans. *The Chinese Classics: The Works of Mencius*. Hong Kong：Hong University Press，1960，p. 150.
⑥ Watson, Burton, trans. *Records of the Great Historian of China Volume I: Early Years of the Han Dynasty*，209 to 141 B.C. 台北:新月图书股份有限公司,1971 年,第 21 页、52 页。

As we can see from these examples，English translation of Chinese passive structure is flexible. What translators need to do is to discern the Chinese passive structures and put them into idiomatic English sentences，either active or passive.

3.5　Paratactic structures

Contrastive linguistics studies reveal that one major difference between Chinese and English is that the former relies on parataxis to achieve coherence while the latter uses hypotaxis to attain it. In paratactic structures，phrases or clauses are placed one after another without using coordinators or subordinators；whereas the logic of hypotactic sentences is outwardly expressed by using coordinating and/or subordinating structures. Parataxis is more prominent in classic Chinese than it is in vernacular Chinese as the latter has been Westernized to a certain extent. Due to this difference，translators often need to use coordinators and subordinators in translating Chinese paratactic sentences. For example，Luo Jingguo put the paratactic sentences "落霞与孤鹜齐飞，秋水共长天一色" and "穷且益坚，不坠青云之志" into the coordinated sentence："A solitary wild duck flies alongside the multi-colored sunset clouds，and the autumn water is merged with the boundless sky into one hue" and the subordinated sentence："Poor as one is，he is all the more determined in adversity and by no means gives up his ambition."[①] The conversion of Chinese paratactic sentences into English hypotactic ones requires a thorough understanding of the original sentences and English proficiency on the part of translators.

3.6　Repetition

Repetition is used as a means of cohesion in classic Chinese，but English prefers substitution to achieve variety. This difference，like the difference between parataxis and hypotaxis，calls for linguistic change in Chinese-English translation. For instance，in the Chinese sentence "古之学者必有师。师者，所以传道授业解惑也，" the character 师 is repeated，but in English translation by Luo Jingguo，the second 师 is replaced by "one" as in："In ancient times those who wanted to learn would seek out a teacher，one who could propagate the doctrine，impart professional knowledge，and resolve doubts."[②]

---

① 　罗经国译:《古文观止精选:汉英对照》,北京:外语教学与研究出版社,2005 年,第 39 页,42 页。

② 　罗经国译:《古文观止精选:汉英对照》,北京:外语教学与研究出版社,2005 年,第 62 页。

◇ A Short Summary

In this chapter, we've discussed the value, history, difficulties, methods, and skills of classics translation. Chinese classics serve as the most important means of preserving Chinese cultural identity and the translation of them can promote cultural exchange and mutual understanding. Starting from the late 17th century, the English translation of Chinese classics has developed over 300 years and many classics have been translated and retranslated into English. Before the 20th century, sinologists were the main force in rendering Chinese classics into English. After the 20th century, Chinese translators began to take the initiative and focused on the English translation of literary classics. Currently, English translation of Chinese classics is carried out on a larger scale and more Chinese translators are making their contributions. Master translators often form their own views on the criteria, strategies, and methods of classics translation and their practice can provide guidance for the English translation of Chinese culture-specific characters, interchangeable characters, polysemes, passive structures, paratactic structures, and repetitions.

◇ Reviewing Questions

1. What are the functions of Chinese classics?

2. What is the value of classics translation?

3. What are the major translators, their representative works, and their views on translation in the history of Chinese classics translation?

4. What are the difficulties of translating Chinese classics?

Chapter 11

Translation of Literary Works

 Objectives

➢ Understand the features of literary language and their implications for translation

➢ Understand the elements of literary texts and their implications for translation

➢ Understand the criteria of literary translation

➢ Understand the qualities of a good translator of literary works

➢ Be able to translate simple literary texts into proper English

1. The Features of Literary Language and Their Implications for Translation

Maxim Gorky asserts that language is the primary element and "material of literature,"[1] but in what ways is language used artistically in literature or what are the features of literary language? From our own reading experience, we know that the language used in literature differs from that used in daily speech. Viktor Shklovsky, distinguishing poetic language from everyday language, argues that poetic language is impeded and distorted while everyday language is easy, economical, and correct.[2] What Shklovsky means is that poetic language is used in such a way as to create a challenging and refreshing reading experience for readers. Unlike everyday language whose meaning can be easily understood, poetic language is implicit and indirect and requires intellectual efforts to decipher it. Such a distinction foreshadows Shklovsky's concept of estrangement or defamiliarization, which, simply put, refers to the anti-habitual use of language in literature to create a fresh and aesthetic effect. Generally, literary language, in contrast with everyday language, is self-referential, indirect, and fiction-referential. Let's exemplify the features of literary language and discuss their implications for translation.

1.1 Self-reference

By self-reference, we mean that literary language usually foregrounds itself in terms of phonetics, grammar, register, etc., to achieve stylistic, rhetorical, and/or aesthetic effects.

1.1.1 Phonetics

The self-referential feature of language in terms of phonetics is often the most apparent in poetry. In daily conversation and writing for practical purposes, we usually do not pay much attention to the phonetic effects of our speech and writing. We simply focus on expressing ideas and passing information. However, in poetry, an art form that highly relies on phonetic devices for its aesthetic effect, poets often resort to the phonetic features of language, such as sound, rhyme, and tempo to attain a musical effect and express feelings or thoughts. Let's illustrate it with a stanza from Yeats' "The Lake Isle of Innisfree":

---

[1] Gorky, Maxim. *On Literature*. Moscow: Progress Publishers, 1982, pp. 297 – 298.

[2] Shklovsky, Viktor. *Theory of Prose*. Trans. Benjamin Sher. Elmwood Park: Dalkey Archive Press, 1991, p. 13.

I will arise and go now, and go to Innisfree,

And a small cabin build there, of clay and wattles made;

Nine bean-rows will I have there, a hive for the honeybee,

And live alone in the bee-loud glade.

And I shall have some peace there, for peace comes dropping slow,

Dropping from the veils of the morning to where the cricket sings;

There midnight's all a glimmer, and noon a purple glow,

And evening full of the linnet's wings.

I will arise and go now, for always night and day

I hear lake water lapping with low sounds by the shore;

While I stand on the roadway, or on the pavements gray,

I hear it in the deep heart's core. [1]

In the poem, Yeats used end rhyme and iambic meter to create a tranquil atmosphere and express his yearning for an idyllic life. He adopted the rhyme pattern of "abab" to express his unrealizable dream of a secluded life near the lake by creating a recurring feeling and used iambic meter which juxtaposes stressed sound with unstressed sound to imitate the lapping of lake water. The phonetic devices not only exist for the sake of beauty alone, they, as we have analyzed, also help convey the author's thoughts and the poem's theme(s).

In poetry translation, phonetic device is a hard nut to crack. As we have learned in Chapter 10, the rhymes of ancient Chinese verses, according to some translators, are untranslatable and it is for this reason that Waley rendered *The Book of Songs* into free verse, but translators still tend to agree that a good translation of ancient Chinese poetry needs to reproduce the original rhyme. For example, Xu Yuanchong emphasized the reproduction of rhyme pattern in translation, as shown in his English translation of "Thoughts on a Tranquil Night" (《静夜思》) by Li Bai:

Before my bed a pool of light—

O can it be frost on the ground?

Looking up, I find the moon bright;

Bowing, in homesickness I'm drowned. [2]

---

[1]   Yeats, William Butler. *The Collected Poems of W. B. Yeats*. New York: Macmillan Publishing Company, 1989, p. 39.

[2]   许渊冲译:《许渊冲译唐诗三百首》,北京:中译出版社,2021 年,第 269 页。

1.1.2 Grammar

The normal use of written language is usually grammar-bound. In writings for non-literary purposes，deviation from grammatical rules is often taken as a token of poor education. However，literary writings sometimes deliberately deviate from grammatical rules to achieve aesthetic effects. In poetry，enjambment can break the rules of grammar and grammatically incorrect sentences are used in prose to depict characters or express emotions and thoughts. In "A Madman's Diary"，the narrator is in a state of dereliction and horror，which is marked by his incoherent speech—"没有的事？狼子村现吃；还有书上都写着，通红崭新！"[①] However，Yang Xianyi and Gladys Yang's translation，for the purpose of smooth reading，renders the narrator's speech into immaculate English—"What am I talking about? They are eating men in Wolf Club Village，and you can see it written all over the books，in fresh red ink."[②]

In translation，translators need to be faithful to the style of the original text. If they，as Venuti argues，render the original text，regardless of its style，into a fluent English version，they are not only veiling or erasing the style of the author，but also crippling or even sacrificing the expressiveness of the source text. Suppose translators render Jim's black vernacular speech in *The Adventures of Huckleberry Finn* into impeccable English，what would Mark Twain think of such brutal treatments of his novel?

1.1.3 Register

Register as a linguistic term refers to a variety of language used in a specific social setting，such as informal register，scientific register. Usually，the register we use needs to match the situation. For example，in writing a paper on mining technology，we often use objective language，if we use decorative language，it may read awkward. In literature，the convention on register use is sometimes deliberately breached for the purpose of characterization. In "Our Learned Friend"（《高老夫子》），Lu Xun depicted the hypocrisy of the protagonist Mr. Gao through register. Gao，a vulgar man in private，assumes a learned appearance and adapts the register of his speech to the addressee. To his disreputable friend Huang San who discloses Gao's real intention for accepting the teaching post—to peep at girl students，Gao uses vulgar words to dismiss the accusation："你不要相信老钵的狗屁！" When he encounters the dean of the school，he changes his register and speaks in a civilized and pedantic style："瑶翁公事很忙罢，

---

① 鲁迅：《狂人日记》，成都：四川人民出版社，2017年，第16页。
② Yang，Hsien-yi & Gladys Yang，trans. *Selected Stories of Lu Hsun*. New York and London：W. W. Norton & Company，2003，p. 14.

可以不必客气……"① The variation of register was used by Lu Xun to depict the double-faced protagonist and it should be reproduced in translation. Julia Lovell and Li Yiyun translated the two sentences into "Well，Bo comes out with all sorts of crap" and "You must be terribly busy，please don't let me hold you—" respectively，② capturing the register variation.

1.2　Indirectness

In everyday life，we usually express ourselves directly. For example，if we miss a friend，we may simply say "I miss you，" seldom would we express our feelings in poetic lines as Li Bai did in "我寄愁心与明月，随君直到夜郎西。"③ However，if things are all expressed in a matter-of-fact way，the beauty of literature will be substantially compromised. Here，we come to another feature of literary language—indirectness. In literature，language is usually used indirectly and implicitly and that's where the charm of literary language lies. If someone translates a literary text as he/she does with an informative text and only brings out the information，the translation is likely to be awful. Let's suppose "Night Rain：Sent North"（《夜雨寄北》）by Li Shangyin is rendered into "I have no idea when you'll be back and I miss you so much，" we'd rather prefer that the poem not be translated. Fortunately，that's not what Stephen Owen did in his translation. He understood the indirectness of literary language and Li Shangyin's romantic spirit and reproduced the texture of the original poem by retaining the concrete and emotion-loaded images in his translation：

Night Rain：Sent North

You ask the date for my return；
　　　　no date is set yet；
night rain in the hills of Ba
　　　　floods the autumn pools.
When will we together trim
　　　　the candle by the western window
and discuss these times of the night rain

---

① 鲁迅:《狂人日记》,成都:四川人民出版社,2017 年,第 221 页、第 225 页。
② Lovell, Julia & Li Yiyun, trans. *The Real Stories of A-Q and Other Tales of China: The Complete Fiction of Lu Xun.* New York: Penguin Classics, 2009, p. 223, p. 227
③ 李白:《李白诗歌全集》,北京:今日中国出版社,1997 年,第 444 页。

in the hills of Ba? ①

1.3 Fictional reference

By fictional reference, we mean that literary language, particularly the language of novel, does not refer to entities in the real world and that literary language does not express scientific or generally accepted truth, but this does not mean that the fictional world created by language is not convincing; rather, literary language creates fictional reality that operates within the framework of human logic, either cognitive or emotional. Let's illustrate this with examples. In *Moby Dick*, Herman Melville creates a fictional world in which the obstinate captain Ahab takes revenge on the white whale and brings the ship and his seamen to destruction. The story does not happen in reality, but it is still very convincing, because the fictional world operates like the world we inhabit. This illustrates one aspect of fictional reference, but this facet of fictional reference does not affect translation much.

In reading literature, we sometimes encounter descriptions that are probably discrepant with the reality of life. For example, the poetic lines "方宅十余亩,草屋八九间"② by Tao Yuanming may arouse the curiosity and query of careful readers: Did Tao Yuanming really build a residence surrounded by a land of ten *mu* and have eight or nine thatched-roof rooms? We don't know for sure, but it is unnecessary to conduct research to ascertain the statement. Here comes the other aspect of fictional reference—literary language may not conform to hard facts. This aspect of fictional reference can affect translation in that translators may discern the fictional reference and make a liberal translation. This is just what Hightower did in his translation of the couplet: "The land I own amounts to a couple of acres/The thatched-roof house has four or five rooms."③ Fictional reference sometimes can also be interpreted as hyperbole as in "白发三千丈" by Li Bai and this line loses its fictional hyperbolical reference in Xu Yuanchong's translation: "My white hairs would make a long, long cord."④

The demarcation between literary and non-literary language is not clear-cut. The features of literary language can also be shared by everyday language and vice versa.

---

① Owen, Stephen, trans. *The Late Tang: Chinese Poetry of the Mid-Ninth Century (827—860)*. Cambridge: Harvard University Asia Center, 2006, p. 351.

② 陶渊明:《陶渊明全集全鉴》,北京:中国纺织出版社,2020 年,第 38 页。

③ Hightower, James Robert, trans. *The Poetry of T'ao Ch'ien*. Oxford: Oxford University Press, 1970, p. 50.

④ 许渊冲译:《汉英对照唐诗一百五十首》,西安:陕西人民出版社,1984 年,第 36 页。

For example, in speech making, a speaker may rely on phonetic devices for a better delivery. In literature, narrators or characters sometimes pour out their feelings as Lord Byron's characters often do. In biography, the subject and his/her words and deeds often have occurrences in the real world. Meanwhile, literary language can also be informative. It's only that the features of self-reference, indirectness, and fictional reference are more prominent in literary language. This reminds us of Peter Newmark's classification of texts into three broad categories—literary, institutional, and scientific and his idea that literary texts are distinguished from institutional and scientific texts "in being more important in their mental and imaginative connotations than their factual denotations."[1] The characteristics of literary language require that literary translation should bring out the aesthetic effects and information of the original text.

2. The Elements of Literary Texts and Their Implications for Translation

As argued by Gorky, language is the material of literature, but what are the elements of literary text as a language-wrought object of art? Let's review some of the major concepts and theories on the elements of literary texts and discuss their implications for literary translation.

2.1   Wang Bi's concept of language, symbols/imagery, and meaning

Wang Bi (王弼, 226—249), a scholar of the Three Kingdoms period, proposed a three-layer structure of a text based on his study of classics, especially *The Book of Changes*. According to Wang, a text consists of language, symbols/imagery, and meaning which are interconnected and form a hierarchical relationship: "夫象者,出意者也。言者,明象者也。"[2] What he means is that meaning is conveyed through symbols/imagery which in turn are/is created by language. Though Wang Bi's concept is based on his explication of classics, it can also apply to literary texts. Let's illustrate it with "Autumn Thoughts: To the Tune of Sunny Sand" (《天净沙·秋思》) by Ma Zhiyuan (马致远). In the verse, the poet used language to create a series of images like rotten vines, evening crows, small bridge, stream, cottage, ancient road, west wind, lean horse, setting sun, and a heartbroken loner. Through these images, Ma created a desolate and immemorial atmosphere and conveyed the theme of homesickness and loneliness.

---

① Newmark, Peter. *A Textbook of Translation*. Hemel Hempstead: Prentice Hall, 1988, p. 44.
② 王弼:《王弼集校释》,楼宇烈校释,北京:中华书局,1980 年,第 609 页。

2.2 Roman Ingarden's strata of a literary text

Western scholars also attempt to dissect a literary text into its various components. Roman Ingarden, a Polish philosopher and aesthetician, classified a literary work into four strata in *The Literary Work of Art*, namely, the stratum of linguistic sound formations, the stratum of meaning units, the stratum of represented objects, and the stratum of schematized aspects. Linguistic sound refers to the sound of letters or their combinations, meaning units refer to the meaning of language, represented objects refer to the fictional world created by language and schematized aspects refer to the aspects of characters or things represented by the text. These four strata are interconnected. The strata of phonetic sounds and meaning units are used to depict characters or things schematically which in turn constitute the fictional world. [①]

Let's illustrate Ingarden's theory with Alfred Tennyson's "The Eagle":

He clasps the crag with crooked hands;
Close to the sun in lonely lands,
Ringed with the azure world, he stands.
The wrinkled sea beneath him crawls;
He watches from his mountain walls,
And like a thunderbolt he falls. [②]

First, let's discuss the stratum of phonetic sounds. In the poem, Tennyson highlighted the "k" sound and used alliteration ("clasps the crag with crooked hands," "lonely lands") and the end rhyme of "aaabbb" to create a quick tempo and a determined, forceful feeling. These devices belong to the stratum of phonetic sounds and help depict the majestic and fearless image of the eagle. As for the stratum of meaning units, the language, by its conventional signifying function and rule-bound combination, expresses the content of the poem—the eagle's claws, posture, living environment, eyes, and actions. And the world of eagle is thereby built where the eagle proclaims itself king and takes everything under his reign. Please note that Tennyson left out the beak, feature, and size of the eagle, but we still can picture a full eagle's image in our mind. Here plays the role of the stratum of schematized

---

① Ingarden, Roman. *The Literary Work of Art*. Trans. George G. Garbowicz. Evanston: Northwestern University Press, 1973, pp. 29 – 33.

② Tennyson, Alfred. *Tennyson: A Selected Edition*. London and New York: Routledge, 2014, p. 96.

aspects. As we perceive the world in a schematic way, a comprehensive description of the eagle would do nothing but spoil the succinctness of the poem. The four strata of a literary text, as we have analyzed, are interconnected in that they each relies upon one another and contributes to the realization of the literary text as an organic whole.

2.3 Graphology

Graphology is not taken as a stratum of a literary text by Ingarden, but it does play a role in conveying meanings, feelings, and/or thoughts and carries implications for translation. Originally referring to the study of the relationship between one's handwriting and his/her personality, graphology is defined by Seaton as the outward form of written language like typeface, word size, capitalization, etc. Later it also includes other formal aspects of written language, such as enjambment, paragraph arrangement, and text layout. As we know, there are conventions on the form of written language. For example, we usually capitalize the initial letters of one's name and write sentences in a sequential way. If these conventions are breached, the writer often does so for a certain reason, which can be delivering messages, expressing emotions, or achieving aesthetic effects. African American writer and critic bell hooks deliberately puts her name in small letters to show her dissatisfaction with Anglo-American centrism as embodied in "Standard English" and to efface her importance as an author so as to divert the readers' attention to her work. In *Dombey and Son*, Charles Dickens uses irregular punctuations to imitate the ticking of clock, reflecting the dullness of the doctor's speech.

> Grave as an organ was the Doctor's speech; and when he ceased, the great clock in the hall seemed (to Paul at least) to take him up, and to go on saying, "how, is, my, lit, tle, friend? how, is, my, lit, tle, friend?" over and over and over again. [1]

American poet John Hollander makes daring experimentation with form and uses graphology to attain aesthetic effects. In "Swan and Shadow", he arranges the form of the poem in such a way as to mimic the reflection of the swan in the lake, letting the form interact with the content. [2]

---

[1] Dickens, Charles. *Dombey and Son*. State College: Pennsylvania State University, 2007, p. 161.

[2] The original poem can be seen in Hollander, John. *Types of Shape*. New Haven: Yale University Press, 1991. The picture version of it is from https://anagrammy. com/literary/rg/poems-rg18. html.

```
                                  Dusk
                                Above the
                            water hang the
                                     loud
                                     flies
                                     here
                                    O so
                                    gray
                                    then
                            What              A pale signal will appear
                            When         Soon before its shadow fades
                            Where         Here in this pool of opened eye
                            In us      No upon us  As at the very edges
                       of where we take shape in the dark air
                            this object bares its image awakening
                            ripples of recognition that will
                            brush darkness up into light
            even after this bird this hour both drift by atop the perfect sad instant now
                            already passing out of sight
                            toward yet-untroubled reflection
                            this image bears its object darkening
                            into memorial shades  Scattered bits of
                       light          No of water Or something across
                       water           Breaking up No Being regathered
                       soon            Yet by then a swan will have
                       gone                Yes out of mind into what
                       vast
                       pale
                       hush
                       of a
                           place
                           past
                    sudden dark as
                       if a swan
                          sang
```

Poems like "Swan and Shadow" are called shape poems or pattern poems and they are not unique to English. We also have pattern poems in Chinese. Acrostic poetry and picture poetry are two types of them. In Chapter 61 of *Water Margin*，Lu Junyi inscribed an acrostic poem on the wall：

> 芦花丛里一扁舟，
> 俊杰俄从此地游。
> 义士若能知此理，
> 反躬逃难可无忧。①

The initial characters of each line combine to deliver the message "卢俊义反"—Lu Junyi rebels. In "Buffalo," a picture poem composed by Zhan Bing，the poet arranges the lines into the shape of a buffalo.② It's obvious that graphology is conducive to meaning production and is also an external element of a literary text.

2.4   The implications for translation

The elements of a literary text carry implications for translation. Translators

---

①   施耐庵、罗贯中：《水浒传》(第二版)，北京：人民文学出版社，1997 年，第 807 页。
②   王珂：《论台港及海外华文图像诗》，《华文文学》2002 年第 4 期，第 19 页。

should reproduce all the strata or components of a literary text. In other words, a qualified translator of literary works should theoretically recreate the original text in terms of graphology, phonetics, meaning, represented objects, and schematized aspects, but the different strata are of unequal prominence in different genres of literary works. For example, graphology and phonetic sounds weigh more in poetry than in prose, so in discussing the implications for translation, we may cite literary texts of different genres as we see fit.

The stratum of phonetic sounds can pose a great challenge for Chinese-English translators. Unlike French-English translation in which the phonetic sounds of French can be easily put into those of English, the rendition of Chinese phonetic sounds into those of English can even exasperate renowned sinologists like Arthur Waley and Stephen Owen who simply used free verse in translating ancient Chinese poetry because they deemed it's an impossible mission to reproduce in English rhyme-effects similar to those of the original. For example, Owen left out the original rhyme pattern of "Out of the Great Wall" (《凉州词》) by Wang Zhihuan and rendered the poem into free verse:

> Yellow sands rise far away on high among white clouds,
> Silhouette of a lonely fortress on a thousand-foot mountain.
> Why should this nomad flute be playing wrath at the "leaves" of willow,
> Since the wind of spring will never cross Jade Gate Barrier?[1]

Leaving out the rhyme would make translation easier, but many believe a good translation should retain the rhyme effect of the original text and it's partly for this reason that the same poem was retranslated by Xu Yuanchong, who tried to recreate the rhyme pattern of the original poem:

> The yellow sand uprises as high as white cloud,
> The lonely Great Wall lost amid the mountains proud.
> Why should the Mongol flute complain no willow grow?
> Beyond the Gate of Jade spring wind never blow![2]

---

[1] Owen, Stephen. *The Great Age of Chinese Poetry: The High T'ang*. New Haven: Yale University Press, 1981, p. 92. The original poem can also be seen on this page: 黄沙远上白云间,一片孤城万仞山。羌笛何须怨杨柳,春风不度玉门关。Please note that some believe the first line of the original poem is "黄河远上白云间."

[2] 许渊冲译:《汉英对照唐诗一百五十首》,西安:陕西人民出版社,1984 年,第 12 页。

Readers might have discovered that Xu's translation recreates the rhyme pattern of the original poem at the expense of faithfulness. Wang Zhihuan did not say that the mountains are proud or that no willows grow. A possible explanation is that Xu Yuanchong adapted the meaning of the original poem to achieve the end rhyme pattern "aabb" in his translation. A comparison of Owen's and Xu's translations reveals that reproduction of the rhyme effect of the original poem is sometimes achieved at the cost of faithfulness. A good translation should retain both the rhyme and meaning of the original poem，which Xu Yuanchong succeeded in some of his translations. Take his translation of "Willow Trees" (《咏柳》) by He Zhizhang as an example：

> Ten thousand branches of tall trees begin to sprout,
> They droop like fringes of a robe made of green jade,
> But do you know by whom these young leaves are cut out?
> The early spring wind is as sharp as scissor blade. [①]

In this translation，Xu restructured English to recreate the rhyme effect of the original，but without compromising the meaning too much. A good translation should not overlook the stratum of phonetic sounds；rather，it should reproduce the phonetic effect as much as possible and remain faithful to the meaning of the original text.

The strata of meaning units，represented objects，and schematized aspects are closely related and universal to almost all genres of literary works. We discuss their implications for translation together. In most cases，translators would regard the literary work of art as an organic whole and would not dissect it into different strata，but they might be manipulated by ideology，poetics，and patronage and make alterations to the original. Sometimes，the alternations are too substantial to be justified and the translator's ethics is put in a dubious position. Let's discuss some specific cases of literary translations，both good and questionable ones.

Wang Wei usually created word-pictures in his poetry by using fresh and vivid images. In "Crossing the Yellow River to Ch'ing-ho" (《渡河到清河作》)，he used images to visualize the magnificent scene of his journey down the Yellow River. Here the strata of meaning units，represented objects，and schematized aspects are interwoven. Meaning is conveyed through language，the landscape is depicted in terms of water，sky，wave，houses，capital，etc.，and the poetic world is thus vividly

---

① 许渊冲译：《汉英对照唐诗一百五十首》，西安：陕西人民出版社，1984 年，第 5 页。The original poem is："碧玉妆成一树高，万条垂下绿丝绦。不知细叶谁裁出，二月春风似剪刀。"

presented. Let's see Stephen Owen's translation：

> Drift by boat upon the Great River，
> Massed waters touching the sky's very edge.
> Sky and waves suddenly split apart—
> The million houses of a district capital.
> And further on，see walls and market，
> Then clearly appears mulberry，hemp.
> I look back toward my homeland—
> Vast floods stretching to the clouds. ①

Owen remains faithful to all the three strata，without jeopardizing any of them. He reproduces the images，meaning，and imposing scene of the verse and the original viewpoints are also kept.

　　Manipulated by ideology，translators might alter part of the original text. In Chapter 32 of *Water Margin*，Wu Song is mad at the restaurant owner as the authors narrate：

　　　　武行者心中要吃，那里听他分说，一片声喝道："放屁，放屁!"②

Pearl S. Buck rendered the sentence as follows：

> Now Wu the priest longed much to eat，and so how could he be willing to listen to this explanation? He bellowed forth，"Pass your wind—pass your wind!"③

Buck's translation is generally faithful to the original line，except Wu Song's title and his curse. Chinese readers know that Wu Song is not a priest；he is disguised as a monk to escape arrest. Buck was probably influenced by her father's occupation as a missionary and her personal religious belief to accord the appellation "priest" to Wu Song. Her inappropriate translation of "放屁" into "pass your wind" has been

①　Owen，Stephen. *The Great Age of Chinese Poetry：The High T'ang*. New Haven：Yale University Press，1981，pp. 30 - 31. The original poem is："泛舟大河里，积水穷天涯。天波忽开拆，郡邑千万家。行复见城市，宛然有桑麻。回瞻旧乡国，森漫连云霞."
②　施耐庵、罗贯中：《水浒传》(第二版)，北京：人民文学出版社，1997 年，第 414 页。
③　Buck，Pearl S.，trans. *All Men Are Brothers*. New York：The George Macy Companies，Inc.，1948，p. 293.

analyzed by Qian Gechuan. According to Qian, "pass the wind" is a neutral expression of the physiological phenomenon; whereas, "放屁" is a curse in the original.[①] It should be instead put into "nonsense" or "bullshit."

Compared with Buck, Lin Shu took a much liberal attitude to the original text. Lin's translation works, as we have mentioned in Chapter 2, used to enjoy a large readership in China, but they are hardly faithful to the original texts. Here we come to the issue of translation criteria again. For literary translation, the polemics on criteria center on faithfulness, readability, and translator's subjectivity which form an intricate matrix that determines the outcome of translation activities. As can be seen from the above examples, a translator's subjectivity weighs between faithfulness and readability. If he or she opts for the former, the product may not be a fluent translation, but it retains most strata, if not all of the source text. On the contrary, if the translator shows strong subjectivity, and chooses readability over faithfulness, he or she might take liberty with the text and doctor it with the audacity of a surgeon and come up with a fluent translation palatable to target readers. Can translators produce products that are both faithful and readable? The answer is affirmative, but the sad truth is that most Chinese-English translators have to make a choice between fidelity and fluency as the great discrepancies between Chinese and English and their respective cultures make the "both and" criteria hard to meet, which has been demonstrated by the afore-mentioned examples. No wonder many translators complain that literary translation is a hard nut to crack.

Now, let's discuss the implication of graphology for translation. Oftentimes, graphology is not a big challenge for literary translation, as translators can simply reproduce the format of the source text in another language, but acrostic Chinese poems like the one in *Water Margin* can bewilder even the most capable translator. The following is Buck's translation:

> A nobleman stands in a boat on the lake,
> Turns he here or there his fear to slake?
> Turns he here, turns he there, none comes to help or save,
> Robbers, darkness, storm and winds—all he can but brave![②]

Buck failed to reproduce the graphology of the original acrostic poem, but the

---

① 钱歌川:《翻译的基本知识》,长沙:湖南科学技术出版社,1981 年,第 10 页。

② Buck, Pearl, S., trans. *All Men Are Brothers*. New York: The George Macy Companies, Inc., 1948, p. 587.

fortunate thing is that very few acrostic poems attain the status of classic as experimentation with outward form usually compromises artistry and that graphology is not a prominent issue in most literary works.

So far, we've discussed the features of literary language, the strata of a literary work, and their implications for literary translation, but what are the qualities of a good translator of literary works?

3. Qualities of a Good Translator of Literary Works

A popular notion is that translators are language professionals and anyone with bilingual proficiency can be a translator. This is usually not the case. According to Eugene Nida, a complete French-English bilingual translated a text from French to English and the result was a disastrous work, so he believes bilingual proficiency is not enough to make a qualified translator. "Top-notch translators need to have a significant aptitude for interlingual communication, but they also need to be well grounded in the principles of transferring the meaning of a source text into a receptor language."[1] What Nida means is that a qualified translator should be able to reproduce the meaning of the original text under the guidance of translation principles.

3.1 Basic qualities

Some scholars prescribe the basic qualities of a translator—professional ethics, bilingual proficiency, and encyclopedic knowledge. Professional ethics require a translator to be faithful to the original text and unjustified mistranslation, abridgement, omission, adaptation, etc., are held unethical. The Chinese version of Amy Tan's *Saving Fish from Drowning* (《沉没之鱼》) published by Beijing Press is alleged to have made substantial alteration to the original text and the translator's professional ethics is questioned. Bilingual proficiency refers to a translator's fine ability of the source and target languages. Anyone who falls short of bilingual proficiency is unable to work as a qualified independent translator. Encyclopedic knowledge comprises miscellaneous aspects of knowledge related to translation, such as culture, history, literature, geography, linguistics, translation theories and principles. For example, Thomas Pynchon created a labyrinth of allusions, word puzzles, music, hip culture, urban space, cyborg, etc. in his novels, making the translation of his works an intellect-wringing task. Dan Hansong, the Chinese

---

[1] Nida, Eugene A. *Contexts in Translating*. Amsterdam and Philadelphia: John Benjamins Publishing Company, 2001, p. 7.

translator of his *Inherent Vice*, compared the translation of Pynchon's novel to imprisonment in Guantanamo and Abu Ghraib. ① A translator in want of encyclopedic knowledge is likely to spend a lot of time doing the drudgery of searching and checking information, which will compromise his or her working efficiency.

What other qualities does a good translator need pertaining to the translation of literary works? Fu Lei argued that translators of literary works need to be adequate in life experience which can be acquired through observation, perception, imagination, and immersion in life. Scholars summarize some of the key qualities of a qualified literary translator—language sensitivity, rich imagination, intense emotions, and good aesthetic ability.

3.2　Language sensitivity

By language sensitivity, we mean that translators should be perspicacious in detecting the beauty of language and the devices or techniques used to achieve it so that the beauty of the source language can be reproduced in the target language. Take the following stanza from "The Solitary Reaper" by William Wordsworth as an example:

> No Nightingale did ever chaunt
> So sweetly to reposing bands
> Of Travelers in some shady haunt,
> Among Arabian Sands:
> No sweeter voice was ever heard
> In spring-time from the Cuckoo-bird,
> Breaking the silence of the seas
> Among the farthest Hebrides. ②

A sensitive translator should be able to instantly recognize the phonetic devices and metaphors used in the stanza and recreate them in the target language. Translators of literary works are first of all close readers and interpreters. Dullness to the source language can slow down translation and may result in mediocre translation or mistranslation.

---

① 但汉松:《做品钦门下走狗——〈性本恶〉译后》,《书城》2011 年第 12 期,第 87 页。

② Wordsworth, William. *William Wordsworth*. Oxford: Oxford University Press, 2010, pp. 253 - 254.

3.3　Rich imagination

In our discussion of the strata of a literary work，we know that writers create fictional reality through language. As a result，translators should exercise their imagination in savoring the original text by visualizing the scenes and transposing themselves into fictional reality. Ancient Chinese poetry is rich in imagery and even philosophical poems convey thoughts through images. In "On the Stork Tower"（《登鹳雀楼》），Wang Zhihuan created a bird-view scene and expressed the idea of "ascending high to see far" through images. A good translator is likely to visualize the scene and recreate the atmosphere in translation as Xu Yuanchong did：

> The sun beyond the mountains glows；
> The Yellow River seawards flows.
> You can enjoy a grander sight
> By climbing to a greater height. [1]

The same is true for prose translation. The power of literature lies in empathy. Authors and readers alike tend to immerse themselves into the fictional world and identify with the experiences and emotions of characters. When writing *Madame Bovary*，Flaubert burst into tears over the death of Bovary. A literary translator is also likely to "live" in the world of the original text to experience the vicissitudes of characters' lives and then reproduces the fictional world in another language. Fu Lei even went a step further to contend that a translator should choose texts that are akin to his or her temperament so that the style of the original text can be better expressed.

3.4　Good aesthetic ability

Aesthetic ability overlaps with language sensitivity as literary language is also a form of verbal art. Here we mainly use it to refer to the ability to appreciate other forms of art like painting and dancing. As we've discussed in Section 3.3，many ancient Chinese poems are verbal paintings in which the poets reveal their ways of composing the pictures. In "Crossing the Yellow River to Ch'ing-ho"，Wang Wei composed the verbal picture in the sequence of distant view，close view，and distant view and his points of view changed correspondingly from a forward-looking one to a horizontal-looking one and finally a backward-looking one. A qualified translator

---

[1]　许渊冲译：《汉英对照唐诗一百五十首》，西安：陕西人民出版社，1984 年，第 11 页。The original poem is："白日依山尽，黄河入海流。欲穷千里目，更上一层楼."

should be able to discern the way of poem/picture composition and reproduce it in the target language. Liu Zongyuan in "River-Snow" (《江雪》) also composed a verbal painting and the focal point is shifted from the distant tranquil snow-clad view to the close lonely fisherman. Both the picture and its way of composition were reproduced by Witter Bynner in his translation:

> A hundred mountains and no bird,
>
> A thousand paths without a footprint;
>
> A little boat, a bamboo cloak,
>
> An old man fishing in the cold river-snow. [①]

Dancing is another form of art that translators need to be acquainted with if the source text is about dancing. Not a few Chinese poems take dancing as the subject matter, such as "Dancing" (《赠张云容舞》) by Yang Yuhuan (杨玉环) and "A Song of Dagger-Dancing: To a Girl-Pupil of Lady Kung-sun" (《观公孙大娘弟子舞剑器行》) by Li Bai. In "A Song of Dagger-Dancing", Li Bai devoted a proportion of poem to the postures of Lady Kung-sun. If readers are to really appreciate the poem, they need to know about dagger-dancing. Bynner in his translation recreated the postures of Lady Kung-sun. Let's quote part of it as an illustration:

> There lived years ago the beautiful Kung-sun,
>
> Who, dancing with her dagger, drew from all four quarters
>
> An audience like mountains lost among themselves.
>
> Heaven and earth moved back and forth, following her motions,
>
> Which were bright as when the Archer shot the nine suns down the sky
>
> And rapid as angels before the wings of dragons.
>
> She began like a thunderbolt, venting its anger,
>
> And ended like the shining calm of rivers and the sea ... [②]

There are other forms of art like calligraphy, sculpture, and music that translators should be able to appreciate if the original texts involve these art forms.

---

① Bynner, Witter, trans. *The Jade Mountain: A Chinese Anthology Being Three Hundred Poems of the Tang Dynasty, 618—906*. New York: Alfred A. Knopf, 1929, p. 97. Please note that Bynner recognized the fictional reference of "万径" and put in into "a thousand paths", probably to make all the four lines begin with the article words "a" and "an" to achieve an aesthetic effect in form.

② Bynner, Witter, trans. and ed. *The Jade Mountain: A Chinese Anthology Being Three Hundred Poems of the Tang Dynasty, 618—906*. New York: Alfred A. Knopf, 1929, pp. 167 - 168.

Readers may be overwhelmed by the qualities required of a good translator of literary works and it's reasonable for them to have such a feeling as a successful literary translator usually needs language capacity, rich experience, dedication, versatility, and probably some talent.

A Short Summary

In this chapter, we've exemplified the features of literary language, the strata of a literary text, and the qualities required of a good translator of literary works. Compared with everyday language, literary language is self-referential, indirect, and fiction-referential. It possesses autonomy and creates fictional realty in an indirect way. A literary text, constructed with language, has several strata—phonetic sounds, meaning units, represented objects, schematized aspects, and graphology. Qualified translators should be able to reproduce all the strata in translation, but in some cases, some strata are simply untranslatable and translators have to weigh between fidelity and fluency and sacrifice some strata for others. This is a contested issue and reflects the nature and criteria of literary translation. A good translator of literary works should possess versatile qualities, among which are good professional ethics, bilingual proficiency, encyclopedic knowledge, language sensitivity, rich imagination, and good aesthetic ability.

Reviewing Questions

1. What are the features of literary language in contrast with everyday language and their implications for translation?

2. What are the strata of a literary text and their implications for translation?

3. Why is there the ongoing debate between fidelity and fluency in literary translation?

4. What do you think are the qualities of a good translator of literary works?

5. What is your vision for literary translation in the future?

Chapter 12

Translation of Tourism Publicity Materials

 Objectives

➢ Understand the significance of tourism translation

➢ Understand the features of tourism texts

➢ Understand the principles of tourism translation

➢ Grasp the methods and skills of tourism translation

➢ Be able to translate tourism publicity materials into proper English

1. The Significance of Tourism Translation

Tourism, by offering visitors a first-hand experience of the landscapes of China, is an important way of promoting Chinese culture as it is often said that to see something once is better than to hear about it a hundred times. For example, foreigners may have seen images of Terracotta Warriors many times, but they are likely to be awed by the grandeur and artistry of the vast array of real Terracotta Warriors and Horses in Qin Shihuang Mausoleum, a top tourist site in China. To better promote Chinese culture through tourism, it is imperative that tourism publicity materials like signs, brochures, and travel guides be faithfully and smoothly translated so that foreign visitors can get a good understanding of Chinese culture. In this chapter, we limit our discussion of tourism translation to translation of tourism publicity materials which we define as materials that introduce tourism resources for average foreign visitors and translation of tourism monographs will not be discussed. Unless otherwise specified, tourism texts in this chapter refer to tourism publicity materials and tourism translation refers to English translation of Chinese tourism publicity materials.

2. The Features of Tourism Texts

In the history of development, different types of texts have formed their distinctive features which distinguish them from each other and formed generic conventions that both writers and readers conform to.[①] These generic conventions, akin to what André Lefevere terms "poetics," also exert great influence on translation as translators cannot alter the poetic traditions as they wish. Therefore, a discussion of the features of tourism texts can aid the translation of tourism publicity materials. In general, tourism texts possess four distinctive features: multifunctionality, heterogeneity in genre, diversity in content, and a relatively high level of literariness.

2.1 Multifunctionality

Tourism texts often serve multiple functions which include but are not limited to those of informative, aesthetic, and imperative. First of all, tourism texts are informative in that they often present factual information of the tourist attractions.

---

① Abrams, M. H & Geoffrey Galt Harpham. *A Glossary of Literary Terms* (9th edition). Boston: Wadsworth Cengage Learning, 2009, pp. 134 – 136.

For example，the sentence "历史上的天安门高度为 33.87 米，1970 年大修后通高达到 34.7 米" offers factual information of the height of Tiananmen.[①] Besides providing factual information，tourism texts also try to achieve an aesthetic effect by using refined and figurative language. For instance，in the sentence "国家大剧院壳体上面的 '蘑菇灯' 散发的是点点光芒，如同夜空中闪烁的繁星，使国家大剧院充满了一种含蓄而别致的韵味与美感，" figurative language is used to reproduce the beauty of National Center for the Performing Arts.[②] Tourism texts sometimes are also imperative as they resort to imperative sentences to persuade potential tourists to visit the attractions. In a typical tourism brochure，for example，the imperative sentence "现在，请大家入内参观" is often used to invite the tourists for a visit.[③] More often than not，a tourism text possesses all the three functions.

2.2　Heterogeneity in genre

To fulfill their multiple functions，tourism texts usually adopt a variety of genres，particularly description，narration，and exposition. For example，in their introduction to the Grand Buddha of Leshan，the authors combine description with narration and exposition. They describe the location，size，and features of the Buddha，narrate its origin，and expose its process of construction and cultural connotations.[④] These heterogenous genres are jointly used to present the factual information，beauty，and cultural connotations of tourist attractions.

2.3　Diversity in content

Tourism texts can be highly diverse in content as they usually include different aspects of the tourist attractions and involve various branches of knowledge such as history，geography，myth，literature，art，architecture，religion，and ethnology. For instance，an introduction to Shaolin Temple in Henan Province includes the temple's history，kung fu，stone inscriptions，and Buddhist buildings，covering history，martial arts，Buddhism，folklore，and architecture.[⑤]

2.4　Relatively high level of literariness

The literariness of a tourism text is embodied both in the elaborate language and

---

① 洪华:《北京旅游景点与文化》,北京:燕山出版社,2009 年,第 5 页。
② 洪华:《北京旅游景点与文化》,北京:燕山出版社,2009 年,第 186 页。
③ 蒋金奎:《宁波旅游:新编景点导游词》,北京:中国旅游出版社,2008 年,第 57 页。
④ 干福弟,祁彩梅:《中国最佳旅游景点图册》,北京:中国地图出版社,1998 年,第 40 - 41 页。
⑤ 王玉宝:《河南旅游精品景点》,北京:中国旅游出版社,2007 年,第 2 - 12 页。

the literary works embedded in the text. Writers or compilers of tourism texts tend to use decorative language to describe tourist attractions and quote literary works，poems in particular，to add persuasiveness and literariness to the texts. For example，in their introduction to the Yellow Crane Tower，a famous tourist attraction in Wuhan，Li Fengling et al use refined language such as "昔日黄鹤楼轩昂宏伟，辉煌瑰丽，峥嵘缥缈，引来很多诗人墨客登楼吟诗作赋，讴歌这黄鹤楼的壮丽景观"and quote poems written on the tower by Cui Hao，Su Shi，and Liu Haisu. [①]

3. The Principles of Tourism Translation

As tourist attractions and tourism texts are culture-bound，the translation of tourist texts，like the translation of relics or architecture，is essentially a form of cross-cultural activity in which the SL culture and TL culture are mediated by the translator. The principles of tourism translation are based on the criteria of fidelity and readability. By fidelity，it is meant that tourism translation should be faithful to the original text both linguistically and culturally，that is，it should reproduce the Chinese cultural elements as much as possible while remaining faithful to the meaning of the source text since one primary purpose of tourism translation is to help foreign readers understand Chinese culture and promote cross-cultural communication. And by readability，we mean that the "end products" of tourism translation should be smooth and meet the reading habits of target readers even if translators have to make adaptations to the source texts，sometimes even substantially. However，it is not rare that the principle of fidelity and the principle of readability are at odds with each other，in which case，translators need to strike a balance between them or prioritize one over the other. This is a dilemma that translators often encounter in cultural translation.

4. The Methods and Skills of Tourism Translation

Translators usually resort to the methods and skills of transliteration，half transliteration，free translation，addition，omission，rewriting，and cross-cultural substitution in putting tourism texts into English.

4.1 Transliteration

Much has been said about transliteration which is frequently used in rendering

---

① 李凤玲，孙颖，辛建萍：《中国旅游景点文化概览》，济南：山东大学出版社，2002 年，第 100 - 101 页。

culture-loaded words into the target language. In translating the names of tourist attractions，translators often use transliteration and put them into Romanized letters based on Chinese *pinyin*. For example，太和殿，乾清宫，and 三潭印月 are sometimes transliterated as *Taihedian*，*Qianqinggong* and *Santanyinyue* respectively. Transliteration is more frequently used with the increasing influence of Chinese. The replacement of "road" by *lu*（路）in road signs is a case in point. However，as we have previously stated that overreliance on transliteration can impede understanding，the names of tourist attractions are more often half transliterated or freely translated.

4.2 Half transliteration

Half transliteration，as indicated by the name，refers to the method of translation in which one part of the text is transliterated while the other part is freely translated. As for the names of tourist attractions，the proper names are often transliterated whereas the generic names are freely translated. For instance，by using half transliteration，太和殿，乾清宫，and 鹰嘴岩 can be rendered as "Tianhe Hall"，"Qianqing Palace" and "Yingzui Cliff." Half transliteration is denounced by some translators as it often leads to awkward translations by juxtaposing Chinese with English in an unnatural way.

4.3 Free translation

In translating the names of tourist attractions，not a few translators prefer free translation to transliteration and half transliteration，believing that free translation can both demonstrate their translation ability and produce readable texts for target readers. Through free translation，太和殿，三潭印月，寒山寺，紫来洞，and 鹰嘴岩 are put into "The Hall of Grand Harmony，" "Three Pools Mirroring the Moon，" "Cold Mountain Temple，" "Purple Source Cave，" and "Eagle Beak Cliff" respectively.

Currently，transliteration，half transliteration，and free translation are all used in translating the names of tourist attractions，resulting in inconsistency of translated names. It is necessary to standardize the English names of Chinese tourist attractions by promulgating national standards and compiling reference books.

4.4 Addition

Tourism texts are often saturated with Chinese culture and contain a lot of culture-specific terms such as characters' names，historical events，and places which are well-known to Chinese but unfamiliar to foreign readers. In translating these culture-loaded terms into English，translators need to add the background knowledge needed to understand these terms. For example，we can use appositive to add information about 秦始皇 and 西域 to help English readers understand them：Qin Shihuang（秦始皇），the first emperor in Chinese history who unified China in 221 B. C. ；the Western Regions（西域），a Han dynasty term for the area west of *Yumenguan* Pass，including what is now Xinjiang Uygur Autonomous Region and part of Central Asia. Sometimes clauses and notes are added to provide necessary background information. Let's illustrate this with two examples.

> 三官殿里一株茶花树，在寒冬腊月开出一束鲜花，因此又名"耐冬"。
>
> There is a camellia tree in *Sanguan* Palace blooming fully in severe winter，so it is called "*Naidong* ，" meaning it can stand bitterly cold winters.

> 鲁迅纪念馆对外开放场所包括鲁迅祖居、百草园、三味书屋和陈列厅。
>
> Open to visitors are Lu Xun's former residence，including his ancestral home，Baicao Garden，Sanwei Study and the exhibition hall. Note：Sanwei Study is the private school where young Lu Xun studied classics for about five years and Baicao garden is a waste vegetable plot that made a paradise for little Lu Xun.

In the former sentence，a non-finite verbal clause is used to explain *Naidong* and in the latter sentence，a sentence is added as a note to explain Baicao Garden and Sanwei Study. However，it needs to be pointed out that addition should be used according to the principle of necessity.

4.5 Omission

Contrary to addition，omission refers to the process in which information that is not essential in understanding the text or difficult for target readers to understand is left out in translation. Omission can be endorsed by *skopos* theory which advocates the justification of translation process by translation purpose. In this sense，if the purpose of tourism translation is to help target readers grasp the key information of tourist attractions，nonessential information can be omitted. Let's exemplify it with the translation of the sentences：

> 在我国最早的典籍中，即有关于这条河的记载。《尚书·禹贡》："漆沮既从，沣水攸同"，《诗经·大雅》："沣水东注，维禹之绩"，说明沣水在远古就是一条著名的河流。
>
> Records about the river can be found even in the earliest Chinese classics，which proves that the Feng River has been well known since ancient times.

In the translation, quotations from *The Book of History* and *The Book of Songs* are omitted, which can be justified by *skopos* theory. However, we need to realize that omission, though often theoretically and functionally justifiable, can sometimes be taken as an indicator of the translator's incompetence. Competent and meticulous translators would rise to the challenge and properly put the quotations into English however difficult they are.

4.6   Rewriting

André Lefevere regards translation as a form of rewriting and the translation practice of Lin Shu still rings a bell. Rewriting can also be justified by *Skopos* Theory and is frequently used in tourism translation. The structure, content, and style of the source text can all be rewritten.

First, the structure of the source text can be rewritten. Let's compare the structures of the following excerpt and its English translation.

在四川西部，有一处美妙的去处。它背倚岷山主峰雪宝顶，树木苍翠，花香袭人，鸟语婉转，流水潺潺。这就是松潘县的黄龙。

One of Sichuan's finest scenic spot is Huanglong, literally meaning Yellow Dragon in Songpan County just beneath Xuebao, the main peak of the Minshan Mountain. Its lush green forests, filled with fragrant flowers, bubbling streams and songbirds, are rich in historical interest as well as natural beauty.

In the translation, the structure of the source excerpt is rewritten by placing the tourist attraction at the beginning of the sentence, which suits the reading habit and thinking mode of English readers.

Next, the content of the source text, especially description of the beauty of the tourist attraction and quotations can also be rewritten by summarizing their key information. Let's make a comparison of the following sentence and its rewritten English version.

水映山容,使山容益添秀美,山清水秀,使水能更显柔情,有诗云:岸上湖中各自奇,山觞水酌两皆宜。只言游舫浑如画,身在画中元不知。

The hills overshadow the lake, and the lake reflects the hills. As depicted by a poem, the hills and lake are in perfect harmony, and more beautiful than a picture.

In the source text, the author uses four-character idioms and parallel structure and quotes a poem by Yang Wanli（杨万里）, a poet of the Southern Song dynasty, to describe the beauty of the scenery while in the English translation, the poetic description is condensed into two sentences.

The style of the source text can also be changed in the process of rewriting as indicated by the previous example. Let's illustrate it with one more example.

> 黄河奔腾不息,勇往直前,忽而惊涛裂岸,势不可挡,使群山动容;忽而安静如处子,风平浪静,波光激滟,气象万千。
>
> The Yellow River surges ahead through the mountains and at some places flows on peacefully with a sedate appearance and glistening ripples.

The original sentence and its English rewriting are of different styles. The former attains an elaborate and half-classic style by using nine idioms and a parallel structure; whereas the latter exhibits a plain style by summing up the key information of the source text. It can be noticed from the examples that rewriting of any one of the three aspects of the source text—structure, content, and style usually results in the rewriting of the other two aspects.

4.7 Cross-cultural substitution

By cross-cultural substitution, we mean the culture-specific terms in the source text are replaced by terms with similar meanings in the target language and culture. Let's illustrate it with an often-quoted example. In an international conference held in Geneva in 1954, Premier Zhou Enlai introduced *Butterfly Lovers*（《梁山伯与祝英台》） to foreign viewers as the Chinese *Romeo and Juliet* and the foreigners' interest was aroused. This is a fine example of cross-cultural substitution and we have many other examples. For instance, Ji Gong is compared to Robin Hood and Xi Shi（西施）is compared to Cleopatra. In tourism translation, cross-cultural substitution is also used to explain some tourist attractions. For example, we can explain the ancient town of Zhouzhuang by likening it to Venice. Cross-cultural substitution can help target readers get a quick understanding of the tourist attractions.

◇ A Short Summary

In this chapter, we've analyzed the significance of tourism translation, discussed the features of tourism texts, explained the principles, and exemplified the methods and skills of translating tourism publicity materials. Tourism translation plays an important role in promoting Chinese culture by introducing Chinese tourist attractions which are embodiments of Chinese culture to foreign readers. Tourism texts are often multifunctional, diverse in content, heterogeneous in genre and demonstrate a relatively high level of literariness. As tourist attractions and tourism texts are closely associated with Chinese culture, tourism translation is a typical form of cross-cultural activity that involves a successful mediation between SL culture and TL culture. Translations of tourism texts should be faithful and readable. Translators usually use transliteration, half transliteration, free translation, addition, omission, rewriting, and cross-cultural substitution in putting tourism texts into English.

Reviewing Questions

1. What is the significance of tourism translation?

2. What are the features of tourism texts?

3. What are the principles of tourism translation?

4. What are the commonly used methods and skills in translating tourism publicity materials?

Chapter 13

Translation of Chinese Idioms

 Objectives

➢ Understand the definitions and characteristics of Chinese idioms

➢ Understand the relationship between Chinese idioms and Chinese culture

➢ Understand the cultural differences embodied in idioms

➢ Grasp the methods and skills of idiom translation

➢ Be able to translate Chinese idioms into proper English

1. The Definitions and Characteristics of Chinese Idioms

The word "idiom" is derived from the Greek word *idios*, meaning "proper or peculiar to oneself."[1] *Oxford Dictionary of English* defines idiom as "a group of words established by usage as having a meaning not deducible from those of the individual words" or "a form of expression natural to a language, person, or group of people."[2] According to *The American Heritage Dictionary*, an idiom is "a speech form or an expression of a given language that is peculiar to itself grammatically or cannot be understood from the individual meanings of its elements."[3] From its origin and definitions, we know that an idiom possesses some distinctive characteristics. First, it is unique to a particular language, culture, or group. For example, the idiom "明修栈道，暗度陈仓，" involving the historical event of Han Xin's war strategy, is specific to Chinese culture. Second, it consists of several words or characters as exemplified by the idiom 敲山震虎 which is made of four Chinese characters. Third, its meaning usually is not an addition of the meanings of its constituents. For instance, the meaning of 瓜田李下 cannot be obtained by adding the meanings of 瓜田 and 李下. In this chapter, we define Chinese idioms as linguistic chunks made up of phrases or sentences whose real meanings cannot be obtained by adding the meanings of their constituents. Usually, Chinese idioms include proverbs, allegorical sayings, slangs, and jargons. In this chapter we limit our discussion to the English translation of 成语, 俗语，谚语，and 歇后语.

2. The Relationship Between Chinese Idioms and Chinese Culture

The meanings of idioms are conventional and culture-bound. As we've discussed in Chapter 1，language is a medium of culture, and idioms, as culture-specific expressions, are regarded as the essence and gems of a language. The origin of almost every Chinese idiom can be traced to a certain aspect of Chinese culture, such as history，literature，philosophy，mythology，customs，geography，clothing，and politics. For example，望梅止渴，三顾茅庐，and 四面楚歌 are related to history，窈窕

---

[1] Partridge, Eric. *A Short Etymological Dictionary of Modern English*. London and New York: Routledge, 2006, p. 1496.

[2] Stevenson, Angus. *Oxford Dictionary of English* (3rd edition). Oxford: Oxford University Press, 2010, p. 16199.

[3] Soukhanov, Anne H. *The American Heritage Dictionary of the English Language* (3rd edition). Boston: Houghton Mifflin Harcourt, 2000, p. 3616.

淑女，世外桃源，and 江郎才尽 are derived from literature，and 学而不厌，己所不欲，勿施于人，and 巧言令色 have their origins in Confucian classics. It is clear that Chinese idioms are highly rich in cultural connotations and the English translation of them is a typical form of cross-cultural activity which requires a successful mediation between cultures. Therefore，it is necessary that we understand the cultural differences embodied in idioms.

3. The Cultural Differences Embodied in Idioms

According to Nida，culture can be classified into ecological culture，material culture，social culture，religious culture，and linguistic culture. [①] Ecological culture is shaped by geographical conditions. Material culture means the culture associated with things or objects. Social culture includes customs，traditions，folk beliefs，social psychology，etc. Religious culture refers to religious beliefs. And linguistic culture is related to language as a storehouse of culture. Let's exemplify the cultural differences embodied in idioms from the five aspects.

3.1 Differences in ecological culture

Due to their different geographical conditions，China and the West have formed different ecological cultures. It is generally agreed that Chinese culture is earth-bound and rooted in a long farming tradition while Western culture is sea-oriented and originates from an age-old maritime tradition. Many Chinese idioms are related to agriculture，such as 种瓜得瓜，种豆得豆 and 一分耕耘一分收获. On the contrary，many English idioms have something to do with the sea. For instance，when someone wants to take a break，he/she will "rest on his/her oars" and when someone is confused，we can say he/she is all at sea. Some idioms with identical meanings can well illustrate the differences between Chinese culture and Western culture in terms of ecology. For example，in Chinese we use 挥金如土 to describe the unthrift use of money while in English，the idiom "spend money like water" is used to express the same meaning. And Chinese people often use the hyperbolical idiom 骄阳似火 to describe summer heat as summer can be scorching in China while Shakespeare compared his beloved to "a summer's day" in "Sonnet 18" because summer is mild in Britain.

---

① Nida，Eugene. "Linguistics and Ethnology in Translation Problems." *WORD* 1 (1945)，p. 196.

3.2　Differences in material culture

Idioms can also reflect differences in material culture. For example，Chinese idioms like 痛打落水狗，狗仗人势，and 丧家犬 reflect the largely negative cultural connotations of dog in Chinese culture and English idioms like "love me，love my dog," "lucky dog," and "every dog has its day" are associated with the positive implications of dog in English culture. The cultural connotations of animals and the translation of animal terms will be discussed in Chapter 15.

3.3　Differences in social culture

Some idioms have their roots in folk beliefs，social customs，traditions，etc. and can reflect differences in social culture. Chinese idioms like 狐狸精，黑白无常，and 没做亏心事，不怕鬼敲门 indicate superstitious folk beliefs and English idioms like "treat or treat," "white witch," and "it's raining cats and dogs" are related with English festivals，customs，or folk beliefs.

3.4　Differences in religious culture

Different from English-speaking countries that are chiefly religious，China is essentially a secular country，but traditional Chinese philosophies like Taoism and Buddhism are also regarded as religions sometimes. Many idioms are derived from religious beliefs and indicate differences in religious culture. 天，for example，is a key term in "Taoism" and idioms like 天知道 and 天道酬勤 are related with it. In English，idioms with similar meanings are "God knows" and "God helps those who help themselves," both of which have their origins in Christianity.

3.5　Differences in linguistic culture

Language draws extensively from various aspects of culture and is a storehouse of it. Many idioms，as gems in the storehouse，have their origins in history，literature，philosophy，myth，etc. and are culture-specific. For example，both the Chinese idiom 进退两难 and the English idiom "catch - 22" are used to describe a dilemmatic situation，but they have different cultural origins. The former originates from *The Strategies of War* (《卫公兵法》) by Li Jing whereas the latter is from the American novel *Catch - 22* by Joseph Heller. In a like manner，the Chinese idiom 垓下之围 which is often used by Chinese to describe a desperate situation or a fatal war is associated with Xiang Yu who was routed by Liu Bang at the Battle of Gaixia and killed himself；whereas a similarly fatal situation or utter failure is referred to as "one's Waterloo," which originates from Napoleon's crushing final defeat at the Battle of Waterloo. These idioms indicate differences in linguistic culture which should be accorded enough attention in translation.

From our discussion，we know that idioms are deeply rooted in culture，and therefore，the English translation of Chinese idioms requires the mediation between Chinese and English and the cultures associated with them.

4. The Methods and Skills of Idiom Translation

Translators often adopt the methods and skills of literal translation，literal translation with annotation，free translation，substitution，and addition in translating Chinese idioms into English.

4.1   Literal translation

Literal translation is an important way of retaining Chinese cultural elements and introducing them into English. Many Chinese idioms are put into English through literal translation. For instance，雪中送炭 can be translated as "to offer charcoal in snowy weather," 瓜田李下 as "neither adjust your shoe in a melon patch，nor your hat under a plum tree," and 井水不犯河水 as "well water and river water don't mix." These literally translated idioms can bring new cultural elements into English and are not difficult to understand for English readers as there are specific contexts. One more example concerns the translation of 姜太公钓鱼，愿者上钩 in a sentence written by Chairman Mao：

> 美国人在北平，在天津，在上海，都洒了些救济粉，看一看什么人愿意弯腰拾起来。太公钓鱼，愿者上钩。嗟来之食，吃下去肚子要痛的。
>
> The Americans have sprinkled some relief flour in Peiping，Tientsin and Shanghai to see who will stoop to pick it up. Like Chiang Tai Kung fishing，they have cast the line for the fish who want to be caught. But he who swallows food handed out in contempt will get a bellyache. ①

For average English readers，the anecdote of 姜太公钓鱼 is something new，but they can grasp its meaning from the context and understand it as "be willingly to fall into the snare." However，it needs to be pointed out that literal translation should not be used at the expense of readability，i. e.，translators should use literal translation on

---

① Mao，Zedong. *The Selected Works of Mao Tse-tung*，Vol. Ⅳ. Beijing：Foreign Languages Press，1961，p. 437.

the basis of making the text understandable to target readers rather than create obstacles for understanding.

4.2 Literal translation plus annotation

Translators sometimes combine literal translation with annotation in the English translation of Chinese idioms. Let's exemplify this with Yang Xianyi and Gladys Yang's translation of 东施效颦. Mr. and Mrs. Yang first offered a literal translation of the idiom—"Tung Shih imitating Hsi Shih" and then added a note to it: "Hsi Shih was a famous beauty in the ancient Kingdom of Yueh. Tung Shih was an ugly girl who tried to imitate her ways." The sentence "人说'塞翁失马'，未知是福是祸……" from Chapter 40 of *The Scholars* is also put into English through the method of literal translation with annotation. After a literal translation of the idiom as "when the old man at the frontier lost his horse, he thought it might be a bad thing … ,"[①] the translators offered a detailed note to the idiom:

> An allusion to a story popular for more than 2,000 years in China. When an old man lost his horse, neighbors condoled with him. "This may be a good thing," he said. The horse came back with another horse, and the old man's neighbors congratulated him. "This may prove unlucky," he said. When his son, who liked the new horse, rode it and broke his leg, once more the neighbors expressed their sympathy. "This may turn out for the best," said the old man. And, indeed, just then the Huns invaded the country and most able-bodied men were conscripted and killed in battle; but thanks to his broken leg the old man's son survived. [②]

According to Mu Lei, literal translation plus annotation is a good method to help English readers learn Chinese culture and when English readers are well acquainted with the idioms, notes can be left out. [③]

4.3 Free translation

Free translation, as we've discussed before, focuses on the readability and acceptability of the source text. In the process of free translation, the cultural connotations of Chinese idioms are replaced or left out. Goldblatt translated "买卖不

---

① 吴敬梓:《儒林外史》,杨宪益,戴乃迭译,长沙:湖南人民出版社;北京:外文出版社,1999 年,第 959 页。
② 吴敬梓:《儒林外史》,杨宪益,戴乃迭译,长沙:湖南人民出版社;北京:外文出版社,1999 年,第 1307 页。
③ 穆雷:《接受理论与习语翻译》,《外语研究》1990 年第 1 期,第 64 页。

成仁义在么，这不是动刀动枪的地方，有本事对着日本人使去" as："Even if you can't agree，you mustn't abandon justice and honor. This isn't the time or place to fight. Take your fury on the Japanese."[1] The idiom 买卖不成仁义在 highlights the traditional Chinese values of 仁义（benevolence and righteousness），but they are replaced by values that are held dear to Western culture—"justice" and "honor." The cultural connotations of Chinese idioms sometimes are left out in free translation. Let's analyze the English translation of the sentence from *Midnight*（《子夜》）by Mao Dun（茅盾）.

> 他亦未必没有相当成就,但是仅仅十万人口的双桥镇何足以供回旋,比起目前计划来,真是小巫见大巫了!
>
> There，his achievements had not been insignificant；but his scope had been limited by the small population—barely a hundred thousand. His activities in Shaungchiao Town had been mere child's play compared with this present scheme. [2]

In the English translation，the cultural connotation of the idiom 小巫见大巫 which is associated with witchcraft and literally means a lesser witch is outshone by a greater one，is lost.

4.4　Substitution

Concerning the English translation of Chinese idioms，substitution refers to the process in which Chinese idioms are replaced by English idioms. For example，倾盆大雨 can be substituted by "it's raining cats and dogs，" 谋事在人，成事在天 by "man proposes，God disposes，" and 杀人不眨眼 as "kill without batting an eye."

4.5　Addition

Addition is a frequently used skill in cultural translation，whose main purpose is to provide target readers with necessary background information needed to understand the target text. For instance，the English translation of 三个臭皮匠，合成一个诸葛亮—"three cobblers with their wits combined would equal Zhuge Liang，the master mind" explains the status of Zhuge Liang to help English readers understand the meaning of the original idiom. Likewise，the English translation of 班门弄斧—"show off one's proficiency with the ax before Lu Ban，the master carpenter" adds the

---

[1]　Mo，Yan. *Red Sorghum*. Trans. Howard Goldblatt. London：Arrow Books，2003，p. 29.

[2]　Mao，Dun. *Midnight*. Hong Kong：C & W Publishing Co.，1976，p. 119.

profession of Lu Ban so that readers can understand the meaning of the idiom.

These methods and skills, belonging to the strategy of domestication or foreignization, are often used in combination by translators in idiom translation. To achieve a mutual cultural flow in idiom translation, translators should maintain a balance between domestication and foreignization and avoid overuse of either of them.

A Short Summary

In this chapter, we've discussed the English translation of Chinese idioms. As linguistic chunks consisting of phrases or sentences whose real meanings cannot be obtained by adding the meanings of their constituents, idioms are culture-specific. The English translation of Chinese idioms is a cross-cultural activity that requires negotiations between cultures. Translators usually adopt literal translation, literal translation plus annotation, free translation, substitution, and addition in the English translation of Chinese idioms.

Reviewing Questions

1. What is an idiom?

2. What are the characteristics of idioms?

3. What is the relationship between Chinese idioms and Chinese culture?

4. Can you exemplify the differences between Chinese and English cultures as embodied in idioms?

5. What are the commonly used methods and skills of translating Chinese idioms?

Chapter 14

Translation of Color Terms

 Objectives

➤ Understand the classification of language meaning

➤ Understand the cultural connotations of different colors from a cross-cultural perspective

➤ Grasp the methods and skills of translating color terms

➤ Be able to translate color terms into proper English

1. Classification of Language Meaning

Charles Morris, American philosopher and founder of modern semiotics, regards language as a system of signs and associates it with human cognition and behavior. He theorizes language as a system of signs and proposes the key terms of "sign," "interpreter," "interpretant," "denotatum," and "significatum." According to Morris, a sign is something that "is a preparatory-stimulus of the kind specified in our previous formulation," an interpreter is an organism that recognizes and interprets the sign, the disposition to respond in a certain way is called an interpretant, anything that permits the occurrence of interpretant is called a denotatum, and the "conditions which are such that whatever fulfills them is a denotatum will be called a significatum of the sign."[1] Morris illustrates his theory with the experiment of Pavlov's dog:

> So in the example of the dog, the buzzer is the sign; the dog is the interpreter; the disposition to seek food at a certain place, when caused by the buzzer, is the interpretant; food in the place sought which permits the completion of the response-sequence to which the dog is disposed is a denotatum and is denoted by the buzzer; the condition of being an edible object (perhaps of a certain sort) in a given place is the significatum of the buzzer and is what the buzzer signifies.[2]

Morris' semiotics theory is not that easy to understand, but its implication for the classification of language meaning is comparatively easy to grasp. We humans are interpreters; our tendency to interpret signs in a certain way is the interpretant; and the sociocultural context that determines our way of interpretation can be taken as the denotatum. Some scholars simplify Morris' semiotics theory and classify language meaning into referential meaning, structural meaning, and pragmatic meaning. This classification will suffice for our discussion of the translation of color terms.

1.1 Referential meaning

According to Saussure, a sign consists of the signifier and the signified. The

---

[1] Morris, Charles W. *Signs, Language and Behavior*. New York: George Braziller, Inc., 1946, p. 17.

[2] Morris, Charles W. *Signs, Language and Behavior*. New York: George Braziller, Inc., 1946, pp. 17 - 18.

signifier is a vocal or written symbol like a word, a phrase, or an expression and the signified is what the signifier refers to. For instance, "tiger" as a signifier refers to a large ferocious animal that is a member of the cat family. Referential meaning usually is not isolated and is associated with structural meaning and pragmatic meaning. For example, in the sentence "He is an old fox," the word "fox" not only refers to a carnivorous mammal of the dog family with a pointed muzzle and bushy tail, but also indicates the characteristic of "cunning." The referential meaning and pragmatic meaning of "fox" coexist in the sentence.

1.2 Structural meaning

The series of signs of a language, with their own referential meanings, are usually arranged in a certain order to express meaning. The arrangement, be it on a phrase, clause, sentence, paragraph, or text level, usually follows grammatical rules and conventions. Rearrangement can lead to alteration in meaning. For instance, the two sentences "He quit school and got addicted to online games" and "He got addicted to online games and quit school" use the same signs and structure, but their meanings are different due to different arrangements of the signs. This is one aspect of structural meaning. As the translation of color terms mainly concerns pragmatic meaning, we'll leave out other aspects of structural meaning and focus our attention on pragmatic meaning.

1.3 Pragmatic meaning

Pragmatic meaning is context-bound and tied up with culture. It relies on the culture of a certain people, or the denotatum as theorized by Morris as a vehicle for the realization of its meaning. For example, the symbolic meaning of "willow"— friendship and parting is rooted in Chinese culture and the connotation of "Achilles' heel" has its origin in Greek mythology.

Pragmatic meaning is further classified into associative meaning, interactive meaning, and representative meaning. As we've argued in Chapter 1, language is inseparable with culture and reflects the beliefs, values, customs, mode of thinking, etc. of a certain people. Language signs are also tied up with culture and can generate specific meanings or evoke certain feelings for the sharers of a common culture. This is what we call associative meaning. For instance, red double happiness (囍) is associated with good luck and happiness in Chinese culture.

Interactive meaning is also culture-bound and often exhibits discrepancy between language form and its real meaning. Still remember the anecdote of Li Hongzhang in Chapter 1 in which the form of language differs from its real meaning? Formulaic expressions like "你吃了吗?" and "你干什么去?"in Chinese are mainly greetings and should not be taken as real questions and translated literally.

Representative meaning can reveal the age，gender，education，nationality，etc.，of the speaker. For example，the sentence "Kid，don't talk to me like this" is probably spoken by an adult. It indicates that the speaker is probably senior to the addressee. And the sentence "I plan to visit Venice next fall" reveals American nationality of the speaker as Americans use the word "fall" instead of "autumn."

2. The Connotations of Major Colors and Translation of Color Terms

From our discussion，we know that the meanings of color terms are primarily those of pragmatic，especially associative. They are associated with culture. In this sense，the translation of color terms is essentially an intercultural activity. As the connotations of colors are culture-bound，we will elucidate the cultural connotations of some major colors—white，black，red，green，yellow，and blue from a cross-cultural perspective and discuss the translation of color terms.

2.1 The connotations of white and translation of "white" terms

White as an achromatic color of maximum lightness is neutral，but its connotations are culture-bound and vary from culture to culture. There are several cases concerning the cultural connotations or pragmatic meanings of white in Chinese and English cultures.

First，its associative meanings of purity and innocence are overlapping in the two cultures. In Chinese，we have four-character idioms like 洁白无瑕，精白之心，清白无辜 and poetic lines like 旷野白云山，流连白雪意，and 西塞山前白鹭飞. In the West，the bride is clad in white to show her chastity and purity. In *The Scarlet Letter*，the protagonist Hester Prynne's "skill was called in aid to embroider the white veil which was to cover the pure blushes of a bride."[①] Hawthorne uses the associative meaning of white and makes it an implicit contrast to the original meaning of the scarlet letter A，sin of adultery to depict Prynne's redemption and inner purity.

Second，white as a symbol of death and mourning is unique to Chinese culture and in the West，it is black that carries such associative meanings. In *Snow in Summer* (《窦娥冤》)，Guan Hanqing（关汉卿）makes white the dominant hue in the scene of Dou E's execution：

---

① Hawthorne，Nathaniel. *The Scarlet Letter*. Oxford：Oxford University Press，2007，p. 66.

The response was instantaneous. Dozens of people scurried around, and soon came back with a clean mat and the required length of white silk. The chief executioner ordered his assistants to hang the silk from the flagpole and place the mat of Dou E to stand on. All was set for the execution to go ahead.

说话之间,早有人寻来净席、白练,飞奔法场,交给监斩官。监斩官即命刽子手竖起旗杆,挂上白练,又将净席置于窦娥脚下,准备行刑。①

The symbolic meanings of white in the quoted paragraph are twofold. It is a mourning color and symbolizes Dou E's innocence. On the contrary, the meanings of death and mourning are vested in the color black in the West. The plague that claimed over 25 million lives in Europe in the 14th century was called the Black Death. W. H. Auden demands that policemen wear black gloves to mourn his deceased friend: "Put crepe bows round the white necks of the public doves, /Let the traffic policemen wear black cotton gloves."②

Third, some color expressions are dissociated from the associative meanings of white such as 白干, 白吃白拿, and 白开水 in Chinese and "a white day," "a white lie," and "a white-haired boy" in English. In Table 6 we list some "white" terms and their translations.

Table 6　Some "White" Terms and Their Translations③

Chinese	English	English	Chinese
白干	work in vain	a white day	吉日
白开水	plain boiled water	a white light district	不夜区
白菜	Chinese cabbage	a white night	不眠之夜
白搭	no use	bleed white	榨尽血汗
白事	funeral	white wash	掩饰,洗白
吃白食	freeload	white elephant	昂贵无用之物
打白条	issue an IOU	a white lie	善意的谎言
白痴	idiot	a white witch	做善事的女巫
白日梦	fantasy, daydream	a white Christmas	白色圣诞节(圣诞下雪)

---

① 关汉卿:《中国古代悲剧故事:窦娥冤》,杨孝昌改编、Paul White 译,北京:新世界出版社,2002 年,第 197－198 页。
② Auden, W. H. *Selected Poems* (Revised Edition). London: Faber & Faber, 2010, p. 49.
③ 思马得学校主编:《汉英中国文化词典》,南京:南京大学出版社,2005 年。

2.2 The connotations of black and translation of "black" terms

Black is usually associated with negative meanings and emotions like evil, illegality, suffering, bad luck, horror, sadness, and anger. In Chinese, we have expressions like 黑心, 颠倒黑白, 黑市 and poetic lines like 两鬓苍苍十指黑, 黑云压城城欲摧, and 月黑雁飞高. In these expressions and poetic lines, 黑 does not merely refer to the color itself, it reveals the users' and narrators' attitudes and feelings as well. For example, 两鬓苍苍十指黑 implies the old charcoal seller's miserable living conditions and the narrator's sadness. 黑云压城城欲摧 conveys the feelings of constriction and tension. Likewise, black is associated with negativity in English as shown by expressions like "black sheep," "blackguard," and "blacklist." When Jane Eyre's marriage with Rochester was aborted due to his mad wife on the attic, Charlotte Brontë highlighted darkness to reveal the heroine's frustration and despair:

My eyes were covered and closed: eddying darkness seemed to swim round me, and reflection came in as black and confused a flow. Self-abandoned, relaxed, and effortless, I seemed to have laid me down in the dried-up bed of a great river; I heard a flood loosened in remote mountains, and felt the torrent come: to rise I had no will, to flee I had no strength. [1]

In the quoted paragraph, the associative meaning of black is evoked to depict Jane's sadness and helplessness. Writers often use black and its synonyms or variations like gray, darkness, blackness, and blackening to create dangerous, desolate, gloomy, or gothic scenes or atmospheres to reflect the protagonist's state of mind. In Table 7, we list some "black" terms and their translations.

Table 7   Some "Black" Terms and Their Translations

Chinese	English	English	Chinese
黑心	black heart, evil mind	a black letter day	倒霉的一天
黑幕	inside story of a plot, shady deal	black Monday	黑色星期一
黑手	evil backstage manipulator	black despair	绝望
黑市	black market	black sheep	害群之马
黑钱	black money, money earned illegally	look black at sb.	怒目而视

---

[1] Brontë, Charlotte. *Jane Eyre* (3rd edition). New York and London: W. W. Norton & Company, 2001, p. 253.

(**Continued**)

Chinese	English	English	Chinese
黑名单	blacklist	blackguard	恶棍
黑货	smuggled goods	black art	妖术，魔法
颠倒黑白	call white black and black white	a black lie	不可饶恕的谎言
白纸黑字	put it down in black and white	black flag	黑旗，海盗旗

2.3　The connotations of red and translation of "red" terms

Red in Chinese culture is associated with happiness and good luck. During the Spring Festival，couplets are pasted to ward off evil spirits and wish for good luck and children can receive red envelopes from elders as a token of blessing and safety. In a traditional Chinese wedding，the bride is clad in a red wedding dress and red double happiness is pasted to mark the celebration and symbolize the union of bride and bridegroom. Poetic lines like 霜叶红于二月花，百般红紫斗芳菲，and 万紫千红总是春 all use the color 红 to express vitality and a joyful mood，but sometimes red is also used to describe the transience of life and the unlucky fate of women like in 落红不是无情物 and 红颜胜人多薄命. In "Love Seeds"（《相思》）by Wang Wei，red berry is used as a symbol of love or friendship. "Red berries grow in southern land，/In spring they overload the trees. /Gather them till full is your hand，/They would revive fond memories."[1] The associative meaning of red is largely positive in Chinese culture.

In Western culture，red is evocative of evil and sin. In *The Scarlet Letter*，the red letter A is embroidered on Prynne's clothes to mark her adultery with Dimmesdale. Weinstein argued that the letter A in the novel is a cultural marker：

> Whether as the first letter of the English language，the legal crime of adultery that Hester has committed，the red badge that she has turned into a gorgeously aesthetic object，or the object that Hawthorne discovers in the Salem Custom-House among the papers of former Surveyor Jonathan Pue，the "A" is a cultural marker. [2]

As a master of symbolism，Hawthorne accorded different symbolic meanings to the letter A as the narration evolves. Initially，it symbolizes Prynne's adultery with the

---

[1]　许渊冲译：《汉英对照唐诗一百五十首》，西安：陕西人民出版社，1984 年，第 24 页。The original poem is："红豆生南国，春来发几枝。愿君多采撷，此物最相思."

[2]　Weinstein, Cindy. "Introduction." *The Scarlet Letter*. Nathaniel Hawthorne. Oxford：Oxford University Press，2007，p. ix.

young priest. Later，as Prynne serves the community to raise Pearl and redeem herself，the letter A is symbolic of her ability. And finally，it becomes a symbol of Prynne's angelic quality.

We can see that the color red carries different associative meanings in Chinese and English. Table 8 lists some "red" color terms and their translations.

Table 8   Some "Red" Terms and Their Translations

Chinese	English	English	Chinese
红尘	the world of mortals	see red	突然发怒，大怒
红粉	women，the fair sex	to paint the town red	狂欢
红娘	go-between，matchmaker	catch sb. red-handed	当场抓住
红得发紫	enjoying great popularity	redneck	乡下佬
红运	good luck	be in the red	亏空，负债
红包	red paper envelope	red-eye flight	红眼航班
红人	be a favorite	red in tooth and claw	残酷无情，野蛮
红头文件	official document	a red rag to a bull	激起人怒火的事物
红榜	honor roll or board	a red-letter day	喜庆的日子

2.4   The connotations of green and translation of "green" terms

The color green is a sign of safety，permission，and vitality in both Chinese and English. Green light signifies safety and permission to proceed and financially unprivileged students are granted green channel status in registration. Li Qingzhao used 绿肥红瘦 to describe the scene of late spring in which lush green leaves are contrasted with withered red flowers. D. H. Lawrence created a verbal picture of vigor and clear beauty by projecting his feelings to the color green in the following short imagist poem "Green"：

> The dawn was apple-green，
>> The sky was green wine held up in the sun，
> The moon was a golden petal between.
>
> She opened her eyes，and green
>> They shone，clear like flowers undone
> For the first time，now for the first time seen. [1]

---

[1]   Lawrence，D. H. *The Complete Poems of D. H. Lawrence.* New York：Penguin Books，1977，p. 216.

Though the implications of green are sometimes identical in different cultures，we need to note that the associative meanings of green in Chinese can differ from those in English. 眼红 and its English equivalent "green-eyed" are often cited to illustrate the different cultural connotations of color terms. We have more examples. In Chinese，绿 sometimes means blue. For example，the narrator's father in "The Sight of Father's Back"（《背影》）by Zhu Ziqing hobbled "towards the railway track in his black skullcap，black cloth mandarin jacket and dark blue cotton-padded cloth long gown."（我看见他戴着黑布小帽,穿着黑布大马褂,深青布棉袍,蹒跚地走到铁道边,慢慢探下身去,尚不大难。）① Bai Juyi（白居易）shed tears over the plaintive tune of the *pipa* player："Of all the company at table who wept most?/It was none other than the exiled blue-robed host."（座中泣下谁最多,江州司马青衫湿。）② In expressions like 青天大老爷 the color 青 implies justice. In English，green can be indicative of money as the dollar is green. It can also imply inexperience as in "green hand." In Table 9，we list some "green" terms and their translations.

Table 9　Some "Green" Terms and Their Translations

Chinese	English	English	Chinese
绿水青山	green mountains and blue waters / lucid waters and lush mountains	green power	金钱的力量
灯红酒绿	red lanterns and green wine / scene of debauchery	a green thumb	园艺高手
绿色食品	green food	greenhouse effect	温室效应
绿化带	green belt	green old age	老当益壮
花红柳绿	bright red blossoms and green willows	give the green light	批准,开绿灯
说白道绿	comment on vicious things without restraint	green room	演员休息室
绿豆糕	mung-bean cake	green salad	蔬菜沙拉
绿帽子	cuckold	green winter	暖冬

2.5　The connotations of yellow and translation of "yellow" terms

The connotations of yellow in Chinese differ significantly from those in English. Yellow in China is a symbol of imperial power and a signifier of pornography；whereas in the West，it is associated with cowardice and despicability. The dragon robe of a Chinese emperor is yellow and imperial yellow mandarin jackets are conferred upon officials to acknowledge their achievements. We call pornographic

---

① 　张培基译：《英译现代中国散文选（一）》,上海：上海外语教育出版社,2007 年,第 51 页。
② 　许渊冲：《许渊冲译唐诗三百首》,北京：中译出版社,2021 年,第 681 页。

movies 黄色电影 and pornographic publications 黄色读物；whereas in English the color blue is used to denote phonographic stuff as in "blue jokes" and "blue films." Yellow is also used to express cowardice and despicability in English. The demeaning expression "a yellow dog" refers to someone who is despicable. As yellow is the color of gold，it is also associated with wealth. In Chinese we have expressions like 黄白之物 and in English "yellow boys" refer to gold coins. Table 10 lists some "yellow" terms and their translations.

Table 10　Some "Yellow" Terms and Their Translations

Chinese	English	English	Chinese
黄包车	rickshaw	yellow page	黄页
黄道吉日	propitious date	yellow fever	黄热病
黄历	lunar almanac	yellow line	黄色标线,禁止停车线
黄粱美梦	a pipe dream	yellow belly	胆小鬼
黄脸婆	faded old woman	yellow back	黄金债券
黄毛丫头	silly little girl	yellow jacket	大黄蜂,胡蜂
黄泉	the world of the dead	yellow flag	黄旗,检疫旗
面黄肌瘦	emaciation with sallow complexion	yellow card	黄牌

2.6　The connotations of blue and translation of "blue" terms

While blue is relatively neutral in Chinese，it is associated with low feelings, pornography，and nobility in English. Since we've mentioned blue as a symbol of pornography，we'll exemplify the association of blue with sadness and noble blood here. In Section 2.1 of this chapter，we've cited Auden's "Funeral Blues." As a genre of sad music with strong rhythms developed by African American musicians in the southern US，blues derives its name from the melancholy connotations of the color blue. And we use blue blood to refer to a person of noble birth. Some "blue" terms and their translations are listed in Table 11.

Table 11　Some "Blue" Terms and Their Translations

English	Chinese	English	Chinese
in a blue mood	情绪低落	black and blue	遍体鳞伤
out of the blue	突然地,意外地	a bolt from the blue	晴天霹雳
blue in the face	脸色发青	blue-collar workers	蓝领工人
once in a blue moon	千载难逢	blue talk	下流言论

From our discussion, we can find that the associative meanings of color terms generally fall into three categories from a cross-cultural perspective. First, the cultural connotations are identical in Chinese and English. Second, the cultural connotations are different. And third, the meanings of color terms don't have much to do with the colors themselves. In translating color terms, we need to keep a cross-cultural awareness and pay special attention to the second and third categories.

A Short Summary

In this chapter, we've discussed the connotations of different colors and the translation of color terms from a cross-cultural perspective. The cultural implications of colors in Chinese and English can be identical or different. Sometimes, the meanings of certain color terms don't have much to do with the colors themselves. The translation of color terms is a process of cross-cultural communication. We need to maintain a cross-cultural awareness and pay attention to the cultural connotations of colors.

Reviewing Questions

1. What is the pragmatic meaning of language and its relationship with culture?

2. What are the cultural connotations of white, black, red, green, yellow, and blue in Chinese and English?

3. What are the methods and skills used in translating color terms?

Chapter 15

Translation of Animal Terms

 Objectives

➤ Understand the cultural connotations of animals from a cross-cultural perspective

➤ Grasp the methods and skills of translating animal terms

➤ Be able to translate animal terms into proper English

1. Translation of Animal Terms as a Form of Cross-Cultural Activity

Like color terms, animal terms are also tied up with culture and the same animal may carry different associative meanings in different cultures. For example, owl is regarded as a bird of ill omen in Chinese culture, but in the West, it is a symbol of knowledge and wisdom. Therefore, the translation of animal terms is a typical form of cross-cultural activity in which the cultural connotations of source texts and target texts are negotiated. As what we've done in Chapter 14, we'll discuss and exemplify the associative meanings of different animals from a cross-cultural perspective and list some of the animal terms and their translations. For the convenience of discussion, we group animal terms into four categories: those having identical cultural connotations in Chinese and English, those possessing different cultural connotations in Chinese and English, different animal terms with identical meanings in Chinese and English, and animal terms without equivalent animal terms in the other language.

2. Translation of Animal Terms with Similar Cultural Connotations

Some animals possess similar cultural connotations in Chinese and English, such as fox, tiger, wolf, pig, parrot, bee, and pigeon.

2.1 Fox

Fox is associated with cunningness and evil. In Chinese, we have the expression 老狐狸, which can be literally and suitably translated as "old fox." And the cunningness and evil of fox are wisely expressed by some English proverbs and sayings. "A fox may grow gray, but never good." "Old foxes want no tutors." "When a fox says he is vegetarian, it's time for the hen to look out." However, some "fox" terms, such as 狐狸精, are unique to Chinese culture. Maxine Hong Kingston tries to reveal the characteristics of "fox spirit" through the narrator's mother's admonition of a ghost in *The Woman Warrior*:

That must be just what you are—a Fox Spirit. You are so hairy, you must be a fox that doesn't even know how to transform itself. You're not clever for a Fox Spirit, I must say. No tricks. No blood. Where are your hanged man's rotting noose and icy breath? No throwing shoes into the rafters? No metamorphosis into a beautiful sad lady? No disguises in my dead relatives' shapes? No drowned woman with seaweed hair? No riddles or penalty games? You are a puny little boulder indeed. Yes, when I get my oil, I will fry you for breakfast. [①]

Kingston constructs the image of fox spirit from movies, books, and tales and accords it the characteristics of cunningness, cruelty, and seduction. The image of fox spirit in Kingston's novel is deeply rooted in Chinese culture. Currently, pop culture in the West is seemingly reshaping the image of fox. For example, in *Zootopia*, the fox Nick is depicted as a loyal, responsible, calm, and resourceful character, but don't forget other people's stereotyped view of it at the beginning of the movie—lazy, cunning, and unreliable.

2.2　Tiger

Tiger is a symbol of ferocity and strength. In Chinese, we use 虎狼之师 to describe an army with exceedingly combative competence and strict discipline. Xin Qiji used 气吞万里如虎 to express his admiration of the valiancy of Liu Yu, a statesman, strategist, and reformer during the Eastern Jin and the Southern and Northern dynasties. Western culture also associates tiger with might and ferocity. English poet William Blake eulogized tiger in his titular poem "The Tiger": "Tiger, tiger, burning bright/In the forest of the night, /What immortal hand or eye/Could frame thy fearful symmetry?" [②] But in Chinese, tiger is sometimes used as a metaphor for tyranny as in 苛政猛于虎, meaning a tyranny is even more to be dreaded than tigers. In Table 12, we list some "tiger" terms and their translations.

Table 12　Some "Tiger" Terms and Their Translations

Chinese	English
虎毒不食子	even a hungry tiger doesn't eat its own cubs/kindred feelings are irresistible
虎狼之国	country like a hungry tiger and predatory wolf/aggressor or aggressive country
虎落平阳被犬欺	a tiger on level ground may be bullied by a dog
虎头蛇尾	with a tiger's head but a snake's tail/in like a lion, out like a lamb
龙潭虎穴	dragon's pool and tiger's den/dangerous place

---

① Kingston, Maxine Hong. *The Woman Warrior*, *China Men*, *Tripmaster Monkey: His Fake Book*, *Hawai'i One Summer*, *Other Writings*. New York: Library Classics of the United States, Inc., 2022, p. 63.

② Blake, William. *Blake: The Complete Poems* (3rd edition). London and New York: Routledge, 2007, p. 221.

2.3 Wolf

Both Chinese and English cultures regard wolf as a cruel，cunning，greedy，and ungrateful animal. The fable "Mr. Dongguo and the Wolf" and expressions like 狼子野心，引狼入室，狼吞虎咽，狼心狗肺，and 子系中山狼，得志便猖狂 all attest to the cruelty，greed，craft，and ingratitude of wolf. These qualities are also shown in some English "wolf" idioms：the big bad wolf，wolf in sheep's clothing，greedy as a wolf … . We list some "wolf" terms and their translations in Table 13.

Table 13　Some "Wolf" Terms and Their Translations

Chinese	English
狼心狗肺	ungrateful
声名狼藉	infamous，notorious
引狼入室	set the wolf to keep the sheep
狼狈为奸	act in collusion with each other
鬼哭狼嚎	wail like ghost and cry like wolves/let loose cries and screams
English	**Chinese**
cry wolf	发假警报
have a wolf in the stomach	饿极了
a lone wolf	孤僻的人，独行侠
see a wolf	张口结舌，说不出话来
keep the wolf from the door	免于饥饿，勉强度日

2.4 Pig

Pig is a nasty animal for Chinese and English speakers and often appears in curses and slurs. Expressions like 猪狗不如 and "filthy swine" indicate the nastiness，dirtiness，laziness，uselessness，and gluttony of a pig. In *Journey to the West*，Zhu Bajie，though not without his adorable qualities，is basically a lazy，gluttonous，and grouchy character.

2.5 Parrot

The connotation of parrot as lack of originality and initiative derives from the imitating and mechanical nature of the bird. People keep parrots as pets mainly for amusement as their imitation of human speech can be funny and entertaining. The nature and connotation of parrot are well reflected in phrases and expressions like "parrot-fashion" and 鹦鹉学舌.

2.6 Bee

Bee is a symbol of diligence, hard work, and sacrifice as in the expression "as busy as a bee" and the couplet "采得百花成蜜后,为谁辛苦为谁甜" by Luo Yin, a poet of the late Tang dynasty. In Chinese, teachers are also compared to bees to acknowledge their sacrifice.

2.7 Pigeon

Pigeons in China used to be messengers whose role was performed by ravens in medieval Europe. Pigeon as a symbol of peace probably originates from the Old Testament. When the flood that destroyed the world receded, the pigeon set by Noah brought back an olive branch. Since then, the image of a pigeon carrying an olive branch has become a symbol of peace.

3. Translation of Animal Terms with Different Cultural Connotations

Animals like dragon, dog, sheep, owl, bat, fish, bear, and magpie carry different cultural connotations in Chinese and English.

3.1 Dragon

Dragon, a mythical and zodiac animal, is a symbol of power and auspiciousness in Chinese culture. The emperor is referred to as 天子 (son of heaven) and wears 龙袍 (dragon robe). Contrary to its positive associations in Chinese culture, dragon is regarded as an incarnation of demon and associated with evil and cruelty. *Beowulf*, a medieval British epic, narrates the heroic deeds of the Scandinavian hero Beowulf who ventures into the dragon's den and slays the vicious animal. Dragon can also mean a shrew as in the expression "dragon lady." To avoid the negative associations of dragon in English, some scholars advocate that we transliterate 龙 as "loong" and "dragon" as 杜拉更 or add the determiner "Chinese" before dragon to differentiate it from "English dragon." In Table 14, we list some "dragon" terms and their translations.

Table 14 Some "Dragon" Terms and Their Translations

Chinese	English
龙的传人	descendants of the dragon
龙飞凤舞	like dragons flying and phoenixes dancing
龙凤呈祥	the dragon and the phoenix bringing prosperity

Chinese	English
龙生九子	The dragon had nine sons and each of them was different from others.
龙生龙，凤生凤	dragons beget dragons，phoenixes beget phoenixes
龙争虎斗	fighting between a tiger and a dragon
龙套	actor playing a walk-on part
龙舟节	the Dragon Boat Festival

3.2 Dog

The cultural associations of dog are different in Chinese and English. In Chinese，it symbolizes indecency while in English，it indicates loveliness and loyalty. Many vulgar expressions in Chinese are related to dog，such as 狗东西，狗屁不通，狗腿子，and 狗眼看人低. On the contrary，English culture takes dog as a lovable and loyal being as attested to by such idioms and sayings as "Every dog has its day" and "Love me，love my dog." Some "dog" terms and their translations are listed in Table 15.

Table 15 Some "Dog" Terms and Their Translations

Chinese	English
狗不嫌家贫，儿不嫌母丑	As a dog does not shun a home however poor, a son does not loathe his mother however plain.
蝇营狗苟	swarm as flies do for good or hang round as dogs do for food/ concentrate on making profits/ingratiate oneself with sb. to gain one's ends
狗急跳墙	a dog will leap over a wall in desperation
狗拿耗子，多管闲事	a dog trying to catch mice/poke one's nose into other's business
狗屁不通	unreadable rubbish
狗头军师	person who offers bad advice
狗尾续貂	join a dog tail to a sable/make an unworthy continuation of a great work
狗眼看人低	act like a snob
狗仗人势	a dog threatens people on the strength of its master's power/ be a bully with the support of a powerful person
狗咬吕洞宾，不识好人心	snarl and snap at Lv Dongbin, one of the eight immortals in Chinese mythology/wrong a kind-hearted person
狗嘴吐不出象牙	no ivory can come out a dog's mouth

（Continued）

English	Chinese
work like a dog	拼命工作
dog days	三伏天
put on the dog	摆架子,装腔作势
as sick as a dog	病得很重
lazy dog	懒汉,懒家伙
dog food	一文不值

3.3   Sheep

Though a symbol of timidity in both Chinese and English，sheep implies foolishness and lack of judgement in English. The Chinese idiom 羊入虎口 contrasts the weakness of lamb with the ferocity of tiger and the English word "sheepish" is associated with the meekness of sheep. The similes "as silly as a lamb" and "follow like sheep" are used to describe people who are in want of judgment and initiative. If we add "black" before "sheep," we have "black sheep," a member of a family or group who is regarded as a disgrace to it. We list some "sheep" expressions and their translations in Table 16.

Table 16   Some "Sheep" Terms and Their Translations

Chinese	English
羊肠小道	a narrow winding trail
羊入虎口	lamb falls into a tiger's mouth/certain death or ruin
羊毛出在羊身上	The wool still comes from the sheep's back. / In the long run, whatever you're given, you pay for it.
English	**Chinese**
a wolf in sheep's clothing	披着羊皮的狼
follow like sheep	盲从
sheep without a shepherd	乌合之众
stand out like a camel in a flock of sheep	鹤立鸡群
separate the sheep from the goats	区分善恶,区分好坏人
cast sheep's eyes at sb.	对某人抛媚眼

3.4   Owl

Chinese people，especially the older generations，are afraid of hearing the hooting of owls，believing it a sign of bad luck；whereas Westerners regard owl as a symbol of knowledge and wisdom. The Chinese expression "夜猫子进宅,无事不来" and the English expression "as wise as an owl" attest to the different cultural connotations of owl. However，owl，usually called 夜猫子 in Chinese，can refer to someone who sleeps late both in Chinese and English.

3.5　Bat

Fans of vampire movies will instantly recognize bats as lurid nocturnal animals. Armed with sharp teeth and ears，they remind Westerners of ugliness and evil. Some informal expressions are associated with such implications，such as "old bat"（an unattractive nasty woman）and "like a bat out of hell"（very fast and wildly）. As bat has poor eyesight，it also implies senselessness in English as in "as blind as bat." In Chinese，bat，a homophone of 福，is associated with blessing and good fortune.

3.6　Fish

The idioms 年年有鱼（余）and 鱼跃龙门 indicate that fish in Chinese culture is a symbol of abundance，but sometimes it is also associated with oppression and poor quality as in 鱼肉百姓 and 鱼目混珠. In English，fish is usually used to refer to an unpleasant person，thing，or situation. Some "fish" expressions and their translations are listed in Table 17.

Table 17　Some "Fish" Terms and Their Translations

Chinese	English
鱼龙混杂	Fish and dragons jumble together. /Good and bad people mix up.
鱼米之乡	land of fish and rice
鱼目混珠	pass off fish eyes as pearls/pass off something sham as genuine
鱼肉乡里	cruelly oppress the people in the locality
鱼水情深	be as close as fish and water
鱼死网破	either the fish dies or the net gets torn/a life-and-death struggle
鱼雁往来	incoming and outgoing of epistolary correspondence
English	**Chinese**
a poor fish	可怜虫
a loose fish	放荡的人
a big fish	大人物
drink like a fish	豪饮
fish in the air	白费力,缘木求鱼
like a fish out of water	不自在,不适应

3.7　Bear

Bear in Chinese culture is associated with good-for-nothingness. For example, we use 瞧他那个熊样 to express our disdain for someone who is worthless. But bear paw is regarded as a rarity and 鱼和熊掌不可兼得 is used to describe a dilemmatic situation. Mencius says

鱼,我所欲也;熊掌,亦我所欲也。二者不可得兼,舍鱼而取熊掌者也。生,我所欲也;义,亦我所欲也。二者不可得兼,舍生而取义者也。

I like fish, and I also like bear's paws. If I cannot have the two together, I will let the fish go, and take the bear's paws. So, I like life, and I also like righteousness. If I cannot keep the two together, I will let life go, and choose righteousness. [1]

In English, bear usually refers to an uncouth or cumbersome man and is also a nickname for Russia.

3.8　Magpie

The tale of Magpie Bridge is well-known in China. In Chinese culture, magpie is believed to be a bird that can bring happiness and good fortune. 鹊报, the chattering of magpie, is interpreted as a good omen and 鸠占鹊巢, literally meaning "the turtledove occupies the magpie's nest," indicates the nobility of magpie in contrast with the abjection of turtledove. In English, magpie is used figuratively to refer to someone who collects things obsessively or chatters idly.

4. Translation of Different Animal Terms with Similar Meanings

Due to cultural differences, different animal terms are sometimes used to express the same meaning. For example, in Chinese we use 胆小如鼠 to express timidity and cowardice while in English the same meaning is expressed by such expressions as "timid as a hare." Similarly, the meanings of 热锅上的蚂蚁, 拦路虎, and 力大如牛 are expressed by "like a cat on hot bricks," "a lion in the way," and "as strong as a horse" in English respectively.

---

[1]　Legge, James, trans. *The Chinese Classics: The Works of Mencius*. Hong Kong: Hong Kong University Press, 1960, p. 411.

5. Translation of Animal Terms Without Equivalent Animal Terms in TL

It's difficult，if not impossible to put some animal terms into equivalent animal terms in Chinese or English. For example，English animal terms like "rain cats and dogs," "let the cat out of the bag," and "bell the cat" have no equivalent Chinese animal terms. Likewise，Chinese animal terms like 牛头不对马嘴，风马牛不相及，and 小肚鸡肠 also lack proper equivalent English animal terms.

As we can see from the above discussion，the meanings of animal terms mainly derive from the biological and habitual features and cultural associations of animals. In translating them，we need to heed their cultural connotations.

A Short Summary

In this chapter，we've discussed the connotations of some animals and the translation of animal terms from a cross-cultural perspective. The cultural connotations of animals and animal terms generally fall into four categories. First，some animals，such as fox，wolf，bee，are of similar connotations in Chinese and English. Second，animals like dragon，fish，and bat possess different cultural implications in Chinese and English. Third，people use different animal terms to express the same meanings in Chinese and English. Fourth，some animal terms have no equivalent animal terms in the other language. The translation of animal terms is a form of cross-cultural activity. We need to maintain a keen cross-cultural awareness and pay attention to the cultural connotations of animals.

Reviewing Questions

1. How do you understand the translation of animal terms as a form of cross-cultural activity?

2. What are the cultural connotations of fox，sheep，dragon，owl，and dog in Chinese and English?

3. What do you think 龙 should be translated?

Chapter 16

Translation of Movie Titles

 Objectives

➢ Understand the importance of movie titles

➢ Understand the translation of movie titles from a cross-cultural perspective

➢ Understand the principles of translating movie titles

➢ Grasp the methods and skills of translating movie titles

➢ Be able to translate movie titles

1. The Importance of Movie Titles

According to Genette, title is an important form of paratext that can influence readers' perception of the text and serve as a threshold through which readers can access and interpret the text.[①] The title of a movie can influence potential viewers' impression of it. In a mass consumer society as the one we are living in, people tend to make quick decisions about movie-seeing and movie titles can impact and sometimes even determine the box office. Except series of blockbusters like *The Lord of the Rings*, *The Avengers*, and *Harry Potter* which are well-known to a worldwide audience, the title of a mew movie must be well chosen and well translated, otherwise the box office is likely to be impacted. For example, *Catch Me If You Can*, a 2002 Hollywood movie directed by Steven Spielberg and starring Leonardo DiCaprio and Tom Hanks was quite successful in the US, but it met its Waterloo in the Chinese market. The low box office in China was partly due to the translated title《猫鼠游戏》. Rather than indicate the genre and content of the movie as a suspension and gangster, the Chinese title might remind Chinese viewers of *Tom and Jerry*, a phenomenally successful animated TV series. It is true that real gold does not fear the test of fire, but a good movie still needs an apt and appealing title to capture audience's attention and lure them to the theater.

2. The Translation of Movie Titles as a Cross-cultural Activity

Movie, as a form of visual art that represents reality, either physical or fictional, is closely associated with culture and is an important medium of representing and promoting beliefs and values. For instance, *Zootopia* offers an implicit satire of American political correctness, *Coco* explores the meaning of death while depicting American multiculturalism, *Green Book* examines American racism, *Superman* promotes individualism and heroism, and *The Pursuit of Happyness* depicts American Dream. The beliefs and values of movies are sometimes reflected by the titles. The tile of *Zootopia*, for example, is a blending of "zoo" and "utopia," a Western political concept which means an imaginary place where everything is perfect. It indicates the genre and content of the movie as a political satire. *The Pursuit of Happyness*, implicative of the American value of individualism and evocative of *The Declaration of*

---

① Genette, Gérard. *Paratexts: Thresholds of Interpretation*. Trans. Jane Lewin. Cambridge: Cambridge University Press, 1997, p. 76.

Independence which states that "all men are created equal, that they are endowed by their Creator with certain unalienable Rights, that among these are Life, Liberty and the pursuit of Happiness."[1] As American movies are associated with American culture, Chinese movies are reflections of Chinese culture. For example, *Raise the Red Lantern*, a movie directed by Zhang Yimou, reveals the decadent feudal way of life and the title implies that the story happened in a wealthy and influential family since only privileged families can hang big red lanterns on the high doorframes. And the title *Farewell, My Concubine*, alluding to the tragic love between Xiang Yu and Yu Ji, foreshadows the tragic love between the protagonists.

As movie titles are inseparable from culture, the translation of them is a form of cross-cultural activity that requires the mediation between SL culture and TL culture. However, unlike some other aspects of culture, movies are highly commercialized and carry aesthetic values and the translation of movie titles often has to consider other factors besides culture.

3. The Principles of Translating Movie Titles

What are the factors to be considered in translating movie titles? To answer this question, we need to understand the functions of title. Genette believes that the title of a text usually has five functions—to designate the text, to reveal the theme, to imply the connotations, to tempt readers, and to indicate the genre.[2] The title of a movie has similar functions and a good title should be able to indicate the theme, content, and genre of the movie, provide aesthetic pleasures, and lure viewers to the theatre. Therefore, the translation of movie titles should pay attention to information, culture, aesthetics, and box office, and follow the principles of value of information, value of culture, aesthetic value, and commercial value.

3.1　Value of information

The translation of movie titles needs to adhere to the criteria of fidelity and readability. A good translation should, first of all, reveal information of the content, genre, and theme of the movie, and translation that is off the point or remote from the subject will probably mislead viewers. For instance, *Anna Karenina* and *True Lies* are translated by some translators as《爱比恋更冷》and《魔鬼大帝》which can be

---

[1]　Marcovitz, Hal. *The Declaration of Independence*. San Diego: ReferencePoint Press, 2015, p. 9.

[2]　Genette, Gérard. *Paratexts: Thresholds of Interpretation*. Trans. Jane Lewin. Cambridge: Cambridge University Press, 1997, pp. 76 - 103.

misleading. The former title seems to indicate the movie as a tragic romance，but it can hardly remind readers of the world classic by Leo Tolstoy. In this case，a transliteration of the title as《安娜·卡列尼娜》will suffice. The latter title implies the genre of the movie as a fantasy or horror，which actually is an action comedy starring Arnold Schwarzenegger. These unaptly translated titles，as thresholds of interpretation，may misguide viewers and cause them to hold wrong expectations. Therefore，translators should not be too liberal in translating movie titles and let their imagination run wild；rather，they should preview the movie，grasp its genre，content，theme，and tone，and then come up with a translated title that matches the movie well. For example，《喋血街头》and《纵横四海》directed by Wu Yusen（吴宇森）are translated as *A Bullet in the Head* and *Once a Thief*，which are concise and match the genres，contents，and themes of the movies.

3.2　Value of culture

Value of culture requires that the translated title convey the cultural connotation，underlying emotion，and philosophy of the original title. Let's exemplify it with the Chinese translation of the movie title *Seven*—《七宗罪》. "Seven" refers to the seven deadly sins in Christianity—envy，gluttony，avarice，lust，pride，sloth，and wrath and each of the serial murders in the movie is committed against one of the sins. The movie title is highly religious and evocative of Christian tradition，but the number "seven" will not evoke same religious feelings among Chinese. As a result，a literal translation of the title as《七》would compromise the religious connotation of the original title and doesn't make much sense to Chinese viewers，so the translator puts it as《七宗罪》to bring out the religious meaning of the original title. A translated movie title，as we can see，can serve as a bridge connecting SL culture with TL culture.

3.3　Aesthetic value

Naming is a form of art. A good movie title can give viewers a sense of beauty and evoke their emotions and sensibilities by resorting to phonetic devices like alliteration and/or drawing upon the associative meaning of language. For example，*Pride and Prejudice* uses alliteration and sounds catchy；*Mona Lisa Smile* reminds viewers of the eponymous painting by Leonardo da Vinci and readers are likely to attribute their impressions and feelings of the painting to the movie；and《花样年华》can strike the sentimental mind of a Chinese and evoke his/her feelings of youth，love，innocence，and vitality.

Different languages have different aesthetic forms and people from different cultures differ in sentimental structures. For example，English is concrete and direct while Chinese is vivid and elusive. English speakers are direct in expressing love; whereas Chinese are comparatively reserved. Translators of movie titles need to consider these differences and make their translations suit the aesthetic habit of target language and the sentimentality of target readers. For instance, the translation of *Ordinary People* as《凡夫俗子》, *Singing in the Rain* as《雨中曲》,《黄飞鸿》as *Once upon a Time in China* and《顺流逆流》as *Time and Tide* sound artistic for target readers.《凡夫俗子》as a four-character idiom often used by Chinese to describe the ordinariness, triviality, and helplessness of everyday life, sounds catchy and well matches the theme and content of the movie.《雨中曲》can evoke a romantic atmosphere. *Once upon a Time in China* imitates the title of the American movie *Once upon a Time in America*. And *Time and Tide* alludes to the English proverb "Time and tide wait for no man." These translated titles shift the aesthetic form and sentimentality of the source langue and culture to those of the target language and culture.

3.4 Commercial value

Box office is the overriding measure for the success of commercial movies and the impact of movie titles on box office should not be overlooked since potential movie-goers tend to make their decisions upon movie titles. Poorly translated movie titles might prove disastrous to the box office. For example, the phenomenally successful movies *The Shawshank Redemption* and *The Matrix* were once translated as《刺激1995》and《二十二世纪杀人网络》. The translations might have ruined the box office in domestic market had it not been the high quality of the movies. Good translations, on the contrary, can take advantage of viewers' psychological expectations and tempt them to the theater. For example, the Chinese translations of *Gone with the Wind* as《乱世佳人》, *The Bridge of Madison County* as《廊桥遗梦》, and *Ghost* as《人鬼情未了》appeal to Chinese viewers' aesthetic habit and sentiment, and partly conduce to their success in China. However, we need to realize that the commercial value should not be obtained at the cost of other values. A good movie title, original or translated, should meet all the four values—the value of information, the value of culture, aesthetic value, and commercial value.

4. The Methods and Skills of Translating Movie Titles

Guided by the principles of value of information, value of culture, aesthetic value, and commercial value, translators often use the methods and skills of transliteration, half transliteration, literal translation, free translation, and addition in the translation of movie titles.

4.1 Transliteration

Some movies are named after proper names，especially people's names and places. For these movies，the titles are often transliterated. For example，*Jane Eyre* is transliterated as《简·爱》，*Titanic* as《泰坦尼克》，and *Aladdin* as《阿拉丁》. As these proper names are well established and known to Chinese viewers，their transliterated titles are easy to be accepted and can avoid inconsistencies caused by new translations.

4.2 Half transliteration

Unlike English movies，few Chinese movies are solely named after proper names. The titles may include the names of people or places，but the proper names，as is often the case，are usually collocated with other phrases or expressions，such as《鉴真东渡》and《梦断楼兰》. Such titles are usually half transliterated. For example，《火烧圆明园》，《鉴真东渡》，and《梦断楼兰》are translated into *The Burning of Yuanmingyuan*，*Jian Zhen Sails to the East*，and *Dream Broken at the Ancient Town of Loulan* respectively.

4.3 Literal translation

Literally translated titles are usually faithful to the original ones，linguistically at least and many movie titles are translated literally. As for English-Chinese translation，《教父》，《沉默的羔羊》，《复仇》，and《第八页》are literal translations of *The Godfather*，*The Silence of the Lambs*，*Revenge*，and *Page Eight*. Chinese movie titles are also literally translated into English，such as《红高粱》(*Red Sorghum*)，《青春之歌》(*The Song of Youth*)，《饮食男女》(*Eat Drink Man Woman*) and《黄土地》(*Yellow Earth*).

4.4 Free translation

Unlike literally translated movie titles through which we can know the original ones，freely translated titles usually differ significantly from the original ones，both in linguistic forms and surface meanings. Many successful movie titles are the "products" of free translation，such as *My Fair Lady* (《窈窕淑女》)，*Leon* (《这个杀手不太冷》)，*Cleopatra* (《埃及艳后》)，《霸王别姬》(*Farewell，My Concubine*)，《东邪西毒》(*Ashes of Time*) and《辣手神探》(*Hard-Boiled*). The purpose of free translation is primarily to enhance the aesthetic effects of movie titles，but translators should not go to extremity and drop into the pitfall of farfetchedness.

4.5   Addition

Addition is also used in the translation of movie titles. Sometimes，information that is implied by but not contained in the title is added to make the translation more acceptable to target readers. The added information can be about the identity of the main character as in《巴顿将军》(*Patton*)，the subject matter of the movie as in《钢琴别恋》(*The Piano*)，or the genre of the movie as in《少年派的奇幻漂流》(*Life of Pi*). Information sometimes is also added for rhetorical purpose. For example，the Chinese translation of *Speed*—《生死时速》conforms to the aesthetic tradition of Chinese and can evoke viewers' sense of tension and excitement.

A Short Summary

In this chapter，we've discussed the translation of movie titles. Movie titles can indicate the genres，contents，and themes of movies and affect viewers' perception of them. The translation of movie titles，as a cross-cultural activity，usually follows the principles of value of information，value of culture，aesthetic value，and commercial value and translators，guided by these principles，often resort to the methods and skills of transliteration，half transliteration，literal translation，free translation，and addition in the translation of movie titles.

Reviewing Questions

1. What are the functions of movie titles?

2. How do you understand the translation of movie titles as a form of cross-cultural activity?

3. What are the principles of translating movie titles?

4. What are the methods and skills of translating movie titles?

Conclusion

Translation is associated with people's urge and need to communicate with others who are from different cultures and use different languages. Since language is a medium of culture, translation is a form of cross-cultural communication. A qualified translator should be able to negotiate between languages and cultures. In this book, we've used cultural translation in three senses. First, we've discussed it from a theoretical perspective, taking it as an approach to translation studies that emphasizes the factor of culture. Second, we've used it as the translation of culture and culture-specific elements. Third, we've discussed it as an adaptation-like strategy of dealing with culturally heterogeneous texts or elements. Besides, we've also investigated cultural translation from the perspective of the contested strategies of domestication and foreignization. Though our focus in the book is culture, we nevertheless still take language as our starting point and firmly believe that discussion of translation from whatever perspective should acknowledge the foundational position of language. Translation has essentially been and will remain an activity that involves text-based transference of one language into another. Even the neurolinguistic approach to translation studies, which investigates the performance of neurons when translation activities occur gives enough consideration to language.

We've carried out our discussion in terms of history, theory, text, and practice. These four aspects help construct a panoramic view of cultural translation and construct it as an organic activity. The theoretical and historical discussion influences our perception of the nature and purpose of cultural translation, presents its genealogy, and offers insights into translation strategies, methods, and skills. The texts serve as experimental sites where theories and strategies, methods, and skills of cultural translation are applied and tested. And practice concretizes theories and helps their betterment by offering applicatory feedback. Such a paradigm to translation incorporates the major aspects of translation into an interactive chain and implies a methodology in translation and translation studies. The theory of translation influences the purpose of translation, the purpose of translation determines translation strategies, methods, and skills which find their application in texts, and translation practice in turn offers feedback to translation theories, strategies, methods, and skills. Besides its methodological significance, the paradigm is also conducive to improving readers' translation competence.

Our discussions have revealed some of the core issues of cultural translation, or translation at large, the most central of which concerns the purpose of translation, as it determines other aspects of translation. From our discussions in Chapters 1—3, we've known that if the purpose of translation is to retain the styles and cultural elements of the source texts, translators would make their translation activities orient towards SL and SL culture and adopt the strategy of foreignization. On the contrary, if translation is positioned to produce smooth target texts, translators would be likely to efface the distinctive styles of the source texts, domesticating them to satisfy the tastes of target readers. The contested purposes of translation lead to the polemics between foreignization and domestication. Though Venuti offers a harsh criticism of domestication which has long dominated the Anglo-American translation world as epitomized in his figurative expression "translator's invisibility" and advocates the strategy of foreignization as resistance, fluent translation is still tacitly regarded as the norm and foreignization as resistance still largely remains theoretical. The well-accepted and highly-acclaimed translations of Chinese classics, as we've discussed, are predominately the products of domestication. We have to admit that smooth domesticated translations do help spread Chinese culture in foreign lands, but the unique cultural elements, particularly those unpalatable to foreign readers are pitifully/deliberately smothered or erased. Foreignization on other hand can retain the cultural elements of source texts, but the products of foreignization oftentimes are not cordially accepted. This dilemma is rooted in the imbalance of comprehensive national power between countries, particularly that of culture. If Anglo-American centrism were subverted, which postcolonial critics are discussing earnestly and the power of discourse were shifted from English to Chinese, the situation might have been changed, but the polemics are likely to continue.

The translation strategy set according to translation purpose determines translation methods. Literal translation, also referred to as direct translation and transliteration are often adopted to keep the original flavors of the source texts; whereas free translation or indirect translation is employed to produce smooth target texts. What needs to be pointed out is that these methods imply cultural orientations and are therefore associated with the purpose and strategy of translation as we've explained. Literal translation, as we've discussed, emphasizes the reproduction of the phonetic, syntactic, and stylistic features of the original texts while free translation puts emphasis on the recreation of readable target texts. More often than not, advocators of free translation, especially sinologists, tend to maintain that the phonetic and/or syntactic features of Chinese classics are simply irreproducible and literal translation will inevitably lead to misunderstandings. Here again arises the highly debated issue of faithfulness versus smoothness, which is almost universal to all types of translation. Although it is generally a consensus that good translation should be faithful to the target text, both in form and content and highly readable, fidelity and smoothness are sometimes, if not always at odds with each other. In his translation of Mo Yan's *Red Sorghum*, Goldblatt, aiming to produce a smooth reading for English readers, takes the liberty of deleting and rewriting the source text. Xu Yuanchong, though succeeding in reproducing the end rhyme of ancient Chinese poetry, sometimes compromises the meaning of the source texts, thus sacrificing fidelity to a certain text. The contestation between fidelity and smoothness has long been extant and will continue into the future.

Is there a solution to the controversy? Probably not, but our discussion has indicated that a combination of literal translation and free translation based on the genre and translatability of source texts can reduce the polemics. If the source texts are primarily scientific or institutional as classified by Peter Newmark, literal translation can be adopted as the major method and used with free translation jointly. If some terms in the source texts are culturally unique and of great importance, transliteration or translation plus free translation can be employed to retain their meanings and cultural connotations. As for literary texts, free translation predominates as literal translation often results in unreadable target texts. In most cases, literal translation, transliteration, and free translation are used in combination to meet the criteria of faithfulness and smoothness.

In the book, we've examined the translation of traditional Chinese clothing, Chinese cuisine, traditional Chinese architecture, Chinese relics, traditional Chinese medicine, traditional Chinese festivals, traditional Chinese thoughts and philosophies, Chinese classics, literary works, tourism publicity materials, Chinese idioms, color terms, animal terms, and movie titles after discussing the definitions, theories, and concepts of cultural translation. The latent problem is that the translation of other aspects of Chinese culture are left undiscussed. We'd like to reemphasize that a discussion of every aspect of Chinese culture is neither possible nor necessary as the aspects of Chinese culture are numerous and the strategies, methods, and skills used in translating different aspects of Chinese culture are almost identical. So long as translators grasp the theories, purposes, criteria, principles, strategies, methods, and skills of cultural translation, they are able to apply them in the translation of every aspect of Chinese culture.